ALSO BY PETER QUENNELL

Biography

BYRON: THE YEARS OF FAME

CAROLINE OF ENGLAND: AN AUGUSTAN PORTRAIT

THE PROFANE VIRTUES: FOUR PORTRAITS
OF THE EIGHTEENTH CENTURY

JOHN RUSKIN: THE PORTRAIT OF A PROPHET

THE SINGULAR PREFERENCE

HOGARTH'S PROGRESS

Fiction

THE PHOENIX-KIND

Byron in Italy

by

PETER QUENNELL

*"I've taught me other tongues, and in strange eyes
Have made me not a stranger . . ."*

NEW YORK · THE VIKING PRESS

COMPASS BOOKS EDITION
ISSUED IN 1957 BY THE VIKING PRESS, INC.
625 MADISON AVENUE, NEW YORK, N.Y. 10022

SECOND PRINTING JUNE 1966

DISTRIBUTED IN CANADA BY
THE MACMILLAN COMPANY OF CANADA LIMITED

PRINTED IN U.S.A. BY THE COLONIAL PRESS INC.

Byron in Italy

Foreword

THIS BOOK deals with Byron's career between 1816 and 1823—from the moment when he left England as a social outcast to the last restless, regretful months he passed at Genoa, preparatory to leaving Italy bound for Greece and death. The volume is intended to constitute an independent study; but, since in the minds of some readers the details of Byron's early life may have grown a little dim, I append a brief recapitulation of its more salient episodes.

When Byron returned from the Near East in July 1811, his spirits were low and the prospect that faced him was not encouraging. From his granduncle he had inherited two impoverished, neglected, and much encumbered estates; the friends of Harrow and Cambridge were estranged or scattered; though intensely conscious of his dignity as an English peer of the realm, he had no position in London and had already aroused some enmity by his early satirical squib. Within a short time the gloomy premonitions that had assailed him as he lay becalmed off the French coast were fully justified. His mother died; and soon afterward he learned of the extinction of Matthews and Edleston, both intimates to whom in different ways he had been deeply devoted. Solitude in London increased his misery. Then, without warning and contrary to all his expectations, the appearance of *Childe Harold,* Cantos I and II, during March 1812 raised him from complete obscurity to the heights of fame. He was the social lion of the year, courted, flattered, besieged. But fame, he soon discovered, had its attendant embarrassments. His love-affair with Lady Caroline Lamb (daughter-in-law of Lady Melbourne and wife of Queen Victoria's future Prime Minister) brought him nothing but discomfort, and he was glad to escape at last into the protective maternal arms of the slightly faded but still fascinating Lady Oxford. By the spring of 1814, Byron's health and habits were giving his friends cause for serious apprehension. He announced, and they had reason to believe, that he had now embarked on some adventure of a particularly dangerous and unconventional kind. Lady Melbourne and Augusta Leigh, his half-sister (whose own reputation had been imperilled by the rumours that Byron's habitual lack of reticence had helped to propagate), were determined that as soon as possible he must be married off. The victim finally selected was Lady Melbourne's blue-stocking niece, Annabella Milbanke; and, after many delays and, on Byron's part, endless procrastination, the ceremony took place at Seaham in January 1815. The circumstances of Byron's married life have been described at length in a brilliant and sympathetic biography of Lady Byron by Miss Ethel Colburn Mayne. The marriage lasted just a year. From the first day it had been unhappy; but Lady Byron seems to have hoped for better things until (according to her subsequent account) she learned through her husband's medical attendants that her belief that he might be temporarily insane had no foundation in fact. At this point, with characteristic firmness, she decided that for her daughter's sake she must insist upon a separation. Byron's immediate response was one of indignation and aggrieved bewilderment. He admitted his faults, but would not admit that he had committed any offence against his wife that could justify her conduct. Annabella, however, refused to change her mind and, at the same time, refused to specify the "charges" that she had intimated in the last resort she was prepared to bring. A deed of separation was eventually signed in April 1816; and meanwhile the clouds of scandal which had been gathering since 1814 broke like a thunderstorm over the poet's head. At Lady Jersey's party he was cut by the majority of his former acquaintances. On April 25 he left England, destined for a life of exile.

In the present volume I have attempted to re-trace his career and portray the development of his character during the years that followed. I have attempted also to give some account of the Romantic Movement as a force that exercised a profound influence on the nineteenth century and, through the nineteenth century, on the configuration of the age we live in. Byron himself was a Romantic *malgré lui.* He despised Romanticism, but, thanks to the peculiar degree of self-awareness (a quality very different from self-knowledge) with which he had been born, his life crystallized many important aspects of the Romantic genius. In the preparation both of this book and of its predecessor, *Byron: The Years of Fame,* I have been indebted to Sir John Murray and to his nephew, John Grey Murray, for much invaluable assistance. Though it is possible that Sir John Murray's view of the poet's character is not always mine, he has generously allowed me to examine the magnificent collection of Byronic archives still preserved at 50 Albemarle Street, and has given me permission to publish an extract from a letter written to Byron by Harriette Wilson.

PETER QUENNELL

Chapter One

THE OTHERS had gone below; only Dr. Polidori remained on deck. A young man, handsome, romantic, conceited, he had recently registered a double triumph: Lord Byron, the greatest poet of the age, had appointed him his personal travelling physician, and Mr. John Murray, Lord Byron's publisher, had promised him a sum of five hundred guineas if he would render an exact account of their foreign journey. This evening, then, he preferred to remain on the deck of the packet boat. It was April 26, 1816. His employer, at the last moment, had limped aboard; Hobhouse, the poet's closest friend, had hurried down the jetty waving and smiling, to which Byron had replied with gesticulations of his gold-trimmed travelling cap; the "barren-looking" cliffs had slipped away till Dover Castle in the distance showed small and miserable; now everything and everybody "wore an aspect of grief." Other passengers retired to the crowded cabin. John Polidori, alone and exalted, looked out over the phosphorescent swirl of the waters, peered into the star-lit obscurity of the sky above. No sound reached him but "the sullen rushing of the vessel" and the hoarse cries of a sailor heaving the lead.

13

There was no illumination except a crepuscular dimness; but "a beautiful streak" followed the lead through the waves. Next morning, they arrived in Ostende harbour, and Lord Byron disembarked with his attendants and carriage.

Having passed through the customs, they withdrew to an inn. And here Byron, for whom foreign travel had a psychological significance which his travelling companions could not long ignore, suddenly revealed himself in an unfamiliar aspect. "As soon as he reached his room [recorded Dr. Polidori] Lord Byron fell like a thunderbolt upon the chambermaid." [1] In his own room, the doctor was disturbed by a smell of fresh paint and by the fact that the tea provided was of a perfumed variety; and he was not sorry when he awoke to set out through the town. There booksellers' windows disconcerted him by displaying volumes of "the most obscene nature"; he saw "little girls of all ages" wearing remarkable head-dresses, "women with wooden shoes," and "men of low rank basking in the sun." He dashed into a café, where the waiters were very civil, and thence into a shop where no one spoke French. He tried German, but "half a dozen women burst out laughing," and he was eventually obliged to buy two books he did not want "because I let a quarto fall upon a fine girl's head while looking at her eyes."

That afternoon, the cavalcade, which included Byron, Polidori, Fletcher, Byron's querulous English valet, Bob Rushton, his North Country sparring partner, and Berger, a Swiss, set off in the direction of Ghent and Antwerp. Byron and Polidori enjoyed the comforts of the enormous travelling carriage ("copied from the celebrated one of Napoleon taken at Genappe") which Byron had commissioned before leaving Eng-

[1] This sentence was cut out of Polidori's manuscript by a female descendant, but restored from recollection by her nephew, W. M. Rossetti, Polidori's editor, who was confident that he remembered "the precise diction of it."

land and which among its other amenities contained "a *lit de repos* . . . a plate chest, and every apparatus for dining." Through Bruges they rumbled with its "long roof-fretted streets" and so on to Ghent, where the gates were shut against them and only bribery enabled them to enter the town. The landscape of the Low Countries proved displeasing. At its best, Polidori decided, it was "tiresomely beautiful." The tile-roofed, whitewashed cottages looked very neat; but fine trim avenues led to ugly churches, and the prospect seemed "as unchangeable as the Flemish face. . . . All evenness, no genius, much stupidity." They yawned and dozed, and were vastly relieved to arrive at Antwerp. Dutifully they paid a visit to the Cathedral, which still showed signs of its spoliation by French republican soldiery who had destroyed or removed as much of the fabric as they could lay their hands on, leaving five feet of piled-up rubbish to encumber the floor. At Rubens's canvases they gazed with interest but little edification. Polidori tried his hardest to be properly appreciative; but the poet, who knew nothing of the plastic arts, soon admitted his discontent with Rubens's models, their high colourings, heavy shoulders, and deeply dimpled flesh. It might "all be very fine"; but he was bored and satiated. Van Dyck he preferred "a hundred times over. . . ."

From Brussels they took horse to the field of Waterloo; and here at last was a scene that Byron found stimulating. To Napoleon's, his own career had often been likened—and not by hyperbolical admirers alone; for he, too, in his stormier and more arrogant moments saw and admitted a parallelism between their destinies. He had been "damned sorry" when he had heard the news of Napoleon's fall. Now himself fallen, defeated, in exile, he rode slowly with Polidori across that pastoral upland where the peasants were whistling as they worked in the fields, and only patched plaster on farmhouse walls showed the effects of artillery fire. The farm of Hougoumont, however, was still in ruins. Fifteen hundred Englishmen had been slaughtered just beyond its garden. Here the Scots Greys had parted their ranks to allow a masked battery to pour its broadsides into the waves of furiously advancing cuirassiers. There, through a gap in the garden hedge, the French had charged again after dreadful losses. "A little further on [noted Polidori] we were shown the spot where Colonel Howard, my friend's cousin, was buried before being carried to England." For Byron the memory of this young man had a double interest, since Howard was the son of his guardian, Lord Carlisle, whose neglect had done so much to embitter his boyhood, to whom he had consecrated one of the savagest couplets of his early satire. In the poem he was already preparing he would make amends. . . . Meanwhile, peasant boys with glittering handfuls of buttons ran beside their stirrups. There were French cockades on sale, swords, eagles, and helmets, breastplates scarred by bullets, dinted and seamed by lance or sabre. Always a great collector of tokens and trophies, Byron made some purchases to send back to England. Then they turned their horses' heads and galloped homeward, helter-skelter over the springy turf of the battlefield, Byron chanting the refrain of a Turkish song.

Leaving Brussels, the travellers moved on to the Rhineland. Through Cologne they went. Then Bonn rose before them, crowned with pinnacles. Meadows and steep vineyards climbed up toward castellated crags; the Rhine rushed at their feet "with its massy swells"; rain-black hills lowered in the far distance. From some peasant girls whom they met upon the highroad Byron accepted a bunch of violets which he immediately sent back to his sister in England, accompanied by a long lyrical address. Unlike the stanzas he had composed at Waterloo, the verses were not shown to Polidori (no doubt because the feelings they expressed were too painful for immediate publication), though a fair copy was afterward inserted in *Childe Harold*. Finally, they crossed the frontier into Swiss territory. For more than half a century this small rocky corner of monarchical Europe had been the refuge and the playground of revolutionary thought. To an entire generation it was the "home of freedom"; and from the sepulchral pyramid that marked the battlefield of Morat, where the Swiss burghers had defeated Charles the Bold, Byron pulled out some mouldering fragments —enough bones to have made "a quarter of a hero." On May 25 they reached the shores of the Lake of Geneva and dismounted in the suburb of Sécheron at the Hôtel d'Angleterre. Among other details jotted down in the hotel register, Byron described himself as aged a hundred years.

It was a typical stroke of Byronic bravado; but, as in so many Byronic outbursts of the same kind, there was an element of sincerity and a pang of deep feeling beneath the surface. Life (he had always considered) was not a matter of years; only in the sufferings of heart and head could the passage of human existence really be measured; and, judging by these standards, he had exceeded his appointed span. Nor was this idea of particularly recent growth. From a much earlier period, the feeling that he had "anticipated life" (which seems to have originated in some mysterious childhood experience, now and then vaguely alluded to in his notebooks and journals) had pursued him through a bewildering series of adult conquests. It was as if the capital of emotion had already been squandered: he had been overdrawn on life before life began. Henceforward he would live as it were in retrospect. . . .

He was twenty-eight. And yet his hair was already greying.

Not without a kind of desperate satisfaction he considered the astonishing completeness of his personal destiny, which had transported him in a moment to the heights of fame, then plunged him back with almost as little notice to the depths of disaster. That disaster, it was true, he had perhaps exaggerated. The injury to his pride had been extremely severe; the appalling scene at Lady Jersey's party where half fashionable London had assembled to cut him and he had stood lonely and defiant amid a collapsing world was the kind of episode that it is not easy to live down; both his love and his self-love had been cruelly mangled; but he had still friends, prodigious celebrity, health, and freedom. Hobhouse at least, the prosy devoted friend to whom Byron showed always his most amenable side [2] and who took a resolutely common-sense view of the "dear fellow's" vagaries, declared afterward that there "was not the slightest necessity even in appearance for his going abroad" and that his fears of being hissed in public were entirely unfounded. But then, Hobhouse was more affectionate than perspicacious; and even though it might have been possible for Byron to stand his ground, to have dared the disapproval of the London *beau monde,* and confuted the many scabrous legends he had been made the hero of, entrenching himself behind barriers of contempt and solitude, the practical operation of such a plan would have been exceedingly difficult. His financial affairs were still in a state of the utmost chaos; and having suffered eleven executions of judgment during the course of his married life, sacrificed his library, and lost his furniture—even the birds and the tame squirrel had been seized by the bailiffs—he had escaped from Piccadilly Terrace with

[2] "I do not write to you in good spirits, and I cannot pretend to be so. . . . I only request you will say nothing of this to Hobhouse, as I wish to wear as quiet an appearance with him as possible." Byron to Mrs. Leigh, September 14, 1816.

only minutes to spare. And, as it happened, he had long intended to go abroad again. During his wife's pregnancy he had discussed the project with Tom Moore; for, though his affections were rooted in London and Newstead, the memories of that early tour through the Near East—of his sensuous bohemian life at Athens and the azure calms and white squalls of the Aegean Sea—month after month had beguiled and teased him as he laboured beneath an increasing burden of domestic miseries. Besides, some instinct ordered him to complete the circle —to round off the course of his fate by a dramatic gesture, leaving England just as he had left it when he was an ingenuous nineteen, but with prospects and preoccupations that were very different. It was not that he hoped or expected to escape from his memories: they were more actual and far more vivid than the landscapes around him.

Like a sleep-walker, then, he strayed through Europe, reached Sécheron, dismounted at the Hôtel d'Angleterre, and renewed the daily business of half-hearted sight-seeing. At the hotel he had been preceded by another English party. Byron had had a suspicion he might possibly find it there; but no encounter appears to have taken place till May 27, when, as he alighted from the boat in which he had been rowed over to Diodati (where he considered taking a property beside the water), he was confronted by a young Englishman and his two companions. An immediate introduction was somehow effected. At Piccadilly Terrace, several months earlier, he had occasionally been at home, but more often had been obliged to deny his door, to a dark-haired, enthusiastic girl named Mary Jane Clairmont—personally she preferred the Christian name of Claire or Clara—who described herself as the step-daughter of William Godwin. She had proved talkative, passionate, an uncommon nuisance—determined not only that he should make her his mistress (which Byron after much pestering had eventually consented to do) but that he should become the confidant of all her aspirations and private perplexities. It seemed that her step-sister Mary had had a runaway love-affair; and this sister one day had been brought to the house— a blond slender intellectual girl with aquiline features—and had gone home again much impressed by the poet's "gentleness." The two girls, Jane Clairmont and Mary Wollstonecraft Godwin, now confronted him as he stepped ashore from the rowboat. Accompanying them was Mary's lover, Percy Shelley, the rebellious son (as Byron had already heard) of the exceedingly respectable Member for New Shoreham, and himself a Godwinian atheist and an apostle of free love.

Byron knew him already by reputation. Indeed, among other brief and teasing lectures delivered to Miss Clairmont at Piccadilly Terrace, interspersed with impatient pleas that she would not bother him, he had produced a serious warning against the principles of this quasi-brother-in-law. The reformer's notoriety was as nothing beside his own; but Shelley's pranks at Eton and his expulsion from Oxford had created in their small way sufficient stir, and his seduction of Godwin's daughter had completed the scandal. Like many professional libertines, Byron had a deep regard for the domestic proprieties; and Shelley's particular brand of social theorizing—all green tea and fine feelings and high-flown radicalism—was of a kind that he found distasteful from every viewpoint. Yet Shelley, met face to face, had an extraordinary charm; and it is just that quality of fascination—difficult to analyse after the lapse of a century, yet experienced very strongly by those around him—that makes him so elusive and so remote a figure. Even his physical likeness is hard to arrive at. The legend that grew up round Byron entailed distortion but solidified in a recognizable and definite outline, in which the lineaments of the real man are not hard to distinguish; Shelley's legend had developed as a kind of luminous blur. All his literary portraits (to borrow a photographic image) would seem for some reason to have been overexposed, so that a misty aura of "halation" obscures the features. Of actual portraits, the best known is the most enigmatic. Miss Curran was a well-meaning but untalented amateur; and no human being who had read and thought and suffered could wear quite the expression of that pantomime Ariel, with its large intense feminine eyes and its sexless mouth. Mary Shelley's pencil portrait from recollection, which follows the general attitude of Miss Curran's daub, returns the same baffling reply to a modern questioner.

Shelley's appearance at Sécheron is not easy to visualize. Byron's portraits, both literary and pictorial, are so detailed and so persuasive in their verisimilitude that hardly an aspect of his physiognomy remains unfocused. Small, pale, and compactly built—he was an aspiring, slightly self-conscious five foot eight—Byron had fine abundant reddish hair, darkened by the lavish use of macassar oil, which curled on the brow and around the temples, a straight classical line of nose and forehead (the tip of the nose a little too solid when observed in profile), a sulky sensuous mouth, and a heavy chin. It was about the mouth that his emotions often revealed themselves. When he was bored, discontented, or ill at ease, the upper lip (as Annabella Milbanke had once noticed) would wrinkle upward into an expression of "impatient disgust." His lips fell "singularly at the corners"; and even when he smiled he seemed contemptuous—at least, while he played his Byronic role at a London party, for in smaller companies he could be boisterous and almost schoolboyish, fond of laughter and wine and convivial hubbub. Among strangers he was supercilious because suspicious, on guard against some affront to his feelings and dignity, and, as long as the suspicion lasted, affected and haughty—a mood which might again dissolve into jocular friendship. His lameness was perceptible but not disfiguring— it gave to his walk a curious gliding or slithering movement. Of his beringed hands—white and woman-sized—he was exceedingly proud.

Admiration, affection, passion—he might evoke them all; but at a first encounter distrust was apt to predominate, since he himself evidently distrusted the world about him. Shelley's approach was one of enthusiasm, if not of confidence. His very gait was somehow enthusiastic; for his was a big-jointed but shambling body, with fragile rounded shoulders and hollowed chest, the head being thrust forward with questing eagerness. Whereas Byron strained on tiptoe to achieve his full height, Shelley's vague stooping unself-conscious carriage caused him to appear much shorter than in fact he was. There was something headlong about him, wild, precipitate, a mixture of clumsiness and delicacy, of speed and violence, that made his ascent of any staircase a series of tumbles. His voice was shrill, feminine, extremely discordant, his eyes very large and very bright, his fine skin roughened by neglect and exposure, his thick brown hair long and always tousled. A skull that was unusually small in circumference, a small sensitive mouth with a pouting underlip, a long nose that seemed to appeal for assistance and sympathy, completed a face that, not strictly handsome, was oddly captivating. If Byron's face was a mask composed from within, which betrayed feeling involuntarily or dramatized it for the especial benefit of some chosen observer, Shelley's was a transparency that revealed his inner life and the various characteristics that governed his intellect—his gullibility, his swift enthusiasm, his erratic ardour. His pecul-

iar temperament had bestowed upon him an air of agelessness.
Chronologically or personally, he refused to be classified.

Of his social origins, however, the traces were clearly
marked. Byron was quick to notice—and noticed with gratitude
—that Shelley retained the manners of the patrician class and
was "as perfect a gentleman as ever crossed a drawing-room."
Shelley's opinions might be perverse and his behaviour eccentric, his clothes might be rumpled and stained and tattered,
but he had inherited a grace and a *savoir vivre* that Byron appreciated—envied perhaps, for his own manners were shy and
awkward; he had been brought up by a dram-drinking mother
in provincial obscurity. Not that Shelley would have paid
homage to any social law. Indeed, there was nothing that he
considered more despicable than the *beau monde* "with its
vulgar and noisy *éclat*"—the world from which Byron had so
lately fallen and to which he looked back afterward with such
longing eyes—but the effects of breeding and association were
still apparent.[3] Glad already, no doubt, to meet a fellow-
reprobate, another exile cast out by English society, Byron was
doubly glad to meet him on the footing of a man of the world,
though Shelley himself might be insensitive to their common
ties. True, the situation was not altogether clear or simple.
Claire expected that he should take her seriously as *maîtresse
en titre*, the companion of his soul, as Mary of Shelley's; and
he neither loved her nor had any appetite for romantic philan-
dering. Could she not understand that he had succumbed
through boredom, that his sensuality was diffuse and uncontrollable—easily aroused, quickly satisfied—and that there
was no possible link between desire and affection: that all the

---

[3] Hobhouse, however, thought otherwise. And in his presentation copy of
Moore's *Life*, against a passage in which Moore suggests that Shelley was "an
aristocrat by birth and . . . also in manners and appearance," he retorts: "Not
the least, unless to be lean and feeble be aristocratical."

love he possessed was disposed of elsewhere? Still, something must be done about this assiduous concubine; it was not like him to be unkind, when kindness was easy, even though temporary kindness might have permanent consequences. Very soon he would slip back into a passing love-affair. Meanwhile, he had decided to settle at Diodati, where John Milton had once stayed on his travels through Switzerland.

Whether Shelley and Mary had yet learned of the connexion between Claire and Byron is not apparent from the records they have left behind. Mary was dominated by her lover's theories. Shelley was enthusiastic rather than common-sensical; and if they knew of it they made no objection and raised no protest. There was no cloud over the charm of their lakeside meeting. Across the gloomy gulf of so many years, the words that they exchanged have failed to reach us—only the inflexion of their very different voices: Byron's low and musical, Shelley's a high-pitched recurrent scream. Their attitude was cordial if a trifle guarded:

> Yet still between his Darkness and his Brightness
> There passed a mutual glance of great politeness

and the pact was sealed by a common interest in literature and a common preoccupation with the cause of freedom. On the evening of their first meeting Shelley was invited to dine; and Polidori, who during the earlier part of the day had been out alone in a boat nursing a fit of temper, had his first glimpse of the author of *Queen Mab*—"bashful, shy, consumptive [he noted] . . . separated from his wife; keeps the two daughters of Godwin, who practise his theories; one L.B.'s." Next morning, Shelley returned the invitation and Polidori was presented to the poet's mistress. All dined together on May 29 and, the following day, met for breakfast after rising late. Shelley talked at length of his early sufferings; and Polidori heard that he had "gone through much misery," that his father had attempted to confine him in a madhouse, and that, under the impression he was a dying man, he had "married a girl for the mere sake of letting her have the jointure that would accrue to her," but had then recovered and "found he could not agree." In fact, Shelley was not and had never been consumptive; nor was there much foundation for the statement that he had married Harriet because he believed that his case was desperate and only decided to leave her when he recovered his health. The truth was somewhat cruder and less romantic; but Shelley, though in many respects remarkably shrewd, was on the whole of an exceedingly gullible temperament and just as often deluded by himself as deceived by others.

Soon the breakfasts and dinners became a habit; Mary, always eager to improve her mind, construed Italian verse with Polidori; and the five of them were rowed on the lake till the sun had gone down. Claire, who had a pretty voice, would be asked to sing, and diurnal reality dissolved into crepuscular sentiment; or they listened in silence to the drip of the oar-blades, breathed the "living fragrance" of lakeside meadows, which drifted out with the stridulation of summer insects, while mysterious sounds murmured in the woods above:

> There seems a floating whisper on the hill,
> But that is fancy . . .

Once, when a sudden squall ruffled the waters and the boatmen were struggling against a north-east wind, Byron, to whom a hint of danger was always exhilarating, proposed that he should render an Albanian song. ". . . Be sentimental," he shouted, "and give me all your attention." But "it was a strange, wild howl that he gave forth," afterward laughing at his companions' disappointment; they had expected a dulcet Eastern melody in the manner of Southey or Tom Moore. Now and then they landed to stroll by the water's edge, and Byron, on these occasions, was inclined to lag behind—he hated walking because it drew attention to his lameness—and "lazily trailed" his sword-stick with an abstracted air. Through the dank chill of an Alpine evening, they would row back to Sécheron, and there finish the day with tea and politics and verse and ghost-stories.

At the end of May, Shelley, Mary, and their household, which numbered, besides Claire, their child and its nursemaid, moved from the hotel to a small property five or six minutes' walk from the Villa Diodati, known as Campagne Chapuis or Campagne Montalègre. Byron transported his more cumbrous retinue to Diodati some fortnight later; and on June 23, leaving the women and Polidori—the latter most fortunately had sprained his ankle—Byron and Shelley set sail in the boat they shared, having determined to circumnavigate the Lake of Geneva. It was an expedition through the literary past they had both inherited; for on the twenty-fifth, coasting along the southern shore, they ran before a fresh gale to the village of Meillerie and entered the poetic landscape of *La Nouvelle Héloïse*. Byron had had the forethought to bring the novel with him; Mrs. Byron had once discovered a resemblance to Rousseau in her equally difficult and exacting son and, though Byron had often disclaimed the parallel, he was deeply moved by the misfortunes of Julie and Saint-Preux and stirred, in spite of himself, by his earliest glimpses of Clarens and Chillon, beneath their chestnut woods and black pine forests and glistening snow-peaks. After dining at Meillerie, they re-embarked; but the storm had risen, the waves on the lake had grown more turbulent, sheets of foam danced in front of them and streamed behind them; their vessel, half swamped, was on the point of sinking; and Byron began hurriedly to strip off his coat. He was a good swimmer. Shelley, who had never learned to swim, though he was passionately devoted to rowing and sailing, followed his example, but then folded his arms and otherwise declined to budge. Fear (he explained subsequently) had been a subordinate feeling. In its place, he experienced a "mixture of sensations" which would have been less painful had he not been alarmed and humiliated by a conviction that Byron might risk his life by attempting to save him. "Positively refusing" any offer of help, he sat down (according to another account) upon a locker, stubbornly grasped the rings at either end, and announced that he proposed to sink "without a struggle." Shelley's attraction to and courtship of death must be analysed elsewhere; for the moment his gesture remained indefinite. In a few minutes the boat had been got under control again, the sail—released by a frightened boatman—had been recaptured, and they drove back, shaken but stimulated, to the port of Saint-Gingoux.

Next day they sailed out as far as the source of the Rhône. The weather had broken among the mountains; the "live thunder" leapt and reverberated from crag to crag; and the big rain thrashed down onto the water's surface which, after dark, seethed with a phosphorescent glow. For two rainy dismal days they were storm-bound at Ouchy; but they visited, nevertheless, the Castle of Chillon (where Bonnivard's dungeon proved immensely impressive), paid a passing tribute to the shade of Voltaire:

> The one was fire and fickleness, a child
> Most mutable in wishes, but in mind
> A wit as various—gay, grave, sage or wild—
> Historian, bard, philosopher, combined;

> He multiplied himself among mankind,
> The Proteus of their talents: But his own
> Breathed most in ridicule—which, as the wind,
> Blew where it listed, laying all things prone—
> Now to o'erthrow a fool, and now to shake a throne,

and ventured into the deserted garden of Gibbon's house, where Byron plucked rose- and acacia-leaves to send home to Murray. A melancholy place, dishevelled and derelict; yet it was on this terrace and in this summer-house (now fallen into ruins) that the third member of the mighty Genevan trinity had

> . . . Shaped his weapon with an edge severe,
> Sapping a solemn creed with solemn sneer

—piling up antithesis against weighty antithesis, elaborating an endless series of splendid paragraphs, dignified yet full of the movement and drama of history, each sentence concisely turned yet expressive and fluent; till an evening came when the gigantic work was at length concluded, and Gibbon, uplifted by an immense relief but suffering at the same time a feeling of enormous loneliness, walked out along the moonlit paths of his garden:

After laying down my pen, I took several turns in a *berceau*, or covered walk of acacias, which commands a prospect of the country, the lake, and the mountains. The air was temperate, the sky was serene, the silver orb of the moon was reflected from the waters, and all nature was silent. I will not dissemble the first emotions of joy on the recovery of my freedom, and, perhaps, the establishment of my fame. But my pride was soon humbled, and a sober melancholy was spread over my mind, by the idea that I had taken an everlasting leave of an old and agreeable companion, and that whatsoever might be the future fate of my *History*, the life of the historian must be short and precarious.

It was here, too, that—fascinated by the beauty of Lady Elizabeth Foster, whom Byron knew as an antiquarian Duchess

—the writer had slumped onto his knees and proposed marriage, only to discover, the proposal refused, that his corpulence made it quite impossible to rise to his feet again. Shelley had little use for the graces of Gibbon—his cool Augustan mastery of the English language, in which sense dictated the choice of every epithet and yet sober common sense assumed the quality of inspiration; he preferred the romantic vagaries of Julie and Saint-Preux. During the early morning, while Byron still lay in bed, he would be scrambling uphill among rocks and meadows, gathering such flowers as he had never seen in England and "hunting the water-falls" which dropped in ravelled threads from the cliffs above. . . . Finally, "after two days of pleasant sailing," on Sunday the thirtieth of June they returned to Montalègre.

Polidori greeted them with the announcement that he had fallen in love. Neither of the poets was impressed or interested; for, so overstimulating had been the effect of Byron's society that the doctor's behaviour had grown more impossible with every passing week, and both his employer and his new friends were now heartily sick of him. He had proved touchy, bumptious, arrogant, overreaching; and the fact that he was not unaware of his own deficiencies, and sadly noted in his journal the confusion they caused, made it no easier for him to reform his conduct. So entirely out of his depth, he could not help but flounder, exploding into impertinent remarks that he at once regretted, then retiring to meditate in solitude on his woes and grievances. Absurdity dogged him from morning to midnight. Even his sprained ankle had had a ridiculous history; for the accident had occurred when Byron had suggested that he ought to jump down from the low balcony on which they were both standing and give his arm to Mary Godwin, who was walking up the hill. Polidori executed a precipitate jump, but tripped and stumbled. Byron helped to carry him indoors, had prescribed cold water for the swollen joint, and had limped up to his bedroom to fetch a pillow. "Well, I did not believe you had so much feeling," was Polidori's only response to this unusual kindness.

There had been other scenes as unnecessary and as disagreeable—for instance, when Polidori out on the lake, by clumsy mismanagement of the oar he was handling, had struck Byron a sharp blow across the knee-cap. Byron had winced with pain and had turned away, then observed that he wished Polidori would be more careful, for the misadventure had hurt him a great deal. "I am glad of it," ejaculated the doctor. "I am glad to see you can suffer pain." "Let me advise you, Polidori," retorted Byron, in "a calm suppressed tone" but with not unnatural emphasis, "when you, another time, hurt anyone, not to express your satisfaction. People don't like to be told that those who give them pain are glad of it; and they cannot always command their anger. It was with some difficulty that I refrained from throwing you into the water and, but for Mrs. Shelley's presence, I should probably have done some such rash thing." This, according to Moore, was said "without ill temper"; but the snubs and checks that he occasionally administered did not prevent the young man from becoming violently jealous of Shelley and, at one moment, actually challenging him to fight a duel. Shelley, as a convinced pacifist, had laughed and refused; but Byron, half laughing and half angry, had felt obliged to remind Polidori that, although his friend might have scruples about duelling, he himself had none (as he had already proved) and would be willing at any time to act as Shelley's substitute!

Yet it is difficult not to sympathize with the feelings of Polidori—tormented by desires and ambitions he could never satisfy, baffled by the dazzling superiority of Byron's talents. Sometimes he revolted against his spiritual servitude. What could Byron do, he had inquired furiously, that was beyond his power? "Why, since you force me to say," answered Byron, "I think there are three things . . ."; and when Polidori demanded that he should name them: "I can swim across that river—I can snuff out that candle with a pistol-shot at a distance of twenty paces—and I have written a poem of which fourteen thousand copies were sold in one day." [4] No wonder that, after a particularly humiliating squabble, Polidori had rushed up to his room, selected a phial of poison from his medicine chest, and was only hesitating over the composition of a farewell letter when Byron tapped on the door and entered with extended hand. Poor Polidori had burst out crying, and he admitted afterward that nothing could have exceeded Lord Byron's kindness "in soothing his mind and restoring him to composure." But dark thoughts of suicide still hung about him, and he moved fretfully and unhappily through their daily routine, clinging yet cantankerous, aggressive yet diffident. When he submitted a tragedy he had begun to the assembled circle and Byron volunteered to read it aloud—halting, now and then, to praise it "most vehemently" but usually winding up his praises with the somewhat tepid declaration: "I assure you, when I was in the Drury Lane Committee, much worse things were offered to us"—while Polidori's eyes wandered anxiously from face to face, always on the look-out for an incipient smile, he failed to achieve the triumph his conceit demanded and sank into even profounder depths of nervous misery. It is characteristic of such a condition that one should long

[4] Byron was referring to the success of *The Corsair*, published in 1814.

to please—that the heart should be overflowing with affection and good-will—but that the means of pleasing should grow more impracticable as the desire increases.

His fate might be ignominious; it was by no means tedious. Shelley's irresponsible and hectic fervour and the half-imaginary tale of his early sufferings, Byron's dark moods and teasing wit, Mary's exalted devotion to Shelley, and Claire's much more interested yearning for Byron, were all mirrored on the troubled surface of the young man's mind. Names and images crowded his imagination; and the journal which he had begun in such an ambitious style—it represented literary fame and five hundred guineas—little by little grew more brief and more fragmentary. How could he hope to do justice to such remarkable subject-matter? For instance, in mid-June, just before Byron and Shelley had set out on their expedition round the lake, the whole party had sat down to exchange ghost-stories, prompted by the translation of a German book they had all been reading.[5] It is a significant, and perhaps a disturbing, fact that, to counterbalance their dissimilarity on the moral plane, the two poets (from whom nineteenth-century literature was to derive so many of its poetic standards) were both of them profoundly superstitious and suffered from violent accesses of persecution mania which ebbed and flowed with the waxing and waning of their inward crises. In Shelley's case, the crises were accompanied by hallucinations; his mysterious persecutors were visibly present and, at least once, he had attempted to retaliate with the help of firearms. That, at any rate, seems the most plausible explanation of the strange midnight episode at Tremadoc which preceded his headlong flight to Dublin. Peacock, a sensible and trustworthy witness, had

[5] This work was entitled *Fantasmagoriana, ou Recueil d'Histoires d'Apparitions, de Spectres, Revenans, etc.*, which fell into their hands while they were kept indoors by bad weather.

noted these ebullitions of Shelley's fancy and had come to the conclusion that the perils he complained of were largely base-less. As to Byron, it is on record that, even for the purpose of a short journey from London to the suburbs, he made a point of travelling heavily armed; that he had a dagger often or always about him; that his weapons were placed within reach when he retired to bed; and that he was the victim of inexplicable midnight terrors. Laudanum and brandy may have aggravated his nervous plight; but Shelley, who abhorred any kind of stimulant, led, comparatively speaking, a blameless existence, and his spiritual maladies had a deeper and less objective origin—in some fundamental disequilibrium of the poet's psyche. Though at times he was apt to prove himself uncommonly sensible, his grasp of reality was often precarious; and the long conversations that he enjoyed with Byron on such subjects as the first principle of life, the possibility of reanimating a dead body, galvanism, and other exciting and alarming topics, scattered sparks on his combustible imagination till it blazed up into a nerve-storm of unusual violence. Polidori was the startled witness of these curious happenings and in his diary made a brief note of the scene and its background.

Twelve o'clock was the hour, on June 18. The evening had been spent in ghostly gossip, and at midnight Byron helped further to obscure the atmosphere by repeating certain lines from Coleridge's *Christabel*:

> Beneath the lamp the lady bowed,
> And slowly rolled her eyes around;
> Then drawing in her breath aloud,
> Like one that shuddered, she unbound
> The cincture from beneath her breast;
> Her silken robe, and inner vest,
> Dropt to her feet, and full in view,

> Behold! Her bosom and half her side—
> A sight to dream of . . .

He was interrupted by a piercing shriek from Shelley. Grasping his ruffled head between desperate hands, the poet staggered to his feet, caught up a candlestick, and flitted through the door into darkness beyond. Followed and pacified with a douche of cold water and a whiff of ether, he presently explained that he had been gazing at Mary when he remembered a story he had been told of a woman who "had eyes instead of nipples, which taking hold of his mind horrified him. . . ."

Byron did not confine himself to the relation of ghost-stories. He also talked, vaguely but expansively, of his early life, divagated on his adventures in Eastern countries, and described how, when he was living in Constantinople, he had had an unfaithful concubine sewn up in a sack and tossed into the Bosporus. "Thirza" (he said) was a girl whom he had seduced and by whom he had had two children. When he refused to marry her, she had committed suicide; and Byron added that he had "fretted very much . . . but nothing, not even that, would have made him marry her because she was of mean birth." Though Shelley hastened to assure his companions it was "all untrue" [6] and derived merely from "a childish love of astonishing people and creating a sensation," he was himself a little shocked by Childe Harold's heterodoxy and, on July 17, gravely reported to Peacock that Lord Byron was "an exceedingly interesting person" but "a slave to the vilest and most vulgar prejudices, and as mad as the winds." He might not approve; to withhold his admiration he found impossible. The force of Byron's genius seemed to overwhelm him, till he had begun to lose faith in the existence of his own abilities. But so

[6] Byron had remained in Constantinople for a little more than two months—from May 14 to mid-July 1810.

generous was his nature that he felt no bitterness. To him, as to the other members of the circle, Byron was an object of absorbing interest, changeable, fascinating, pettish, intolerant: very masculine in his attitude toward the opposite sex (whom he professed to regard sometimes as vassals and playthings), yet feminine, too, in his susceptibility and his need for affection. One moment he would be rendering an Albanian ballad (by his friends he was at this time nicknamed "Albé") and the next trying the effect of some perverse opinion, with illustrations and embellishments deliberately designed to appal. Bad enough that he should have been responsible for murder and suicide—these offences had a fine colouring of romantic frenzy —but he had refused to marry his mistress because her birth was humble!

So, indeed, were the origins of his present favourite. But even though marriage had not been out of the question, Claire would scarcely have expected that Byron should make her his wife, since she laughed at the conventional ties imposed by society. Nor did she hope that he would remain exactly constant. Here again, her views were advanced and altruistic; and already, before Byron arrived at Sécheron, she had informed him that, were he to fall in love with Mary (who, she admitted, was "very handsome and very amiable") and be "blest in his attachment" (as no doubt he would be), he need have no fear that he would find her jealous or obstructive. Quite the contrary —"I will redouble my attentions to please her. . . ." What she did expect was some conspicuous tribute to her romantic self-esteem, that she should be allowed the conviction that she was enacting a distinguished role. But this small mercy her lover persistently declined to grant. He neither pretended to a degree of passion he did not experience nor troubled to disguise the acute boredom from which he often suffered. *"Poor thing,"* he had called her in his "most gentle tone," but *"little fool"* or *"little fiend"* when she pursued and badgered him.

He was lazy: he "hated bother": he distrusted sentiment. Besides, the shattering events of the last year had been such as to disable him for effusive feeling: they had left his heart bruised to numbness, his emotions exhausted. Who was Claire that she should imagine that she could bring him to life again? Tact was not a quality she had ever boasted. He abhorred women who ran after him—as women were apt to do—yet no sooner had he arrived at the Hôtel d'Angleterre than his mistress was pestering him with impatient notes, demanding to know how he could be "so very unkind" and reminding him that he could no longer allege, as once in London, that he was "overwhelmed with business" and had not a moment free. "I have been in this weary hotel this fortnight" (she lamented); but Byron was in no hurry for a private reunion. Would he not go "straight up to the top of the house . . . at half-past seven and I will infallibly be on the landing place and show you the room. Pray do not ask any of the servants to conduct you for they might take you to Shelley's room which would be very awkward." Thanks more to Shelley's charm than to her own attractions, she soon succeeded in re-establishing her place as bed-fellow; but the relationship was hardly flattering or satisfactory. He endured her importunate attentions: he did not welcome them. And, when she had hurried up from Chapuis to Diodati, as likely as not she would find Polidori continuing to hold the floor. Could not Byron (protested Claire) get rid of the doctor? He might be deputed to compile a dictionary "or visit his ladylove." But the poet remained curiously impervious either to hints or to pleas. He was difficult of access; his doctor omnipresent. Byron's apathy grew more pronounced, and his interest fainter.

Yet as a literary copyist Claire was useful. The poems that he was finishing needed transcription; and from time to time she walked up from the vineyards below to make a fair draft of his scrawled and disordered manuscripts. Once Byron had checked her with an abrupt inquiry. Did she not think, he had asked, that he was "a terrible person"? No, Claire replied loyally, she would not believe it. He had then unlocked a cabinet and had spread a number of his sister's letters upon a table. He had opened some and had invited her to read them. But, although "the beginning was ordinary enough—common news of their friends, her health"—these passages were followed by "long spaces written in cyphers which he said only he and she had the key of—and unintelligible to all other people." They had begun to collect the letters and put them aside, when Byron had suddenly announced that there was one letter missing and had accused Claire of having stolen it: "He was extremely agitated." Claire, however, protested that she had done nothing of the sort and begged that Byron would look through the papers again, which he did until he had found the missing document and immediately apologized for having suspected her. "I mentioned the cyphers to Mary and Shelley but the latter said they most likely were used to convey news of his illegitimate children—I supposed so too and thought no more of Mrs. Leigh. . . ."

Though his relationship with its inmates remained his chief diversion, Campagne Chapuis was not the only house that Byron visited. For example, he was often to be found at Coppet, where an old London acquaintance, Germain de Staël, was passing the last months of her exhilarating and troubled career. Her daughter Albertine, whom she had tried unsuccessfully to market in England—"a beautiful, dirty-skinned woman [Polidori noted]; pleasant, soft-eyed speaker; dances well, waltzes"

—was now married off to the Duc de Broglie. And with her daughter and her son-in-law and her own youthful and exceed‑ingly good-looking second husband, Madame de Staël con‑tinued to preside over crowded gatherings, packed with Ge‑nevan dignitaries and fashionable foreign tourists. Her energy and her love of life were still undaunted. Hers was the volubil‑ity that only Death can quiet. Death, indeed, was preparing his supreme extinguisher; but meanwhile, squat, courageous, in‑defatigable, she poured forth the same overwhelming flood of talk that had deafened and delighted her English audiences. Toward Byron her attitude was both admiring and critical. With the hardihood that is the concomitant of a certain insensi‑tiveness, she even lectured him on his behaviour to Lady Byron;[7] and Byron listened patiently and nodded obediently. Madame de Staël (he knew) was a generous and good-hearted woman; and for the spoiled celebrity who had sat through din‑ner parties with half-closed eyes, whom she had once declared to be a demon in human shape, she now revealed an almost maternal kindness. No doubt she was not displeased that at least one of his visits should have been distinguished by a scene in the romantic manner. He had been invited, as he thought, to a family party; but when he entered he saw that the room was crowded with strangers, who had come to stare at him (he com‑plained bitterly) "as at some outlandish beast." Mrs. Hervey, aged sixty-five, a sister of Beckford, had swooned away with the wild emotions induced by seeing him!

Later, she rallied sufficiently to return for a closer view. But Byron, though he appreciated Madame de Staël, was never quite at his ease in the Coppet circle—it expected far too much in speech and sentiment. True (as he told Augusta) the hostess

[7] With Madame de Staël's encouragement he made an abortive attempt at reconciliation.

had been "particularly kind and friendly . . . and (I hear) fought battles without number in my very indifferent cause." He was amused to have her impressions of *Glenarvon*, Caroline Lamb's pathetic and preposterous story—concerning which she reported "marvellous and grievous things"—and glad to observe the Duchesse de Lauzun's happiness—"nothing [he remarked pensively] is more pleasing than to see the development of the domestic affections in a very young woman"; yet he was not sorry to descend to less exalted spheres. English acquaintances suited him better. During the early part of August there arrived in Switzerland, on his way home from the huge plantations he had inherited in Jamaica, Matthew Gregory Lewis, a slight, wispy, boyish-looking man, with large, bulging, curiously flattened eyeballs which projected from his cranium like the eyes of an insect. Strange that this unimpressive and often tedious person should have produced one of the most shocking best-sellers of the age in which he lived! Byron's susceptibilities were easily ruffled; and, after "reading the worst parts of *The Monk*" in 1813, he had remarked that they "might have been written by Tiberius at Caprea . . . the *philtered* ideas of a jaded voluptuary . . . all the sour cream of cantharides," and that it was inconceivable that Lewis should have composed such a work before he was twenty-one. In private life the author was prosy and sentimental. But, "damned bore" though he might be, Byron was fond of him and, after presenting Lewis to Shelley on August 14, he joined him in a short pilgrimage to the house of Voltaire. On the eighteenth, there was another meeting at Diodati and the company plunged deep into a discussion of spiritualism. Neither Byron nor Lewis would admit that he believed in ghosts; but Shelley, who since boyhood had been the familiar of phantoms, adopted a point of view that was more irrational and more poetic. He did not agree that it was impossible to believe in ghosts without believing in God—personally he was both a spiritualist and a convinced agnostic—and he did not think "that all the persons who profess to discredit these visitations, really discredit them; or, if they do in the daylight, are not admonished, by the approaches of loneliness and midnight, to think more respectfully of the world of shadows." Under the influence of his revolutionary acquaintances the rich slave-owner decided that he should change his will; and according to a codicil dated August 20, 1816, and witnessed by Byron, Shelley, and Polidori, he laid down that the inheritor of his Jamaican estates must pass at least three months every three years upon the property, that not a single Negro should be sold or disposed of, and no "comforts or indulgences" abrogated that he had himself decreed.

Byron at the time was expecting Hobhouse and Scrope Davies; and it was perhaps just as well that the appearance of John Cam should have been preceded by the departure of the Shelley *ménage;* for though Hobhouse might not have disapproved of the association on the grounds of morality—he was above all things, he liked to assure himself, a hard-headed man of the world—he had as much Tory prejudice as could be squared with Whiggish principles. His liberalism had been acquired at Cambridge and in the school of Holland House. Shelley's Cockney friends and Godwinian fantasies were equally abhorrent to this staunch scion of the English upper middle class who was afterward to earn the execration of the British army, and become notorious through the ranks as "Bloody Jack," by his persistent refusal to abolish flogging. He would have appreciated neither the ghost-stories nor the irreligion, and might have displayed little patience with Shelley's theory that mankind, being at bottom naturally good, at any moment, by a common exertion of will-power, could restore to earth the reign of peace and happiness. But Shelley during August had received a summons from his lawyer calling him back to London and, in the last week of that month, he set out with his household, travelling to Paris by way of Dijon and pausing to visit Versailles and Fontainebleau, which inspired him to appropriate reflexions on "the hollow show of monarchy" as he explored the vast solitudes of park and palace. Among the responsibilities that he took to England—together with a load of Byron's manuscripts, which he had been commissioned to deliver to Mr. Murray—was one at least that the friend he left behind might have more suitably shouldered: the immediate problem of Claire Clairmont and the child she was carrying.

Just when she had discovered that she was pregnant we cannot exactly tell—nor in what manner the news was conveyed to Shelley. There was some explanation, however, between Shelley and Byron; and Shelley, by whom the difficulties of persons he liked or loved were as a matter of course taken over to increase his own, immediately volunteered to escort Claire homeward and to harbour and protect her until she had borne her child. Naturally, it was an arrangement that suited Byron. There could be no question of allowing Claire to become a fixture; and, since he had never welcomed her assiduities and demonstrably had done nothing to raise her hopes, he considered that he was under no obligation to respect her feelings. Besides, she had involved him in yet another scrape. It was bad enough to be pursued by English tourists, to be obliged to edge past their carriages on some mountain road and see the green veils lifted and the eyebrows raised. It was intolerable to learn that with the help of spy-glasses they had scanned the façade of the Villa Diodati and had mistaken some tablecloths hanging from a balustrade for "robes and flounces"—an indication

of the populous seraglio within its walls! He learned, moreover, that news had gone back to England that he and that notorious atheist, young Mr. Shelley, had established a satanic
"league of incest" and were living with two sisters "in pro-
miscuous intercourse," though on the whole his way of existence had been mild and reasonable. And, when he received a
flurried letter from Mrs. Leigh, who had several motives for
alarm at the rumours circulating, he dispatched a succinct account of his latest love-affair:

. . . As to all these "mistresses" [he protested on September 8],
Lord help me—I have had but one. Now don't scold; but what could
I do?—a foolish girl, in spite of all I could say or do, would come
after me, or rather went before—for I found her here—and I have
had all the plague possible to persuade her to go back again. . . .
Now, dearest, I do most truly tell thee, that I could not help this, that
I did all I could to prevent it. . . . I was not in love . . . but I
could not exactly play the stoic with a woman, who had scrambled
eight hundred miles to unphilosophize me. Besides, I had been re-
galed with so many "two courses and a *desert*" (Alas!) of aversion,
that I was fain to take a little love (if pressed particularly). . . .

The sequel he reserved for a later missive:

I forgot to tell you that the demoiselle who returned to England
from Geneva went there to produce a new baby B. . . .

Thereupon, he turned to the society of the new arrivals.
After the stimulating yet exhausting companionship of Shelley,
Hobhouse's solidity and Davies's cynicism came over him like
a breath of his carefree London past—a whiff of fog and steam-
ing "Regency punch" and midnight candle-grease. He was determined they should not find him changed or saddened; and
Hobhouse, always resolute in his pursuit of the commonplace
and eager to discount his friend's extravagances, was able to
send a reassuring report to England. ". . . Your excellent
relative [he told Augusta] is living with the strictest attention

to decorum. . . ." The tablecloths, he could promise, had *not* been petticoats; and "in sober sadness I can give you very good accounts from this place, both as to morals and other material points. A considerable change has taken place in his health; no brandy, no very late hours, no quarts of magnesia, nor deluges of soda water. Neither passion nor perverseness . . . he seems as happy as he ought to be; by this of course you will see that I mean, as happy as it is consistent for a man of honour and common feeling to be after the occurrence of a calamity involving a charge, whether just or unjust, against his honour and his feeling."

Davies was in a hurry to get back to England; but he had time enough, with Byron, Hobhouse, and the doctor, to make an expedition from Diodati to Chamonix, during which Byron, opening the visitors' book at Montavert and finding Shelley's name followed by the self-description: *atheist*,[8] thought it worth his while to remove the entry. . . . Davies's departure coincided with the doctor's dismissal. The experiment of engaging him had been a failure from start to finish; but again Byron was not regardless of the young man's *amour propre*. And he had "determined upon our parting [wrote Polidori], not upon any quarrel, but on account of our not suiting. Gave me £70. . . ." In a letter to Murray several months later, Byron's references to his attendant were fair and charitable. The doctor, he explained, understood his profession well and had no want of general ability. "His faults are the faults of a pardonable vanity and youth. His remaining with me was out of the question. I have enough to do to manage my own scrapes; and, as precepts without example are not the most gracious homilies, I thought it better to give him his *congé:* but I know no great harm of him, and some good." Subsequently, however,

[8] Shelley's original inscription was in Greek.

addressing the same correspondent, Byron's animadversion upon poor dear "Pollydolly" was a trifle more splenetic. In retrospect he wondered that he had been able to endure him; for "I never was much more disgusted with any human production than with the eternal nonsense and *tracasseries* and emptiness and ill-humour and vanity of that young person: but he has some talent, and is a man of honour, and has dispositions of amendment in which he has been aided by a little subsequent experience, and may turn out well."

Polidori took his leave on September 16; and, as soon as they were free of him, Byron and Hobhouse set out on an extended tour. For thirteen long stormy exciting days, often drenched to the skin, in danger of tumbling down precipices, among "Glaciers, Clouds, and Summits of eternal snow," they wound their way through the pinnacles of the Bernese Alps. It was such scenery as stirred Byron to the depths of his consciousness. The vacancy and inhumanity of mountain landscape, untrodden by man and untainted by the reminder of human virtues and vices, afforded his towering egotism the scope it needed. Yet only in intensity—not in attitude—are Byron's descriptions of the scenes he passed through to be distinguished from the eloquent and romantic letters that Gray and Walpole had sent home almost eighty years earlier. "Not a precipice, not a torrent, not a cliff" but was pregnant with ideas of "religion and poetry," wrote Gray in anticipation of *The Prelude;* while Walpole, the less philosophic of the two companions, who was apt to regard the Alps as a prodigious picture-gallery hung with masterpieces in the style of Salvator Rosa, fell into ecstasies over the "silver speed" of water-falls, mountainsides "obscured with pines or lost in clouds," desolate ruined hermitages and tottering foot-bridges. The Romantic point of view had certainly preceded the Romantic Movement; and the essence of Byron's genius was not a manner of feeling so much as the sheer energy with which he felt and suffered—his incomparable aptitude for self-projection, combined with a degree of self-absorption no less extraordinary.

Beneath an air of apparent calm, he was living at the time in a state of almost continual nervous tension; and very unlike Hobhouse's reassuring report to Mrs. Leigh is Byron's own account of the condition of his mind and heart during the summer and autumn months of 1816. Incessantly he turned over thoughts of his late disaster. And now he raged furiously against his wife, the authoress (he sometimes persuaded himself) of all his miseries. Now remorse tortured him and he felt that he had accomplished the total ruin—impelled who could say by what ancestral curse?—of the human being he had loved most tenderly and most unselfishly.[9] Now he came face to face with an appalling conviction that he could neither justify nor repent of the harm he had done, and stared down as from a cliff's edge into the moral void.[10] He was alarmed, yet fascinated, by the conflict within him. Even by the exercise of rigorous self-control—a quality he had seldom troubled to display—it seemed a nearly hopeless task to keep hold of his sanity;

[9] She was like me in lineaments; her eyes,
Her hair, her features, all, to the very tone
Even of her voice, they said were like to mine;
But soften'd all, and temper'd into beauty:
She had the same lone thoughts and wanderings . . .
Pity, and smiles, and tears—which I had not;
And tenderness—but that I had for her;
Humility—and that I never had.
Her faults were mine—her virtues were her own—
I loved her, and destroy'd her!

[10] There is a power upon me which withholds,
And makes it my fatality to live,—
If it be life to wear within myself
This barrenness of spirit . . .
　　　　　　　　For I have ceased
To justify my deeds unto myself—
The last infirmity of evil.

and there were moments when he felt that his grasp was weakening. He had been "half mad," he declared later of this period, "between metaphysics, mountains, lakes, love unextinguishable, thoughts unutterable, and the nightmare of my own delinquencies. I should, many a good day, have blown my brains out, but for the recollection that it would have given pleasure to my mother-in-law. . . ." Yet, as once before, the interest of self-observation—and to some extent, perhaps, the charms of self-dramatization—proved stronger than the impulse that counselled suicide; and, like Manfred, he started back from the lip of the precipice. The tempest that had been gathering at Diodati, and had had its origins in the now far-off days at Piccadilly Terrace, exhausted its vehemence among the crags of the Jura. He returned to the lakeside refreshed and reconciled.

With him he brought the journal he had kept from day to day —a strange document, fragmentary, unself-conscious, in which every image reflects the mood of the writer and every flash of poetry has a certain colouring of desperation. His sense of beauty was instinct with a sense of terror—reflected even by the cold glassy surface of a lonely mountain lake, "in the very nipple of the bosom of the Mountain." The clouds which boiled up from the valleys below, "curling up perpendicular precipices," were "like the foam of the Ocean of Hell, during a Springtide . . . white, and sulphury, and immeasurably deep. . . ." A torrent, as it leapt from a rock, suggested "the *tail* of a white horse streaming in the wind, such as it might be conceived would be that of the '*pale* horse' on which *Death* is mounted in the Apocalypse. . . . Neither mist nor water . . . its immense height . . . gives it a wave, a curve, a spreading here, a condensation there, wonderful and indescribable." A glacier was compared to "*a frozen hurricane*"; and, the same day, when they passed *"whole woods of withered pines, all withered*; trunks stripped and barkless, branches lifeless . . . their appearance reminded me of me and my family." During the greater part of the expedition, Byron rode a mare he had recently purchased—"young and as quiet as any thing of her sex can be—very good-tempered, and perpetually neighing when she wants any thing, which is every five minutes . . . a very tame pretty childish quadruped"; but the steeper slopes he sometimes ascended on foot, struggling along gallantly in his companion's footsteps, till the sweat rained from his forehead onto a patch of snow, "making the same dints as in a sieve." Regularly an avalanche roared down the mountainside; and, when the reverberation of its passage had died away, his ear would catch the piping of a shepherd—"very different from *Arcadia* (where I saw the pastors with a long Musquet instead of a Crook, and pistols in their Girdles). Our Swiss Shepherd's pipe was sweet, and his tune agreeable." On September 25, the party arrived at Thun and the more interesting stages of the tour were finished. On the twenty-ninth Byron completed his journal with a postscript addressed to Augusta Leigh, by whom, for reasons that will afterward become clear, it was received with somewhat mixed and painful feelings: ". . . In all this [he wrote]—the recollections of bitterness have preyed upon me here; and neither the music of the Shepherd, the crashing of the Avalanche, nor the torrent, the mountain, the Glacier, the Forest, nor the Cloud, have for one moment lightened the weight upon my heart, nor enabled me to lose my own wretched identity. . . . I am past reproaches; and there is a time for all things. . . . *To* you, dearest Augusta, I send, and *for* you I have kept this record. . . . Love me as you are beloved by me."

Chapter Two

THAT autumn, in a symbolic as well as in a geographical sense, Byron turned his back upon the mountains. From lakeshores and pine-forests and radiant snow-peaks— and the ardours of thought and the extremes of suffering with which in his imagination they had become associated—he dropped down to a warmer and more prosaic level. On October 6, accompanied by Hobhouse, he left Diodati, crossed the Simplon, and emerged among the vines and poplar trees of the Lombard plain. A dull but easy journey brought them to Milan, the rich, busy, music-loving metropolis that Henri Beyle (now tired of a military life and somewhat satiated with Napoleonic grandeurs since he had endured the long-drawn-out horror of the retreat from Moscow) was to describe as the gayest and pleasantest in the whole of Italy. Nowhere else (considered that supremely romantic realist) could the Italian way of living and the many genial qualities that flourished in the Italian soul be observed more commodiously or to greater advantage. Here the Italian system of sentiment was carried to perfection. Less priest-ridden than the aristocracy of the Papal States, not so vitiated by sunshine as the inhabitants of Naples on whom weighed the rule of a Bourbon despot, less frivolous and less depraved than the Venetians, the Milanese were friendly, vivacious, passionate, devoted to music and eloquence and the arts of love, the latter being cultivated with a peculiar thoroughness and dignified with an almost religious ceremony. Thus, violent jealousy might be permitted to the lover, but was ridiculous and unbecoming when displayed by the husband, whom decency enjoined to respect the lover's rights. Here reigned a kind of ordered promiscuity which, in Beyle's opinion, gave scope to some of the finest qualities of heart and intelligence. Better still, since Italian society disdained concealment and deep passion for its own sake was condoned and recognized, Milan from the point of view of an itinerant novelist suggested the convexity of a crystal beehive, swarming from within with strange stories and dramatic anecdotes.

The central chamber of the hive was the splendid opera house; and to the Scala Byron resorted soon after his arrival. He noted the cliques, the air of intrigue, the constant whisper and ceaseless coming and going between gilded boxes; and he was a little taken aback when in a conspicuous part of the house a mother and son were pointed out to him and pronounced by his informant to be "of the Theban dynasty. . . . The narrator (one of the first men in Milan) seemed to be not sufficiently scandalized by the taste or the tie." At Milan, moreover, who should reappear but Dr. Polidori! Evidently much relieved to have escaped from Byron's shadow, the doctor was cutting a decided dash in Italian society (where his swart good looks and his glib tongue were important assets) and, but for his gift of making the wrong move, might have continued to do so. Alas, his fatal genius pursued him even to the opera house. Byron had received him with particular kindness and had gone to the trouble of correcting an English essay which he intended to publish in *The Pamphleteer*. The bad impression he had made at Diodati was almost forgotten, till one night, in a party at the Scala, Polidori, Hobhouse, and a young Italian acquaintance happened to descend into the pit to watch the ballet, while Byron remained talking in a box above. Lombardy, at the time, was an Austrian vassal state; and between Polidori and the dancers on the stage there arose the tall figure of an Austrian officer, wearing his great-coat and a grenadier's shako. Polidori, by tradition at least, was an Italian patriot; and, touching the intruder upon the arm, he requested firmly that he would be so kind as to remove his head-covering. "You would like me to?" said the Austrian. "Yes, I should like you to!" replied Polidori in imperative tones. His antagonist, who, as it most unfortunately turned out, was the officer on guard at the theatre that evening, proposed that Polidori should accompany him; to which Polidori, delighted at the prospect of a duel, immediately consented—only to be shoved and hustled through the guard-room door. Declamations followed, protests, floods of "Billingsgate German," and much consternation along corridors and among the boxes. Head over heels in a "philosophical argument on the principle of utility," Beyle (who had met Byron some days earlier [1]) saw the poet Silvio Pellico run up "in breathless haste to apprise Lord Byron that his friend and physician Polidori had been arrested." A large company, including a number of Italian *literati*, loyally accompanied them to the near-by guard-room, where Polidori was discovered "beside himself with passion . . . his face red as a burning coal," still declaring violently against the wrong he had suffered. "Byron, though he too was in a violent rage, was on the

---

[1] "*J'ai dîné avec un joli et charmant jeune homme, figure de dix-huit ans, quoiqu'il en ait 28, profil d'un ange, l'air le plus doux. C'est l'original de Lovelace, ou plutôt mille fois mieux que le bavard Lovelace. . . . C'est le plus grand poète vivant, Lord Byron.*" Stendhal, *Correspondance*, 20.X.1816.

contrary pale as ashes. His patrician blood boiled as he reflected on the slight consideration in which he was held." There ensued a wild uproar of conflicting voices: the Austrian summoned his men, who began to seize their weapons; then the poet Monti stood forth and allayed the tumult or, at any rate, produced the formula that rendered it manageable. Some ten or fifteen Italians, two Englishmen, and various Austrians had all been engaged in fierce dispute at uncomfortably close quarters. "*Sortiami tutti!*" he exclaimed. "*Restino solamente i titolati!*—Let us all leave! Let only the noblemen stay!" He was obeyed; and, while the commoners filed from the room, the noblemen inscribed their names and titles, which were handed to the wearer of the obstructive shako, who excused the affront and released Polidori from confinement. But that same evening he received an order signed by the Austrian Governor to quit Milan within the space of twenty-four hours.

Shedding tears of humiliation, "foaming with rage," and swearing that he would "one day return and bestow manual castigation on the Governor," but helpless against authority's offended might, Polidori left the city early next morning. Byron, though the *contretemps* involving a former member of his household had brought him into some discredit with the Austrian secret police, already suspicious of his alleged republican views, remained to explore Milan a few days longer before setting out again in the direction of Verona and Venice. If not contented or acquiescent, he was at least composed; but the autumn rains had given him a touch of rheumatism and—a further reminder of approaching middle age—he suffered from attacks of faintness and giddiness (which made him fear that, like Swift, he might "die at the top" first); while grey strands were multiplying among his chestnut curls. On the credit side, his teeth were in excellent order, firm and white and sound as during his heyday; but sometimes he fancied they were *"looseish,"* and the old horror of any physical blemish returned to plague him, with the old superstitious dread of age and deformity. "Would you not think [he wrote to Augusta on October 28] I was sixty instead of not quite nine and twenty?"

Yet there could be no doubt that he had benefited by his stay at Milan. Old and loyal friends had re-appeared in the persons of Lord and Lady Jersey; new acquaintances had emerged from the Italian literary world—among others, the before-mentioned Vincenzo Monti, renowned author of *La Basvigliana* (in which he had reviled the French), *Mascheroniana* (welcoming the advent of Napoleon), and subsequently of various mythological poems, written to celebrate the return of the Austrian armies. The variability of the sentiments that inspired them was only equalled by the grace and eloquence of the verses themselves; and when, at a dinner party given by the Marquis de Brême, Monti was prevailed on to recite the whole opening canto of *Mascheroniana*, Henri Beyle, still hovering in the background, noticed how Byron's usual *hauteur*—"that kind of haughty look which a man often puts on when he has to get rid of an inopportune question . . . which rather took away from the beauty of his magnificent countenance"—suddenly dissolved into "an expression of happiness. . . . Never shall I forget the sublime expression of his countenance: it was the peaceful look of power united with genius."

Beyle's deep interest in Byron was scarcely reciprocated. But then, Beyle in 1816 was not yet Stendhal—merely an argumentative and inquisitive Frenchman, sharp-eyed, square-faced, bewhiskered, stocky, who had good stories to tell of Napoleon and the campaign in Russia. To these topics he owed the conversations he held with Byron. Both were enthusiasts

for the imperial legend; and, after some preliminary mis-
understanding caused by Beyle's belief that any Englishman
must detest the Emperor, they settled down to a long and im-
passioned colloquy. But if the young Englishman's capacity
for enthusiasm did him credit, and the emotion that he displayed when he listened to poetry and music, his vanity (Beyle
considered) was strange and shocking. He was disconcerted
by Byron's frequent references to his patrician birth, by his
perverse parade of aristocratic prejudices, and by his desire
to be regarded as a dandy and a man of fashion. Brummell no
less than Napoleon was the poet's hero; and so self-conscious
was he on the subject of his own attractions, and so constantly
preoccupied with the effect they made, that there were moments when he seemed oddly impervious to the appeal of the
opposite sex. Positively he had declined an introduction to
"several young, noble, and lovely females," one of whom at
least had been eager to meet him; and, though he had gazed
in the theatre, he had retired in the ballroom, preferring masculine discussions of verse and philosophy, whether from
"pride, timidity, or a remnant of dandyism" it would have
been hard to say. Beyle, too, with many other of Byron's acquaintances, was disconcerted by the manifestations of a mysterious sense of guilt (which he hazarded might have to do
with some death connived at—the assassination perhaps of
an unfaithful Grecian slave). But, whatever the origins of his
trouble, the result was ominous: "it must be admitted that
during nearly a third of the time we passed in the poet's society, he appeared to us like one labouring under an access of
folly," which often approximated to downright madness.

In fact, the crisis was drawing to a slow conclusion. Some
reminiscent pangs, however, were still experienced; and one
day, as he explored the Ambrosian Library, he was intensely

moved by being shown the love-letters that had passed between Lucrezia Borgia and Cardinal Bembo, and a long smooth golden curl from Lucrezia's head. For the sheer satisfaction of seeing them and turning them over he re-visited the library again and again—"to the scandal of the librarian, who wanted to enlighten men with sundry valuable MSS., classical philosophical, and pious." When permission to copy the letters was refused him, he contented himself with getting by heart certain passages; and, since it was impossible to remove the hair, he took surreptitious possession of a single shining thread. Nothing in Milan had given him an equal pleasure—the hair of the dead woman "so long—and fair & beautiful," and her letters and verses "so pretty & so loving it makes one wretched not to have been born sooner to have at least seen her. And pray what do you think is one of her *signatures?* [he concluded; for he was writing to Augusta]—why this + a cross. . . . Is not this amusing?" Mrs. Leigh, he knew, would understand the reference: a cross was among the private symbols they had themselves employed. Whether she would find it amusing was somewhat more doubtful.

The charm of Milan had been exhausted by the end of October. During the first week of the following month, he was again on the road, skirted the Lago di Garda, which the travellers were able to admire "in all its vexation, foaming like a little Sea, as Virgil has described it," and paused for a brief visit to Verona, where the amphitheatre impressed him as "wonderful—beats even Greece." Though (he admitted) but an indifferent and half-hearted virtuoso, he appreciated the Gothic burial place of the Scaliger family and made an expedition to the so-called "Tomb of Juliet," a plain open stone coffin "with withered leaves in it, in a wild and desolate conventual garden, once a cemetery, now ruined to the very graves," bringing away "a few pieces of the granite, to give to my daughter and my nieces." These sights seen and relics gathered, he continued his eastward journey—the East had for Byron a special significance—reaching Venice on the eleventh of November.

There are cities that mark a definite stage in life's development. For no reason that the mind can immediately follow— sometimes through the force of beauty, now and then through the power of their impressive ugliness—they absorb and localize the workings of the imagination, till the outlines of their roof-tops, the colour and configuration of their walls, the changing yet recurrent pattern of odours and street noises, and most of all perhaps the quality of the light that clothes them, damp and concealing or sharp and crystal-clear, become associated with the mood and emotions of a particular period. Such on Byron was the effect produced by Venice. Weary of travel and sick of sight-seeing, he left the mainland, was ferried out from Mestre across the torpid lagoon, and opened his eyes, pleased and bewildered, to a new experience. Monuments, for their own sake, had ceased to interest him. Even in Greece, when he was younger and far more impressionable, he had shocked Hobhouse as they gazed up at the ruined Parthenon by observing glumly that it was "very like the Mansion House"; and since that time he had had an overdose of churches and picture-galleries.

No character, in the ordinary sense, could have been less "Victorian"; yet it is remarkable in how many of his tastes and prejudices Byron anticipated the limitations of the coming age. There was his deep, though thwarted, respect for the domestic proprieties; there was also that strain of æsthetic philistinism which made him completely insensitive to the appeal of the visual arts. In the long brilliant letters he sent back from the Continent, references to works of art are almost entirely lacking, and such references as do occur are flat and perfunctory. He might be interested by the human charm of an epitaph, moved by the memorial of some historic drama; for mere buildings, paintings, statues he had little affection. Not once, during the years he was to spend in Venice, is there any descriptive mention in his letters of its most conspicuous glories. The great murmuring grotto of St. Mark's, where every surface gleams with a smooth subaqueous lustre and the rolling pavement imitates the wave-worn floor of a submarine cavern; Verrocchio's presentation of Colleoni, with its *"vista superba"* and "piercing and terrible" eyes; the vast devotional fantasies of Tintoretto; huge sunny rooms frescoed by Tiepolo and Veronese—if not unregarded, they remained uncelebrated. They did not touch his sensibility and added nothing to the colouring of his imagination. Very different was the view of the city that so quickly captivated him—more mundane yet, in its own way, perhaps more permanent; since its foundations had been laid by Shakespeare and Otway and, behind the fascinating spectacle of its modern inhabitants, moved the tragic Jew, pitiful, proud and cringing, the jealous Moor, Pierre and Jaffier and Belvidera and the cloaked conspirators meeting on the bridge at midnight. Nor was there a dearth of activity in the immediate foreground. Venice was half-way to Greece and Turkey; and though Eastern merchants had long ceased to perambulate the Piazza San Marco, and only a red-capped Greek sailor, lounging here and there, recalled the proximity of the cities of the Levant, Venice had still a hybrid atmosphere neither of East nor of West, just as itself it was neither of earth nor of water but seemed to hover like a mirage in some mysterious middle space where sky met water, and water marble, and buildings and the reflections below them could scarcely be separated, so bright and clean was the inverted imagery of dome and palace front.

Toward the watery element, both Byron and Shelley felt a profound attraction. Shelley, though no swimmer and a clumsy sailor, was seldom happier or more carefree than by sea or stream; even a rivulet or a small pool would inspire and soothe him. Maternal yet destructive, uncontrollable by human will or human reason, the sea is an image of death and eternity; the earth, of the human mind and its finite conquests. The origins of Byron's feeling were partly matter-of-fact; and, if he loved the sea and delighted in Venice, it was because he found water a friendly medium which gratified his liking for speed and his desire for power. On land he moved awkwardly and was aware of his handicap; but when he swam his deformity was not perceptible. The limbs that balked at a dance-floor could traverse the Hellespont; he was daring and self-confident, strong and envied. Here in Venice he could minimize the effort of walking—onto the Piazza San Marco he rarely ventured—but slip indolent, cool, reflective, down endless waterways.

Besides, Venice gave him the privacy he had always wanted. No longer the city of feverish and intricate dissipation where every illicit love had its secret bolt-hole, and noble Venetians, in obscure apartments near the great piazza approached by passages of which even a gondolier could not discover the issue, led nocturnal lives unsuspected by the world and their families, it preserved something of that same atmosphere of adventurous licence which many years earlier had enchanted Beckford. But the gaiety had almost vanished, though the intrigue remained. A traveller who explored the piazza in 1816 would hardly have admired its "thoughtless giddy transport" or noted, at the hour when lamps were lit, that "anything like restraint seemed perfectly out of the question. . . . However solemn a magistrate may appear in the day [Beckford had written in 1780] he lays up wig and robe and gravity to sleep together, runs intriguing about in his gondola, takes the reigning sultana under his arm, and so rambles half over the town, which grows gayer and gayer as the day declines." Nor from his balcony as dawn was breaking could a tourist have looked down onto the Grand Canal full of barges laden to the water's edge with peaches, grapes, and melons, and observed stepping delicately from boat to boat last night's pleasure-seekers, distinguished by their masks and *tricornes*, in search of fruit to cool their palates before they retired to their morning's rest.

Since 1797, the city's decay had been very rapid. Yet even that crucial period of the Republic's agony (when the Great Council, distraught but ineffective, voted for complete submission to General Bonaparte, then threatening them from beyond the lagoon with his troops and warships, and the last Doge, the hundred and twentieth to bear the title, discarded his robes and doffed his cap of office) had merely accentuated the decline of Venetian fortunes. Venice had outlived its utility, if not its dignity. By the fall of Constantinople, the closing of the caravan roads from Asia, the development of modern ports on the western seaboard, the commercial life of the Republic had been slowly strangled, till there remained only the shadow of power without financial substance. Yet the city had derived added splendour from its increasing decrepitude; and, as their ultimate means of livelihood grew more precarious, so Venetians had made fresh advances in the arts of living, cultivating the happiness of the moment and the beauty of the present day. But now Venetian arts had followed Venetian liberty. Transferred by its conquerors to the Austrian Empire, Venice had sunk to the status of an obscure provincial town—doubly sad and doubly silent because its streets were water-paved. The slimy canal flood sucked and gurgled on deserted palace steps; huge escutcheons hung mouldering over empty doorways.

The golden horses of St. Mark's, it is true, had returned to the piazza. Having been mounted on the triumphal arches of Nero and Trajan, led in captivity from Rome to Byzantium, and from Byzantium by the Doge Dandolo to Venice, they had travelled from the Piazza San Marco to the Place du Carrousel (with other spoils of the generalissimo's Italian conquests) and journeyed back again as Napoleon's gift to an Austrian Emperor.[2] But another symbol of Venetian sovereignty had gone for good. In January 1798, "to the surprise and distress" of the Venetian populace, the *Bucentaur*,[3] the long painted and gilded two-decker used every year in the ceremonious espousals of the Republic to the Adriatic Sea, had been stripped and despoiled by their foreign masters. "All the gilt work" had been torn off and burnt in a heap on the island of San Giorgio Maggiore, and the hull degraded to various menial purposes, sometimes employed as a coastguard battery ship, sometimes moored out in the lagoon as a vulgar prison-hulk. In 1816 it still survived, but rotting and derelict: once the *panache* of the Republic's pride, now the emblem of its decadence and humiliation.

To Byron, however, these signs of decay were by no means displeasing. He had expected much of the city; it had "always been," he told Moore "(next to the East), the greenest island of my imagination. It has not disappointed me; though its

---

[2] They had been replaced in their original position a year before Byron's arrival by the Emperor Francis.

[3] This last *Bucentaur* had been built at the Venetian Arsenal in 1722 from the designs of the naval architect Michele Conti. It was finally broken up by the authorities in 1824.

evident decay would, perhaps, have that effect upon others. But I have been familiar with ruins too long to dislike desolation." Venice (he wrote a little later to John Murray) was one of those places that he felt he knew already before he saw them. He appreciated the silence of Venetian canals and "the gloomy gaiety" of quietly passing gondolas. His ear was agreeably touched by the Venetian patois—"very naïve, and soft, and peculiar, though not at all classical"—and he had immediately set to work to acquire its usages. Women of the upper class, he remarked, were not well featured—that was an observation he had made elsewhere throughout the Continent—but among the people he saw many faces that impressed and charmed him—black braids and dark eyes beneath painted eyelids, impudent appraising glances, and jetty eyebrows.

Naturally, he lost no time in beginning a love-affair—this was a method of settling down he had always favoured. It reassured him to be loved and to believe that he loved in turn; but the need was psychological rather than strictly physical, for, though Byron's appetites were impetuous and even greedy, like many other philanderers who make love their business he exploited his gift of attracting women at least as often as he employed it to gain him pleasure. Were the sexual impulse always governed by sexual motives, human relationships would present a somewhat easier study. In fact, the emotions that we find it convenient to describe as "desire" or "love" usually split up under analysis into several component passions, many of them apparently divorced from sexual feeling. Social vanity, for example, may play an exceedingly important part; and men or women who have established their own attraction tend to utilize it as a weapon against society—either as an aggressive weapon to subdue their fellows (now and then by humiliating and torturing a weaker partner) or as a means of upholding their pride and defending their self-esteem. Conversely, love may be a method of self-punishment; but here again the issues involved are far from simple; and the lover (as at times had happened to Byron) may find punishment in an acute consciousness of the harm he is doing or may create a situation in which he is bound to suffer injury, in which betrayal must succeed to confidence as night to day. Unhappy lovers are frequently lovers who seek unhappiness, suffering being the intoxicant they distil from pleasure. The physical satisfaction that the downright "sensualist" considers he aims at may be subordinate to a dozen mysterious motives, beside which the influence of desire is slight and transitory.

No theory, however comprehensive, no type, however detailed and well established, will quite cover any single human being. Infinitely monotonous yet immensely various, nature produces a thousand thousand patterns—the vast majority obedient to an established formula—yet each signed with some minute distinctive oddity. Characteristic merges into characteristic; the peculiarities of a single given type—psychological, glandular, social, literary—are curiously interwoven with the traits of another; and it is one of the most interesting features of Byron's mind and life that very few aspects of his personality (which is not to be confused with the personal legend he himself created) do not rest on some dramatic contradiction. To a combination of tremendous natural gifts and an intellect, comparatively speaking, light and shallow, we owe the absorbing spectacle his career affords us. His native intelligence was quick and strong, but at no period could he have been described as an "intellectual"; and, though his flashes of intuition were extremely vivid, whether applied to his own life or the lives of others, he failed to coordinate them in any general system. His grasp of ideas was often lax; his character, for good or bad, was not of the heroic mould, being disfigured by evasions and spiritual self-deception. Yet through the self-deception ran an astonishing vein of honesty. If there were times when the pretences he dealt in suggested deliberate humbug, there were also times when his openness amounted to shamelessness, and he stepped forth smiling and unabashed, without guile or subterfuge. He believed in the reality of his emotions as long as he felt them deeply; he did not hesitate to discard them as the occasion prompted.

Thus, in Venice, there occurred a complete overhaul of his feelings and point of view. Because his mood had been desperate and almost demented, he saw no reason why he should continue to "sup on horrors" once his nature had begun to incline him to more cheerful prospects. Soon after reaching Venice, he was violently agitated by reminders of England when a report reached him that Lady Byron considered going abroad and proposed taking with her his infant daughter Augusta Ada. Such a move, considering the condition of the Continent, would be selfish and dangerous; and he immediately wrote off several angry letters of protest, finally eliciting from his father-in-law and wife a formal declaration, delivered through his lawyer, that "there never has existed nor does there exist the remotest intention of removing Miss Byron out of the kingdom." [4] Otherwise, he had determined that he would exist in the present. Having touched the rock bottom of gloom and agony, his spirits bounded up again toward the surface, and burst out into the sunshine of an ordinary sensual life. To his surprise, he had discovered that

[4] Byron's letter of protest, to his lawyer John Hanson, is dated Venice, November 11, 1816. The final reply, signed by Anne Isabella Byron and Ralph Noel, was written on January 30 of the following year. He learned at the same time that his daughter had been made a ward in Chancery.

he could still enjoy himself. The transformation was remarkably expeditious; for he did not arrive in Venice till the eleventh of November and by the sixteenth he was already writing to Tom Moore with the information that he had recently fallen in love, "next to falling into the canal . . . the best or the worst thing I could do." Kinnaird received the same news a fortnight later, and an explanation in the letter-writer's most characteristic style—detached in tone yet with a hint of defiant jauntiness. He had intended (he wrote) to "give up gallivanting" when he said good-bye to England, "where I had been tolerably sickened of that and everything else." But, in spite of his resolutions, the old habit had somehow returned and, at the moment of writing, he could not pretend that he was sorry: ". . . I know not how it is, my health growing better, and my spirits not worse, the '*besoin d'aimer*' came back upon my heart . . . and, after all, there is nothing like it." His new mistress was "a very pretty woman," so much so that even Hobhouse thought her attractive, and—yet another advantage—she was securely married. As to the steps by which they had arrived at their present footing, he was a little vague —when he said that he had fallen in love he told no more than the literal truth: his amatory career had been all along a series of spills and stumbles. "Nevertheless . . . we do exceedingly well together."

Indeed, his choice was neither romantic nor ambitious. The "*besoin d'aimer*" had returned—that was the important thing; and very fortunately the wife of his Venetian landlord, a draper who kept a house and shop in the Frezzeria (at the sign of *Il Corno*—a name that had been changed by his apprentices to *Il Corno Inglese*), gave him any encouragement he may have felt he needed. Marianna Segati was twenty-two years old. Described by a later traveller as a "demon of avarice and libidinousness, who intrigued with every resident in the house, and every guest who visited it," she had "large, black, oriental eyes, with that peculiar expression in them . . . which many of the Turkish women give themselves by tinging the eyelid. . . ." Her temperament proved to be all that her eyes predicted. As to her features, they were "regular and rather aquiline—mouth small—skin clear and soft, with a kind of hectic colour—forehead remarkably good"; while her hair was "of the curl and colour of Lady Jersey's." Besides, she was fond of singing and had a pretty figure. But her greatest merit (Byron added, when narrating the episode to John Murray) "is finding out mine—there is nothing so amiable as discernment." Plainly, Marianna was prepared to save him trouble: no assistant could have been better suited to his scheme of forgetting the past and weaning away his fancy from re-morseful retrospect. "I am sick of sorrow [he was to write to Mrs. Leigh a few weeks later] and must even content myself as well as I can: so here goes—I won't be woeful again if I can help it."

His friends were soon made aware of this salutary deter-mination. Though Byron had often resented the publicity to which he was exposed, and loved Venice because it promised him a chance of concealment, he had by no means resigned himself to being completely forgotten. His sister, his acquaint-ances in London, and even his publisher were frequently enter-tained with glimpses of his new liaison; for, apart from his natural communicativeness and his taste for letter-writing, their amusement or disapproval would give the episode the relief it needed. Yet we cannot dismiss Byron as an amatory poseur. At least honest enough to have no thought of conceal-ing his vanity, he was also ingenuous enough to expose his vanity in its very simplest form. And there was something of defiance, too, beneath the apparent bravado. More conscious of—perhaps one might add, rather more in sympathy with—that excellent and self-righteous section of the British public which professed to regard him as an irreclaimable sinner, he paid a tribute to conventional standards by boldly flouting them. Finally, a brilliant narrator and a born spectator, gifted with an appreciation of drama and a sense of comedy, he had been fascinated always by the odd spectacle his life afforded.

He was amused and cheered by these new diversions: he was not obsessed. And because the pleasures of the head must be brought in to supplement those of the heart and senses—his mind (he had discovered) "wanted something craggy to break upon"—he undertook the study of the Armenian language. It was the kind of pursuit that its apparent futility makes yet more profitable. Moreover it imposed routine, created a habit; and, like other persons of an irritable and nervous humour, he found almost any habit supremely soothing and reassuring. Every day, then, he would have himself conveyed to the Armenian Convent on the island of San Lazzaro, where it had been established since the closing decades of the seventeenth century. Within the convent walls he often remained from morning till evening—in the library which looked out across the burnished lagoon, in the closed garden with its cool paths under the tunnelled vine arbours, or in the rooms which the monks had allotted to him for his private use. As a means of repaying the tuition that he received, he undertook the publication of the librarian's Armenian-English grammar, contributing a thousand francs for five hundred copies; and by the latter part of December he had made some progress, mastered thirty out of thirty-eight Armenian characters, and begun to spell his way with Father Pasquale through the Armenian psalms. There his studies faltered, till they were gradually discontinued. Meanwhile, the company of simple and pious celibates—the Superior "a fine old fellow, with the beard of a meteor," and Father Pasquale, who assured him that "the terrestrial Paradise was to be found in *Armenia*"—was a pleasant prelude to the amusements that began when night descended. "Studious in the day . . . dissolute in the evening," his existence did not admit of much variety; but he was calm and composed now as he had not been for many months and years.

It amazed him, when he considered it—the extent of his composure. No doubt it would not last; yet "if I could but remain as I now am [he wrote to Kinnaird on November 27], I should not merely be happy, but *contented*, which in my mind is the strangest, and the most difficult attainment of the two—for anyone who will hazard enough may have moments of happiness." His present way of life was rational and yet voluptuous. Not only had he books and "a decent establishment," "a fine country" and the language that he preferred, but thrown in with them was "a handsome woman," who did not bore him, who had neither prudery nor principles, was neither chaste nor calculating. ". . . I do not tire of a woman *personally* [he explained to his publisher] but because they are generally bores in their disposition. . . ." Marianna was unusually attractive and seemed uncommonly sensible; and, if he grew tired of the intrigues of the Frezzeria, he could always remove himself to some Venetian salon—to the drawing-rooms of the Countess Albrizzi or the Countess Benzoni, where he was received with the consideration due to his rank and fame. Venice lacked nothing—not even respectable company. Madame Albrizzi had been called the Madame de Staël of Italy (though "a very poor copy indeed," wrote John Cam Hobhouse) and her salon was an indifferent replica of the

Coppet gatherings. Here verses were exchanged and literary characters, composed by the hostess, were sometimes read aloud. Men stood; the women sat in a decorous semi-circle; while glasses of punch—Byron had something to say about its flavour—and trays of ices were handed round among the party, and conversation remained elegant and mild and low-pitched, with "none of that snip-snap . . . which makes half the talk of Paris and London." To Madame Benzoni's house—she was Madame Albrizzi's greatest rival—Byron was attracted a little later; and he continued to visit her when Madame Albrizzi had begun to annoy him. "Thoroughly profligate" but "very pleasant and easy" (as Moore observed on being presented to her in 1819), she was to become the indulgent censor of Byron's escapades and extended her patronage to one at least of his Venetian favourites.

For the moment he stood in no need either of advice or of reprobation. At the end of November he had reported himself extremely happy; and during mid-December he was able to confirm his previous bulletin, adding that "the last month has been one of the pleasantest, and withal the *quietest*, in my recollection." Hobhouse had left for Rome; but Byron lingered, still charmed by Marianna, delighting in Venice, and given up to his daily round of pleasures and studies. When spring came, he planned vaguely that he would return to England—it was not that he intended ever again to make a home there, but he wished to support the reform party in the House of Lords and was eager to pay visits to his barber and dentist, Mr. Blake and the incomparable Mr. Waite. Besides, during January came news of the "complete success" of his latest publications. Disposed of through the agency of Shelley (who in this as in other transactions of a similar kind revealed himself unexpectedly brisk and business-like) for a down payment of no less than two thousand guineas, the Third Canto of *Childe Harold* had been published on November 18 and followed on December 5 by *The Prisoner of Chillon and Other Poems.* Murray wrote to describe how at a booksellers' banquet he had taken orders for seven thousand copies of each volume; and his communication, accompanied by a letter from Mrs. Leigh, reached Byron in Venice on the second of January. It was the anniversary, he remembered, of his "accursed marriage."

To most correspondents Byron's replies were full and punctual. But there was one whom, through indolence or impatience, he did not trouble to gratify, since letter-writing was a kind of thinking aloud and he seldom thought of her. Claire Clairmont continued to remind him of her life and feelings—in neither of which could she flatter herself that he retained the smallest interest—and her methods of approach, though impulsive and tender, were not judicious. Particularly ill-chosen were her attempts at light-hearted badinage. Jokes about Byron's fondness for *petits pois* and his regrettable tendency to sit up drinking were accompanied by an unfortunate reference to Augusta. "Don't look cross at this letter [she had warned] because, perhaps by the same post, you expected one from Mrs. Leigh, and have not got it. That is not my fault, dearest." Elsewhere she abandoned the attempt at flippancy and addressed her "dearest Albé," her "dearest dear," in a more pathetic strain, begging for the favour of "a little letter to say how you are, how all you love are, and above all if you will say you sometimes think of me without anger. . . ." Both appeals proved equally ineffective; and Claire's disappointment was so obvious and painful that Shelley, writing on November 20, begged that, even though he did not wish to write to Claire directly, Byron's letter to himself should include some friendly message. He had shown her a previous letter, "which I should have withheld had I been aware of the wretched state into which it would have thrown her. I need not say that I do not doubt that you were as little aware of such an effect. But the smallest omission or the most unpremeditated word often affects a person in a delicate state of health and spirits."

Early in the spring, Byron learned that he was again a father. At the Shelleys' lodgings in Bath, on January 12, 1817, Claire was delivered of a "beautiful girl . . . a creature [wrote Shelley] of the most exquisite symmetry," who was named first "Alba," but afterward "Clara Allegra," and who was said to have betrayed, even at her birth, "a vigour and a sensibility very unusual." The same letter brought the news of the death of Shelley's wife. Bewildered and aggrieved, at odds with her family, Harriet had written a farewell note on November 9, addressed to her sister Eliza Westbrook (whose advice she reproached herself bitterly for having neglected), then slipped off through Kensington to the autumnal Serpentine. A month later her body was recovered. The circumstances of her last days remain mysterious; but at the time of her suicide she was believed to have been pregnant, while Shelley added (in his account of the affair to Mary) that, having been driven by her sister from her father's house, "this poor woman . . . descended the steps of prostitution until she lived with a groom of the name of Smith, who deserting her, she killed herself." There could be no question, he continued with mounting passion, that "the beastly viper her sister . . . has secured to herself the fortune of the old man . . . by the murder of this poor creature." [5] Proof of Shelley's allegations is entirely lacking. Indeed, through the course of the whole episode

[5] It is an odd fact that, three days after this letter to Mary, Shelley wrote to Eliza Westbrook, assuring her that he gave "no faith to any of the imputations generally cast on your conduct or that of Mr. Westbrook. . . . I cannot help thinking that you might have acted more judiciously, but I do not doubt you intended well." See *Shelley's Lost Letters to Harriet*, ed. Leslie Hotson.

(which for a time, according to Leigh Hunt, "tore his being to pieces") his character appears at its least trustworthy and most irrational, in very definite contrast to the aspect it assumed at other periods. All his indignation is reserved for the accursed Westbrooks—for the "libidinous and vindictive" Eliza and her decrepit parent—who, in an attempt to secure command of his children, Charles and Ianthe, had dragged him (he told Byron) "before the tribunals of tyranny and superstition," or in other words had instituted a Chancery lawsuit. There are a few words of sorrow for the unlucky Harriet. But no sense of responsibility is revealed in his attitude—nothing of the humanity that neither questions nor criticizes, and accepts the inevitable interdependence of right and wrong.

It was in this vein that he wrote of Harriet's death to Byron; and since Shelley's character and that of his fellow-poet are often compared—almost invariably to the latter's moral detriment—the ghost of Harriet must be pursued a little further. Her death (Shelley informed Byron) had communicated a shock which he did not know how he had survived, but he admitted that he had not expected it would move him deeply and that it "followed in the train of a far severer anguish"—the death of plain lonely Fanny Imlay (Mary Wollstonecraft's child by Gilbert Imlay, Mary Shelley's half-sister and Godwin's step-daughter), who left home to commit suicide that same lugubrious autumn. Shelley had been fond of her always and regretted her bitterly. It tortured him to think perhaps he had failed her; but that he had failed Harriet—though in a very different degree and more complex fashion—was an idea that would seem never to have troubled his consciousness. No, Harriet had failed *him*—and that was the root of the matter—not by infidelity which he might or might not have tolerated, but by proving unable to outgrow her sister's influence or

develop spiritually and intellectually as he had himself prescribed. "A noble animal," docile, affectionate, feminine, she
could not "feel poetry and understand philosophy." And in
the letters which he wrote her after his elopement with Mary
(which had been preceded by a period of sentimental dalliance
with those two egregious blue-stockings, Cornelia Turner and
her mother Mrs. Boinville) he refers again and again to the
limitations of her spiritual outlook. Regarding his own qualities, the tone is complacent. "It is no reproach to me [he de-
clared] that you have never filled my heart with an all-suffic-
ing passion." And later: "Since I first beheld you almost, my
chief study has been to overwhelm you with benefits. . . .
And it would be generous, nay even just, to consider with kindness that woman whom my judgment and my heart have selected as the noblest and most excellent of human beings." In
this mood he had put forward a sublime suggestion that Harriet should join himself and Mary, and form the platonic apex
of a triangular *ménage*. Measured by the yardstick of Shelleyan
dogma, the project satisfied every requirement of magnanimous
feeling. That Harriet should have thought otherwise was
strange and troublesome. It confirmed him in his contempt for
her mind and principles. . . .

In the "shock," then, that he experienced on hearing of
Harriet's death there was less of human pity than of moral
indignation. Byron's reply to his letter has not been preserved;
nor is there reason to suppose that he wrote to Claire, though he
was pleased enough by the acquisition of a second daughter.
Carnival had begun at the end of January, with "fiddling,
masquing, singing" in Ridotto and opera house, and Byron
had plunged headlong into a vortex of gaiety. The weeks that
followed were feverish and highly enjoyable. Venice seemed
to wake up to its ancient animation; every gondola was bound

on some illicit errand; in every masquerade there was a promise of adventure; and the tempo of the carnival increased as the days went by. In the midst of these diversions and dissipations, he was made the hero of an upsetting but amusing scene. A gondolier brought him a note requesting an assignation. He gave an appointment at his rooms in the Frezzeria, during the evening while his mistress and her husband were out of the house. Ten o'clock arrived; "and in walked a well-looking and (for an Italian) *bionda* girl of about nineteen, who informed me that she was married to the brother of my *amorosa*, and wished to have some conversation with me." Byron agreed, and the talk was progressing favourably, when the door was again burst open, this time to reveal "Marianna Segati, *in propriâ personâ*," who, "after making a most polite curtsy to her sister-in-law and to me, without a single word seizes her said sister-in-law by the hair, and bestows upon her some sixteen slaps, which would have made your ear ache only to hear their echo. I need not describe the screaming which ensued." As Moore knew—for it was to him that Byron related the story, though a brief sketch of it was also given to Douglas Kinnaird —the poet had a long experience of feminine scene-making. No one who had survived the attentions of Lady Caroline Lamb and had weathered the tremendous rumpus at Lady Heathcote's party, where Lady Caroline had attempted to stab herself with a pair of scissors and had succeeded in cutting her hand with a broken custard-glass, could be much dismayed by the evolutions of a Marianna. And, as soon as the slapped visitor had rushed from the room, he grappled with and forcibly detained Signora Segati until, "after several vain attempts to get away," she "fairly went into fits in my arms; and, in spite of reasoning, eau-de-Cologne, vinegar, half a pint of water," continued in that condition past the stroke of midnight.

It was as if Congreve had composed a farce in collaboration with Goldoni! For this was not all. An hour later "in comes— who? why Signor Segati . . . and finds me with his wife fainting upon the sofa, and all the apparatus of confusion, dishevelled hair, hats, handkerchiefs, salts, smelling-bottles— and the lady as pale as ashes, without sense or motion." Moore, however (he added), had no cause for alarm. Jealousy was not the order of the day in Venice; and next morning some plausible explanation was produced, and hysterical wife and ruffled husband were quietly reconciled; "how they settled it, I know not, but settle it they did." One thing, nevertheless, was fairly evident. Marianna was not the quiet and tactful young woman he had expected. The amusements of the carnival had begun to wear him down, and "three or four up-all-nights" in quick succession lowered his vitality and shook his nerves. "The mumming closed [he explained to Moore] with a masked ball at the Fenice." Now Lent was here with its abstinence and sacred music; and suddenly, as the third paragraph of an indifferent letter, he introduced his finest and most famous lyric, the only memorable short poem he would ever achieve, in which every period is like a sigh of weariness and the muse of poetry (who is also the muse of memory) distils a mysterious charm from the immense lassitude of flesh and spirit:

> So we'll go no more a roving
>   So late into the night,
> Though the heart be still as loving,
>   And the moon be still as bright.
>
> For the sword outwears its sheath,
>   And the soul wears out the breast,
> And the heart must pause to breathe,
>   And Love itself have rest.
>
> Though the night was made for loving,
>   And the day returns too soon,

> Yet we'll go no more a roving
> By the light of the moon.

These lines were sent to Moore on February 28, and some days later Byron was confined to his bed. Luckily, his complaint proved not to be "the low, vulgar typhus, which is at present decimating Venice . . . but a sharp gentlemanly fever that went away in a few days." At the end of March, he was once more "very well, with a monstrous appetite," and much amused to learn of a current story (reported to him by Hobhouse, who was still in Rome) that he had latterly eloped to Naples with a Milanese opera-singer. Yet his illness, though now past, had sounded a serious warning. He wanted a holiday from Venice; perhaps, too, he needed a rest from Marianna Segati. During March he continued to play with the idea that he might return to England; but in mid-April he posted a letter to Hobhouse announcing that it was his "indelible purpose" to join him very shortly. In less than a week the promise had been honoured. Once more his cumbrous equipage took the road, passing through Ferrara, Padua, Bologna, Florence, and drawing up in Rome on April 29. The impressions of that journey constituted the material of the Fourth and last Canto of *Childe Harold;* and it is by a re-reading of the poem that they can best be studied. Arqua recalled the shade of Petrarch. In Ferrara, with its "wide and grass-grown streets," he remembered the Estes and visited Tasso's prison-cell. His stay in Florence was irradiated by the Venus de' Medici, whom privately he considered built rather for admiration than for love, but to whom in his public character he paid a glowing and effective tribute. Rome itself inspired other and far deeper emotions. For it was not among picture-galleries that he had to find them; the whole city opened in a vast perspective of decay and splendour which delighted him "beyond everything, since Athens and Constantinople." His days were spent on horseback either riding around the city, to the Colosseum, a lunar skeleton patched with shaggy forest growths, to the Palatine, a jungle ruin half man-made and half natural, or out toward the Alban hills over the Campagna, where the broken aqueducts stepped away across the landscape and Soracte, along the tawny horizon, swept upward in a gentle curve—a long delicate fluid line like an arrested ocean-swell.

Hobhouse accompanied him on many of his expeditions; and when he needed to rest his mind from sight-seeing, and the "strong and confused" impression that it at first engendered, he had the society of some friendly English tourists—the Jerseys again and the Whig magnifico, Lord Lansdowne. Otherwise English visitors to the city were few; but such of his countrymen as he did encounter were by no means well disposed. It was at this time that an English matron, coming face to face with him among her offspring on the roof of St. Peter's, ordered the young ladies to avert their eyes: so deadly was the fascination of the most casual glance he threw! During this same visit, at the request of Hobhouse, he sat for his portrait-head to the celebrated sculptor Thorwaldsen, who was amused to notice that, as soon as Byron had settled down into a chair, he "at once began to put on a quite different expression from that usual to him." "Will you not sit still?" said Thorwaldsen. "You need not assume that look." That was his expression, Byron answered. "Indeed?" said the artist and proceeded to represent him as he wished—a sulky Apollo round whose mouth and nose hovers a shade of petulance and between whose eyebrows runs a vertical impatient cleft but whose luxuriant hair is beautifully ringleted and carefully ordered. The bust pleased his friends and annoyed the poet. It was most unlike, he protested—but not on the obvious grounds that he looked arrogant and ill-natured. His real expression, he wished to point out, was "more unhappy."

For a man who professed to be wretched he was at least extremely active. Not content with the usual round of sights in and around the city, and with seeing "the Pope alive, and a cardinal dead—both of whom looked very well indeed," he took a fancy to attend a Roman execution. It was not the first time that he had witnessed such a spectacle; for in 1812 he had sat up all night with two old school-friends, Baillie and John Madocks, to see the crazy assassin Bellingham "launched into eternity" among the grim and squalid appurtenances of an English public hanging: the sanded drop, the huge ferocious drunken crowd roaring and tossing in dark waves beneath the scaffold, and the yells of execration that greeted the appearance of the hangman. By comparison, the guillotine seemed a merciful instrument, and the whole ceremony dignified and almost hieratic—"the *masqued* priests; the half-naked executioners; the bandaged criminals; the black Christ and his banner; the scaffold; the soldiery; the slow procession, and the quick rattle and heavy fall of the axe; the splash of the blood, and the ghastliness of the exposed heads. . . ." Here was nothing of the "dog-like agony" he had watched in Bellingham; but, although two of the criminals "behaved calmly enough," the first to suffer "died with great terror and reluctance, which was very horrible . . . and the priest was obliged to drown his exclamations by still louder exhortations." Then the knife thudded smoothly down and the scene was over. Byron had a place close to the scaffold; and, being an amateur of strange sights and violent sensations—one, moreover, who was engrossed by the idea of death—he had come as to the theatre equipped with an opera-glass. Now his hand shook so that he could scarcely hold it; and the experience left him, he discovered, "quite hot and thirsty"; but the second and third deaths had little effect on him (though he admitted that he would have saved the men had it been within his power), "which shows how dreadfully soon things grow indifferent": an observation that alone was perhaps worth making.

Rome detained Byron from May 5 to May 28; but before his time was up he had begun to long for Marianna. He returned, however, only briefly to his Venetian rooms; and, while Venice sweltered and stank with the approach of the dog-days, he established his household and received his mistress in a *villeggiatura* that he had taken beside the Brenta, where rich Venetians for many centuries had found a summer refuge and had built the villas that Palladio planned on correct Vitruvian principles and Veronese and Tiepolo had been proud to decorate. La Mira was a pleasant house, if a trifle dusty. There Marianna joined him, released by unknown means from Signor Segati's superintendence, and thither Hobhouse followed at the conclusion of July. He found his friend well and in excellent spirits. Monk Lewis was staying at La Mira when Hobhouse arrived and remained in residence during the next few weeks, annoying John Cam by his contradictiousness and pettish egotistical susceptibility. But listening to Lewis's anecdotes was not their sole diversion; on August 5 Hobhouse recorded in his journal (from which any reference to Marianna has been carefully excised) that he had "passed the evening strolling about on horseback with Byron and making assignations." These evening rides became part of their summer regimen; and as they jogged home the moon would rise clear and honey-pale in one quarter of the heavens while the snow-peaks of the distant Alps were flushed with sunset, and day "died like a dolphin" above the shadowy river-banks.

It was on such a ride, during the summer of 1817, that the

horsemen encountered a group of peasants among whom (wrote Byron) "we remarked two girls as the prettiest we had seen for some time." Byron was already a public personage and, the countryside being just then miserably impoverished, he had contributed to the relief of his peasant neighbours, generosity (he said) making "a great figure at very little cost in Venetian livres. . . ." One of the girls recognized and hailed him, asking why, since he helped others, he did not help them too. *"Cara* [he replied, turning in his saddle] *tu sei troppo bella e giovane per aver'bisogno del soccorso mio."* She answered that if he saw her hut and the food she ate he would not think so. "All this passed half-jestingly"; but a few evenings later they met again; the conversation was renewed, an appointment given and accepted; and, though the smaller of the two girls took fright at Hobhouse—not so much at John Cam himself, as because it transpired she was not yet married; "for here no woman will do anything under adultery"—Byron's choice, after "some bother," proved more easily manageable. He had offered to help her without conditions, supposing, that is to say, she were in genuine want. She explained, however, that on her own account she would not have hesitated—she was married, she observed, "and all married women did it; but that her husband (a baker) was somewhat ferocious." During the course of subsequent meetings her fears were dissipated. Margarita Cogni, otherwise known as the Fornarina, a fierce product of Venetian slums and backways, assumed a dominant position in Byron's household.

For two years that position was jealously guarded; and with her appearance beside the Brenta—a tall black-haired, black-eyed young woman, wearing the *fazziolo* or white Venetian veil that women of the poorer classes still affected—begins a new stage in the history of Byron's moral evolution. Marianna Segati was not swept aside, but she was daunted and crushed by Margarita's wild effrontery; for, when she and her friends ventured to accost the rival and advise her threateningly to refrain from meddling, the other had thrown back her *fazziolo* and retorted in an explosion of Venetian dialect. Marianna was not Byron's wife! she had cried; nor was she herself. "*You* are his *donna,* and *I* am his *donna; your* husband is a cuckold, and *mine* is another. For the rest, what *right* have you to reproach me? If he prefers what is mine to what is yours, is it my fault? . . . Do not think to speak to me without a reply because you happen to be richer than I am." Having thus signalized her victory, she went on her way. Nor did Marianna from that time dispute her ascendancy but appeared content to take the smaller share of Byron's favours. Byron did not entirely neglect the antelope—it was to that graceful beast he had compared his first Venetian favourite—and for the time being she remained his "regular *amica,*" recognized as such by the easy Venetian code; but the wilder mistress attracted him far more profoundly, with her greedy passion, her outrageous naïveté, and strident humour. To "the strength of an Amazon" she added the disposition of Medea—"a fine animal" but, as it turned out, "quite untamable."

For the student of Byron's career she has not only a scandalous, but also a symbolic, interest; since, although Byron dismissed her lightly as a splendid animal—a "gentle tigress" who displayed a snarling contempt for her surly baker husband, trampled on her rivals, and terrorized her lover's lazy and dishonest servants—her fascination was psychological as well as sexual, and the need she satisfied as much of the imagination as of the body. In every artist's nature, more or less acutely developed, there exists the impulse which has been conveniently, if perhaps not very accurately, entitled *la nostalgie de la boue*. With the love of order coexists a feeling for disorder; with the desire for clarity, propriety, and delicate distinctions—lacking which a work of art cannot emerge from chaos—goes a taste for the kind of experience that is gross but lively. So rarefied is the atmosphere in which art is born that the artist, when he transfers his attention from art to life, often chooses to breathe a steamy and relaxing climate, the air of the brothel, the crowded restaurant, the smoke-fogged drinking party. *"Oh, mes amis, que j'ai besoin de m'encanailler un peu!"* Rachel is said to have exclaimed—true, it was between the frigid walls of Victorian Windsor—after a particularly distinguished and moving performance; and many lesser artists have echoed the same impatient cry. Thus, Byron's growing attraction toward debauchery went far deeper than—though, of course, it comprehended— mere time-wasting and superficial self-indulgence: one might almost suggest, indeed, that it had a moral basis. Hitherto he had often struggled against the drift of his nature; now he would resign himself to its control and await the outcome.

What had he to lose—and what to gain? Very little, he told himself with that inborn fatalism which did not preclude ordinary human cheerfulness or deter him from a strenuous pursuit of the pleasures of living. Thank heavens he was in robust health and had vigorous appetites. *Manfred*, his fantastic dramatic poem, sent back to Murray during the spring just before he embarked on his journey to Rome, had helped to exorcize some of his gloomier preoccupations; and the idea of a return to England grew more and more shadowy. By the ninth of August (when it was shown to Lewis) he had completed the Fourth Canto of *Childe Harold* and had finally bidden good-bye to the character in whom so much of his earlier self, both the genuine and the factitious, had originally been embodied. It was a significant farewell, accompanied by a bold outpouring of rhetorical defiance:

> But I have lived, and have not lived in vain:
> My mind may lose its force, my blood its fire,
> And my frame perish even in conquering pain;
> But there is that within me which shall tire
> Torture and Time, and breathe when I expire. . . .

Elsewhere the tone of the canto is more impersonal than that of any of its predecessors. The "gloomy wanderer" of Cantos One and Two is almost lost to sight among the elaborate set-pieces through which the poem moves—the Dying Gladiator, the Pantheon, the Tomb of Cecilia Metilla; he makes his final bow a little languidly and the stage is vacant. For Byron had outgrown Childe Harold, or rather he had absorbed him—had lived up to and had then exceeded his imaginary self-portrait. That autumn he began to play with the idea of novel-writing; and the adventures of Don Julian—otherwise Don Juan—was the theme he chose.

Chapter Three

ON THE whole it had been a pleasant year, and it ended pleasantly. There was a short journey with Hobhouse to Arqua and Padua, followed by a lively meeting with Douglas Kinnaird and his brother at Venice. Byron then returned to his *villeggiatura*, and John Cam presently re-joined him, finding his friend "well, and merry and happy, more charming every day." Till mid-November they remained together in the country—"a strange life [noted Hobhouse]; very tranquil and comfortable." Finally, on the thirteenth, they were ready to leave; and, while Byron resumed his residence in the Frezzeria, Hobhouse established himself in lodgings opposite. This stay lasted through the autumn and winter of 1817. Byron made a habit of rising late; but during the afternoon they were often rowed out to the Lido, the bleak melancholy island beyond the lagoon, occupied only by market gardens and a Jewish cemetery,[1] where Byron had hired a stable in which he kept his horses. Here on the tawny beach, beside the pallid sluggish waters of the Adriatic, they could ride from Sant' Andrea toward

[1] *A Venise, à l'affreux Lido,*
    Où vient sur l'herbe d'un tombeau
    Mourir la pâle Adriatique . . .

Malmocco, "a spanking gallop" of several miles' length over resilient sand. Ferried home again across the lagoon as it flamed with the setting sun, they would prepare to attend the Countess Benzoni or visit the playhouse or dine with Richard Belgrave Hoppner, the English consul. Byron was talkative, calm, good-humoured; and when Hobhouse left him it was with reluctance but without anxiety.

Before he said good-bye they had seen in the New Year. 1818, as far as Byron was concerned, began with the happiest and most prosperous auguries, since he had recently heard from his lawyer of the sale of Newstead [2]—a sacrifice he regretted but to which he had long resigned himself—and was therefore richer by nearly ninety-five thousand pounds. At last he could hope to pay off his creditors, and he had written Hanson a precise and careful letter explaining just how he wished him to arrange a settlement. Other assets, it is true, were still unrealized; but, even so, he was rich enough, if he stayed in Italy, to maintain an establishment suited to his tastes and interests. Besides, the desire to see England again had gradually withered away. He liked his personal independence and the freedom from moral supervision; the ties that bound him to his own race had slowly weakened. The single human being who might have induced him to travel northward—whose summons he would have obeyed at any cost, as he had repeatedly told her—was of all his correspondents the least encouraging.

At this point, both in time and in space, a digression is needed. From 1818 we must revert to 1816, and from Byron magnificently established at the Palazzo Mocenigo—the great gloomy palazzo overlooking the mid-curve of the Grand Canal which he had taken for himself and his dependants early in

[2] The Abbey was sold to a Harrow acquaintance, Colonel Wildman, who proceeded to remodel a large part of the fabric in the very worst traditions of nineteenth-century Gothic.

the New Year—we turn back to a set of small rooms in St. James's Palace and to various hired houses and furnished lodgings, restless resting places of the two women he had most deeply injured. England he might forget, but not his wife and sister—not Annabella because he felt subconsciously that she had proved too strong for him with her cool, obstinate, undeviating sense of duty; not Augusta because she knew so much of his best and worst side, because he loved her as he was firmly convinced he would never love again, and because, after all, she was a part of himself. There had been a period when he still hoped that they might be re-united. Let Augusta give him a sign and he would re-cross the Channel! Or could not he prevail on her to join him in Switzerland, bringing with her a bevy of his nieces and nephews? To these proposals the replies he elicited were oddly evasive. He coaxed; he reminded; she continued to escape him. More and more ambiguous became her answers; more and more nervously did she shrink away into that language which was so peculiarly her own, made up of hints and mysteries and secondhand pietism—Augusta's "damned crinkum-crankum" was her brother's name for it. Now it seemed that Augusta's heart was hardening, though the process of hardening was a trifle fragmentary and between the lines he caught an occasional glimpse of her despair and passion. But there could be no doubt that she was undergoing a metamorphosis—that a new influence had begun to work upon her simple nature. The authoress of such a transformation was, of course, his wife!

In these suspicions Byron had been perfectly justified. Some weeks before the actual separation, Mrs. Leigh at the instance of her friends had left her brother's house in Piccadilly Terrace (where she had been doing her best to calm and comfort him) and had retired to her private apartments in St. James's Palace.

There occupying the strange double position of fashionable attendant to an elderly and extremely strait-laced Queen and heroine of a shattering private scandal, she had watched and waited and hoped desperately to ward off disaster. She knew of the reports that were being propagated. She recognized that, if she were to preserve a vestige of moral reputation and save her struggling household from utter catastrophe, Lady Byron's friendship must be retained. Among her champions was a certain Mrs. Villiers; and, though described by her contemporaries as broad-minded, sympathetic, and intelligent, Thérèse Villiers was not a woman it would have been easy to like. Perhaps she was betrayed by her sense of drama. After all, it was no slight pleasure and privilege, while the rest of London was buzzing with speculation, and Holland House dinner parties were saying this, and Melbourne House satellites were declaring that, and Lady Caroline Lamb was running in furious circles, giving currency to the wildest and most shocking rumours, to be made a confidante of the whole disastrous story. For Mrs. Villiers had remonstrated with Lady Byron; and Annabella, delicately but very definitely, had explained that there were reasons—grave and conclusive reasons—why, fond as she might be of poor Augusta, she could not afford her unqualified support and assistance. Mrs. Villiers was immensely perturbed but intensely interested. If the story were true—and Lady Byron's veracity was so obvious as to be almost alarming—then it was high time to adopt a different viewpoint. Not that she was predisposed to condemn Augusta! But, although Augusta was the victim of her brother's wickedness, to some extent she must be considered his accomplice and, as accomplice, she should be obliged to expiate the wrong she had done. Henceforward Mrs. Villiers was pledged not only to advise and encourage Lady Byron, but to promote the moral redemption of

Lady Byron's sister-in-law; and, as the situation grew more interesting, her fervour increased.

Lady Byron, to her credit, was a reluctant persecutor. In the past, Mrs. Leigh had earned her gratitude; she was always acutely sensitive to the Byronic charm; and during that dreadful visit to Six Mile Bottom, the gloomiest episode of her wretched marriage-journey, and the more protracted anguish of life in London, they had been drawn together by a thousand bonds of fear and suffering. But now at all costs she must learn to throw off sentiment. Doyle and Horton and the solemn Dr. Lushington—the advisers who had been at her side in the separation drama—kept up their warnings against Mrs. Leigh and urged that she should take precautions for any emergency, if possible by extracting a confession of guilt. Lady Byron's response was characteristically deliberate. She was unwilling to be swayed by personal motives; but it hurt her—perhaps it also piqued her—that Augusta, between fits of violent depression when she made muddled miserable references to the state of her soul ("I don't know what *you* may all be, but I am sure *I'm* not prepared for the next world . . ." she had wailed suddenly at a dinner party of Mrs. Villiers), should still sometimes affect an attitude of "conscious innocence"!

And Lady Byron's feelings had yet another side. Mixed with prudence, a tinge of natural irritation, and a touch of the vengefulness that usually accompanies offended virtue—even in a temperament as carefully self-controlled, as minutely self-appraised as that of Annabella—was one of the strongest and most irrational of human emotions, the passionate instinctive jealousy of love rejected. Yes, she was jealous of Augusta and would always remain so. Typical of jealousy in its extremer forms is the belief that, when certainty has been arrived at, as soon as the worst is known and the depths of humiliation have been explored, the intensity of the pain felt may begin to diminish. Thus the suggestions of her counsellors (who now included Mrs. Villiers) she was prepared to meet half-way. For the sake of her own peace she must be *sure*—while now she had merely suspicions not amounting to proof; she must exchange intuitive for positive and definite knowledge; she must hear the tale of Byron's guilt from the guilty partner. Did she hope that full knowledge would bring her understanding; that she would know, at last, why trying so hard she had failed so dismally?

Augusta was rounded up like a beast for the sacrifice, Lady Byron adopting the role of calm high-priestess, grave and determined in the performance of duty, Mrs. Villiers an officious but collected ministrant. Augusta was just then recovering from one of her numerous accouchements; and, as soon as her physical health was on the mend, the two ladies set about her moral well-being. During May Annabella was still hesitant as to the propriety and practical advisability of consummating the sacrifice then and there. The fever of passion (she considered) had not yet subsided; "—it is perhaps the crisis. . . . From all I learn of her present temper, no result but that of precipitate desperation can be expected." Mrs. Leigh might flee the country to join Byron; and there was one point on which the poet's wife and Doyle and Lushington were in entire, though not explicit, disagreement. For their part, they would have welcomed Augusta's flight; by completing the ruin of her reputation, it would effectually have cleared Lady Byron's name of the charges of heartlessness and "implacability" that then and at a later time were brought against her. But Annabella's feelings were somewhat more complicated. She had decided that it was her duty to "save" Augusta; "my great object [she wrote to Mrs. Villiers on May 16, 1816] next to the Security of my Child, is . . . the restoration of her mind to that state which is religiously desirable." She had also decided, impelled by motives that were all her own—motives with which no one else could be expected to sympathize and to which she herself may not have possessed the real and secret clue—that brother and sister must never be permitted to resume their intercourse. What part had instinctive jealousy in this determination? At any rate, the influence of jealousy was carefully sublimated and her apparent motives were such as she could take a pride in, such as her friends and supporters were bound to approve. She must assume control of the weak and erring victim and guide her back through expiation into the paths of virtue, using obligations to chain her and threats to compel. To assist her redemption, she must slay her pride and destroy the last struggling hopes of unlawful happiness.

After due reflection and much consultation with Mrs. Villiers, Annabella opened her campaign on June 3. The letter she composed was wily and diplomatic, meaning and yet deliberately noncommittal, minatory yet couched in a tone of affectionate platitude. Before her confinement "dearest Augusta" was not to be agitated; but, having learned to her satisfaction that Mrs. Leigh was now recovered, Annabella could no longer conceal the existence of "reasons," unspecified in so many words but vaguely alluded to, which "imposed the duty" of *"limiting"* their future friendship. Augusta was alarmed and puzzled by this communication, replying in her usual effusive and flurried manner that, although not *"wholly surprised* at its contents," she was pained and disconcerted by its general terms; for "if I were on my death Bed I could affirm as I *now* do that I have uniformly considered you and consulted your happiness before and above everything in this world." Annabella, on reflection, was far from satisfied; and, discussing the

reply with Mrs. Villiers, she admitted that it contained "no of-
fensive or irritating expression towards me," but observed that
it showed a lack of true contrition: "her assertions are not exactly *to the point*—though it is evident she perfectly under-
stands me." However, it was "perhaps the best letter she *could*
have written"; and one must face the fact that Augusta was not
as other women—at least, not as women like herself and her
friend: her moral principles at the best of times were loose and
hazy: "she did not appear to think these transgressions *of consequence.*" She had meant well and believed that to mean well
was the essence of virtue—a delusion that Annabella must at
once eradicate.

It is unnecessary for the purposes of the present narrative
to describe in any great detail the various epistolary turns by
which Mrs. Leigh was cornered, the different means—some of
them very subtle—that were employed to inject her with a sense
of her former guilt, or the state of humiliation and tremulous
self-abasement to which she was gradually but mercilessly conducted. But from one asseveration she would not budge. Intentionally she had never harmed her brother's wife—a statement
in which Byron himself afterward concurred. "Dearest A——
[she wrote], *I have not wronged you. I have not abused your
generosity . . .*" ; and elsewhere, alluding to her stay in Piccadilly Terrace, she declared that had she at the time "enter-
tained the *slightest* suspicion of any *'doubts'* of yours—I never
could or would have entered your house. . . ." On an additional point—a point extremely important to Lady Byron's
feelings—the testimony of her letters could not be shaken. She
acknowledged (according to the report furnished by Annabella
to Mrs. Villiers) her moral culpability before Byron's marriage—"as much as she could do on paper"—but stoutly main-

tained "her *innocence* since. . . . Finally she entreats me in the most humble & affecting manner to point out in pity to her anything by which she may 'atone for the past.' "

But the old flighty Augusta was not yet extinguished. ". . . You know I am of a sanguine disposition," she had remarked rather pathetically to Annabella; and, when she came up to London for the Regent's Fête, which she was obliged to attend in her official capacity, at her first meeting with Mrs. Villiers—a meeting her friend had "dreaded beyond measure" —the "whole conversation turned on *Gauzes & Sattins*" and she looked "quite stout & well . . . & perfectly cool & easy, having apparently nothing on her mind. . . ." It was during this visit to the metropolis that Augusta and Annabella met face to face. Their interview had been carefully prearranged; its results were all that Lady Byron had anticipated. Exactly what passed we shall never know—what degrees of suffering were endured, what refinements of torture and self-torture were then applied, what reproaches were uttered, what tears were shed. But questions painfully asked were as painfully answered. Mrs. Leigh broke down and told her story, still clinging, however, to her previous assertion that she had not "wronged" Annabella since the Byrons' marriage and that she "had never felt any suspicion of my suspicions except at the time in the summer of 1815 when I evidently wished she would leave us." She had often told Byron, Augusta declared, that he "said such things before me as would have led any other woman to suspect"; but he had always been able to convince her that her fears were unfounded; and Augusta seemed to have acted upon the principle—indeed, it was almost the only principle that had governed her conduct—"that what could be concealed from me was no injury."

Questioned as to whether Byron had displayed remorse, Au-

gusta replied that she had observed no signs of it, except once
—"the night before they parted. . . ." But in a literary form
he had acknowledged his responsibility; and Augusta admitted
that the notorious verses:

I speak not, I trace not, I breathe not thy name . . .

written in 1814, had been addressed to her. Surely there was
now little more that the culprit could add? But the appetite of
jealous passion is not easily satisfied; and, though Annabella
during the course of her visit renewed her questioning of Mrs.
Leigh on several occasions, the unhappy intensity of her private feelings did not decrease. One confession, she decided,
was not sufficient. Mrs. Villiers must also extort her old friend's
secret, but she must do so without letting it become apparent
that her preliminary information was derived from Lady Byron
and must pretend that it *"originated with Lord B."* (who had
assured Augusta that he had never betrayed her confidence)
and reached Mrs. Villiers *"through an authority she could not
doubt."* Mrs. Leigh submitted, though somewhat reluctantly.
During the earlier stages of the long-drawn sacrifice, she had
kept her spirits up, considering the situation, remarkably well;
and there exists a brief note scribbled to Annabella on the mor-
row of one of their momentous interviews, wherein she pro-
fesses herself, in her customary goose-ish vein, "so sorry for
your bad night—& for your *idea* of my *uncomfortableness*—
which is however quite a *fancy of your own*—but I dare say I
looked something or other which made you fancy."

There must have been moments when the two devotees began
to despair of their task. Could Augusta never be brought to a
proper recognition of her appalling moral plight? Would she
still (like a naughty child after a parental talking-to which,
because it has wept and accepted its reprimand, looks **forward**

confidently to complete forgiveness) continue to appear cool and easy and carefree? But even Augusta's buoyancy was at length exhausted. The ordeal of a second confessional interview, accompanied by the information that Byron had blabbed (as, in fact, he had done, though not in the manner suggested), brought down her spirits to a more appropriate level, and it was in deep dejection that she returned to Newmarket and her husband and family. Her friends could congratulate themselves that their work was accomplished. Augusta (reported Annabella) had been reduced to "the humblest sense of her own situation." She had been horror-struck by what she had learned of her brother's treachery; and "all this [commented Mrs. Villiers] will help to alienate her feelings from him." Lady Byron she described as her Guardian Angel; and to that angelic mentor she now submitted Byron's letters—they were *"absolute love-letters,"* Annabella noted—and begged for advice as to "how she can stop them" or how she could best reply to their entreaties and arguments. In finding herself the censor of this correspondence—an eavesdropper on her husband's passionate outpourings—Lady Byron tasted the final bitterness of her Pyrrhic victory.

Youth, spontaneity, peace of mind—she had renounced them all. A young woman of strong passions and lively feelings, who had known the passing savour if not the full enjoyment of normal happiness, she now fell back on the conviction that she was "doing her duty" and on the stern and lonely consolations of spiritual self-love. She was proud; she was intractable; her choice was deliberate. Yet as time went by she was to discover, with increasing perplexity and with a growing sense of the corruption and ingratitude of her fellow-human beings, that her noblest intentions were seldom operative and that the closest attachments she formed were the most disastrous. Her capacity for gaining affection had somehow evaporated. Capable of deep devotion toward those she loved, she was incapable of that real and lasting tenderness which adapts itself to the vagaries of human conduct and, because it is uncritical and makes no moral demands, is rarely disillusioned. A person of more sensitive spiritual fibre, however stern and conventional her moral prejudices, might have recoiled from assuming so exclusive an authority—backed up by subtle methods of intimidation— over a woman to whom she had at one time been deeply indebted and who was now, as they both of them understood, quite at her mercy. Even though she had considered it essential by every religious standard, she might have felt that the "alienation" of Mrs. Leigh's feelings and the substitution of distrust for attachment between brother and sister (whose love had been innocent and confiding as well as passionate) were duties of an exceedingly painful and perhaps a degrading kind. She was unhappy on her own account, gloomy and feverish, moving restlessly from place to place with her child and nursemaid, writing long detailed reflective letters to Mrs. Villiers; but throughout she kept her head clear and her intentions definite. Her pity remained the prisoner of her sense of duty. That sense of duty was not unconnected with her self-esteem.

Soon her counsels and her commands were virtually indistinguishable. Already during July, before their meeting, when (as she explained to Mrs. Villiers) she was leading on Augusta step by step "to promise that she will never resume a confidential intercourse by letter—or any personal intercourse," she had given precise directions as to how Mrs. Leigh should regulate such correspondence as she could not avoid. She must seek to *rectify*, "instead of *soothing* or *indulging*," and above all she must beware of those private signs, those innuendoes, jokes, and personal references, with which Byron's messages were often sprinkled. Let her, therefore, eschew "all phrases or *marks*, which recall wrong ideas to his mind . . . and let me also warn you [Annabella continued] against the levity and nonsense which he likes for the worst reason, because it prevents him from reflecting seriously. . . ." Yet Augusta must not, of course, suppose that her Guardian Angel was anxious to dictate any line of conduct; and it was part of the subtlety of Lady Byron's method that she insisted again and again on Augusta's freedom. At the same time, Mrs. Leigh should remember her family—"both as respects the world's opinion of yourself and still more from the injury young minds must receive in the society of one so unprincipled"—and she need not be offended if her well-wisher added that "I think his mind too *powerful* for you—I could not feel secure that he would not bewilder you on any subject. . . ." Augusta, therefore, must always be on her guard against, and in justice to herself must never encourage, "his criminal *desires*, I think I may add *designs*." Otherwise, she must remember that she was a free agent; "for anxious as I feel to support and comfort you in the recovered path of virtue, I could not hope to do so by an attempt to impose my own opinions. On the contrary, I would, as far as possible, remove every obstacle to independence of conduct on your part." Augusta accepted her friends' "honour system": she had little choice in the matter. The alternative was too black and terrifying to be confronted lightly.

Her character began to change; and the change was disastrous. A shy, startled, diffident, uncertain being, under the pressure of persecution and her well-wishers' vigilance, Augusta grew at first wary, then deceitful, and latterly developed a strain of self-protective humbug. Thus she recollected and exploited her early religious training. Presently she was in correspondence with Francis Hodgson, one of those dim prosaic figures whom Byron befriended because, though admiring and companionable, they were not competitive. Hodgson had recently taken orders, and therefore might be of very great assistance in Mrs. Leigh's moral rehabilitation, with which—at least from the practical viewpoint—she was much concerned. To him she wrote at rambling length of her brother's weaknesses. She was sure, she told Hodgson, without stating her evidence, that he had recollections fatal to his peace of mind, which would have prevented his ever being happy with a woman as spotless as Lady Byron. Nothing could remedy this tragic cause save the consolations to be derived from religious faith, "which Alas! dear Mr. H., our beloved B. is I fear destitute of. . . ."

Something of the same note eventually crept into her correspondence with the exile. Mrs. Leigh's letters to Byron have not been preserved; but from his frequent and often agitated rejoinders—seen and duly commented on by Lady Byron—it is clear that they were neither unambiguous nor satisfactory. Augusta had accepted her fate and had learned her lesson. One promise, it is true, she still refused to give: if "dearest B." returned from the Continent she could not engage that she would decline to see him. For the rest, she bowed meekly before her guardian's wishes and appeared, little by little, to be withdrawing from the Byronic influence. Yet there was a touch of hypocrisy beneath Augusta's flightiness. In the interests of her personal safety and her family's welfare, she advertised her deep contrition and implicit obedience—while to Hodgson she adopted an attitude of superior virtue, loftily concerned with Childe Harold's sins; but the devices and desires of a rebellious heart were not completely neglected. It is obvious that she continued to write to Byron in an encouraging strain; there is no evidence that she attempted to improve or check him, though the letters she continued to receive were often passionate; but she wrote vaguely, mysteriously, with a hint of troubled reserve that exasperated Byron because he could not analyse it. He replied impatiently, sometimes bitterly; he pleaded and joked with her. But time passed and their separation grew more and more definite.

A sense of his isolation was slowly gaining on him. In Byron's nature his relations with Mrs. Leigh had brought out not only the worst of his temperament—those anarchic and self-destructive impulses that made it necessary for him to torture himself and torture others—but also his kindest, steadiest, and most generous traits. Mrs. Leigh had been tormented because she was a part of himself—she too had inherited the blood of the Byrons and for that reason must share in the Byronic doom— but she had been loved as ideally one might love a sister, with a tenderness into which desire had scarcely entered and from which passion eventually might have died away. To a man or woman who has brought out the best in us we are always grateful; a person we have deeply injured it is hard to forget; and Mrs. Leigh had both claims on Byron's memory—she was his chief victim and his closest intimate at one and the same moment. Her love had satisfied him as he had never before been satisfied. On the small packet that enclosed a lock of Augusta's silky dark brown hair and included also a few lines in her handwriting:

> *Partager tous vos sentimens*
> *ne voir que par vos yeux*
> *n'agir que par vos conseils, ne*
> *vivre que pour vous, voilà mes*
> *vœux, mes projets, & le seul*
> *destin qui peut me rendre*
> *heureuse*

had he not inscribed a single sentence: "La Chevelure of the *one* whom I most *loved*," adding the cross that had a special significance in their relationship? He did not know that every letter he wrote to Augusta, after her final subjugation in the summer of 1816, was passed on to Annabella to be read and criticized.

Lady Byron's feelings as she opened them are not easy to conjure up; but it may well have been with a certain masochistic eagerness that she turned over these scrawled impatient letters from Switzerland, from Milan and then from Venice, in which her husband wrote freely and passionately as he had never written to her, consoling Augusta, soothing and reassuring. . . . No, Augusta was not to be alarmed by the prevalent rumours. Who, among their friends, would take seriously the false and wicked inventions of Lady Caroline Lamb—Augusta did not know that she had been one of Byron's confidantes—a crazy strumpet and "seventy times convicted liar"? "Do not be uneasy [he pleaded]—and do not 'hate yourself.' If you hate either let it be *me*—but do not—it would kill me; we are the last persons in the world—who ought or could cease to love one another." This was from Diodati at the end of August. During September 1816 he received intelligence that Lady Byron had been "very kind," and begged leave to take the news with a touch of scepticism. "And so—Lady B. has been 'kind to you' [he wrote] . . . 'very kind'—umph—it is as well she should be kind to some of us, and I am glad she has the heart and the discernment to be still *your* friend." Here and there, he gave indications of normal jealousy, and when he heard from Hobhouse that Lord Frederick Bentinck was often to be found at his sister's house he wrote to demand why "that fool" was a regular visitor: did Augusta suppose that his intentions were amorous? To Lady Byron his references were rarely charitable; and unmindful of the agonies he had himself inflicted he dwelt angrily upon the sufferings he had been made to endure. The separation, he declared illogically, had broken his heart; "I feel as if an Elephant had trodden on it"; and, though it was "a relief—a partial relief to talk of her sometimes to you," he requested that Augusta would not mention her name. Of Lady Byron's conduct she might judge for herself; "but do not altogether forget that she has destroyed your brother. Whatever my faults might or may have been—*She*—was not the person marked out by providence to be their avenger. . . . I do not think a human being could endure more mental torture than that woman has directly or indirectly inflicted upon me—within the present year."

Meanwhile, she was to reflect upon his invitation. The country was beautiful, travelling easy; he would "return from any distance at any time" to see her. The obstacle, he supposed, was his fatuous brother-in-law, "that very helpless gentleman your Cousin," horsy, improvident, perpetually embarrassed, for whom she wrote letters, solicited loans, and warded off creditors. No doubt "the usual self-love of an elderly person would interfere between you & any scheme of recreation or relaxation, for however short a period"; and he raged miserably against the limitations of the married state which had torn them apart and now held them asunder:

What a fool was I to marry—and *you* not very wise, my dear—we might have lived so single and so happy—as old maids and bachelors; I shall never find any one like you—nor you (vain as it may seem) like me. We are just formed to pass our lives together, and therefore —we—at least—I—am by a crowd of circumstances removed from the only being who could ever have loved me, or whom I can unmixedly feel attached to.

Alas, Mrs. Leigh was neither an honest nor an eloquent letter-writer. In her new position she wrote to Byron less and less frequently; and by the mid-autumn he considered that he had cause to remonstrate. A whole month had gone by without a single letter; he mentioned this, he said, "not from any wish to plague you—but because my unfortunate circumstances perhaps make me feel more keenly anything which looks like neglect. . . ." And when letters did arrive, they were not illuminating, full of "mysteries & alarms" and ambiguities, coupled with a suggestion that hurt him deeply. "You surely do not mean to say [he protested on October 28, 1816] that if I come to England in Spring . . . you & I shall not meet? If so I will never return to it. . . ."

Simultaneously, his descriptions of his wife's behaviour grew more extravagant. It is doubtful if at any time he had really loved her—indeed it was to escape from passion that he had embarked on matrimony—but he had esteemed and admired the quiet, serious, unsmiling girl who had pursued him with such a bizarre devotion throughout their months of courtship, who had been so determined to marry the poet and reform the libertine. Conveniently for himself he could usually forget what he did not choose to remember; and his outbursts and nerve-storms during the year of marriage, when he had worried her with mysterious references to his sins and secrets, or left her alone while he sought the comfort of Kinnaird's brandy parties, or talked of suicide or of separation as soon as the child was born, were not permitted to influence his judgment when he discussed her attitude. It was her coolness, her inflexibility, he could not tolerate. That she should have resisted all his entreaties and his supplications, decided on the line of duty, and calmly held to it, reduced him to transports of helpless fury in which he invoked the judgment of heaven or threatened lawsuits or prophesied that he would live to witness her utter downfall. She was his "moral Clytemnæstra," an "infernal fiend." At Diodati a reconciliation had still seemed possible; but from Venice, on March 5, 1817, having heard of the Chancery proceedings with regard to his daughter, he wrote to inform his wife that the hope had been given up. "No one [he concluded] was ever even the involuntary cause of great evils to others, without a requital. I have paid and am paying for mine—so will you."

In Augusta the confidence he had placed was not yet broken. She at least was no "cold-blooded animal," no unbending moralist; but, while his wife's nature was all self-restraint and unflinching rectitude, his sister's was so unfocused as to be quite amorphous—she was a moral opportunist who took any shape that the occasion demanded. She annoyed him; she disappointed him; she seemed to escape him. Yet he looked forward with eagerness to her infrequent letters—only to be puzzled and exasperated when the letters came. If only the "good Goose" were a little less muddle-headed—not quite so flustered by anxieties she declined to particularize, obsessed by sorrows he was often unable to make head or tail of! Thus, acknowledging a bundle of letters received at Venice, he remarked crossly that they were "full of woes, as usual, megrims & mysteries," and added that his sympathy must be held in abeyance, since "for the life of me I can't make out whether your disorder is a broken heart or the ear-ache—or whether it is *you* that have been ill or the children—or what your melancholy & mysterious apprehensions tend to . . . whether to Caroline Lamb's novels—Mrs. Clermont's evidence—Lady Byron's magnanimity—or any other piece of imposture." But love her he did and must, and could never cease to do—"always . . .

better than any earthly existence." Time was smothering but it had not yet extinguished the passion he felt. Though she might recede, he continued to follow; and the summing-up would be not composed till 1819. He had never ceased to feel (he then wrote) "that perfect and boundless attachment which bounds and binds me to you," and rendered him utterly incapable of *real* love for any other human being.

My own XXXX [he exclaimed in the same letter], we may have been very wrong, but I repent of nothing except that cursed marriage, and your refusing to continue to love me as you had loved me. I can neither forget nor *quite forgive* you for that precious piece of reformation; but I can never be other than I have been, and whenever I love anything it is because it reminds me of you. . . . It is heartbreaking to think of our long Separation, and I am sure more than punishment enough for all our sins. Dante is more humane in his "Hell," for he places his unfortunate lovers (Francesca of Rimini and Paolo, whose case fell a good deal short of ours, though sufficiently naughty) in company and, though they suffer, it is at least together. If ever I return to England it will be to see you. . . . Circumstances may have ruffled my manner, and hardened my spirit. You may have seen me harsh and exasperated with all things around me, grieved and tortured with *your new resolution,* and the soon after persecution of that infamous fiend . . . but remember that, even then, *you* were the sole object that cost me a tear. And *what tears!* Do you remember our parting. . . ? They say absence destroys weak passions, and confirms strong ones. Alas! *mine* for you is the union of all passions and of all affections, has strengthened itself but will destroy me.

Such statements may be emotionally accurate at the time of writing; but the element of truth that they contain is strictly relative; and Byron at this period—indeed much earlier— had thoroughly accustomed himself to separation from Mrs. Leigh. She was a symbol of lost love, of frustrated tenderness. Thanks to his own capacity for living in the moment, and

Augusta's incapacity for continuous feeling, she had ceased to be a practical consideration.

> All suffering doth destroy, or is destroy'd
> Even by the sufferer . . .

That was a lesson already learned when he composed the last canto of *Childe Harold*. He had not been destroyed, but the pain had destroyed itself; and, as it did so, he had discovered the virtues of acquiescence, the satisfaction of existing for the present day yet maintaining a separate unflawed identity in the midst of turmoil. Lounging, remembering, making love— yet squeezing the utmost from each spell of creative energy— he had hit on a mode of life that occupied the imagination and engaged the senses.

It is customary to deplore Byron's existence at the Palazzo Mocenigo. Many of the details of his two years' tenancy are still obscure; what we can gather of his intimate life between 1817 and 1819, among his horde of quarrelsome servants and grasping mistresses, suggests a bohemianism verging on extreme disorder; but his critical faculty was undimmed, his genius active. Dissipation is stimulating to some men, to others stupefying; and Byron, though his physical stamina was decidedly limited and he was no debauchee of the heroic eighteenth-century mould—a Casanova, a Maurice de Saxe, or even a Sheridan—would appear to have belonged to the former category. Compromises he did not disdain, but half-measures, at least in his amusements, he had always detested; and, whereas his first Venetian years had been cheerfully dissolute, the second became a race against advancing middle age—on January 22 had he not celebrated his thirtieth birthday?—a headlong career in the pursuit of extreme sensation. Again the Carnival had descended and caught him up. Soon he was "in

the *estrum* and agonies of a new intrigue" with (he explained
to his publisher) he could not tell exactly "whom or what, except that she is insatiate of love, and won't take money, and
has light hair and blue eyes . . . and that I met her at the
Masque, and that when her mask is off, I am as wise as ever."
He was determined, he added, to make what he could of the
remainder of his youth. He would work its mine (he told
Moore) "to the last vein. . . . And then—good night." He
could feel that he had enjoyed and lived.

For so deliberate a debauchee, he proved unusually thor-
ough-going; but here, as at so many stages of Byron's history,
the affectation and the sincerity are hard to disentangle, since
the apparent pose was founded on a real emotion. This year,
when the Carnival had come to an end, there was no slackening
in the whirligig of Byron's pleasures. His establishment was
well suited to the life he led. Presided over somewhat ineffi-
ciently by his English valet, "the learned Fletcher," who hated
foreign countries and had already been dragged to Athens and
Constantinople, and whose frequent escapades bore a certain
resemblance to those of his master, it included "about fourteen
servants," mostly Italian footmen, besides a floating population of Venetian parasites. Unnamed and unnumbered, his
concubines came and went—usually women of the poorer class,
loud and quarrelsome, yet gifted with a power of expression
that often delighted him. Thus, such a one—a rival of Margarita Cogni—announced that there was war to the death between them—a *Guerra di Candia!* And was it not odd (he
asked) "that the lower order of Venetians should still allude
proverbially to that famous contest,[3] so glorious and so fatal
to the Republic?" Other turns of phrase also amused and struck
him. How characteristic of these tall violent-tempered doxies

[3] Candia fell to Turkey in 1669, after a siege that had lasted twenty-five years.

that they should speak, not of their hearts, like a love-lorn Englishwoman, but of their *viscere* or entrails! Visceral, indeed, was his own response to their naïve caresses. Yet there was an intellectual charm, too, in these curious contacts and in the sudden glimpses they brought of manners and characters —some flash of eloquence from the lips of a Venetian prostitute, some movement expressive of passion and pride and dignity in which the splendour of the fallen Republic seemed to have risen again.

Of the English labouring classes he had known little or nothing, though he had been a familiar of the flash world of boxers and fencers, and had taken a paternal interest in the affairs of his Newstead household. But in Venice he surrounded himself with men and women drawn from the very lowest levels of the Italian populace—harlots and pimps and gondoliers and their dependants and families. During the same century, another Englishman—one of very different aspect and moral outlook—was to devote his genius to the declining city and make a temporary home there. But when Ruskin walked the piazza before the great basilica he averted his eyes with shuddering revulsion from the spectacle of the Venetian proletariat —from the knots of men who, in the porch of San Marco, among the columns of jasper, porphyry, serpentine, beneath the delicate interlacements of Byzantine capitals, lay "all day long . . . basking in the sun like lizards"; while "unregarded children,—every heavy glance of their young eyes full of desperation and stony depravity, and their throats hoarse with cursing,—gamble, and fight, and snarl, and sleep, hour after hour, clashing their bruised centesimi upon the marble ledges of the church porch." It is not unreasonable to imagine that, in these savage congeries, were the sons and grandsons of men who had once known Byron, who had run clandestine errands for him in Venetian byways or had enjoyed his hospitality in the servants' quarters of the Palazzo Mocenigo. More philosophic and less intellectual than the Victorian æsthete, Byron had much to learn, he discovered, from the Venetian underworld.

Energy he worshipped; and it was certainly abundant here. The Fornarina, who, though not for some time a regular inmate, strode in and out of his apartments just as it suited her, was the personification of force and greed and animal violence, mixed with animal devotion to her chosen bed-fellow. Regarding his other favourites, when they were out of her sight, she remained indifferent. He might have a hundred, she declared; but to her she knew that he must always return; and such was her physical hold that for many months the boast was justified. Moreover, she made him laugh—an exceedingly important point. ". . . In her *fazziolo* . . . she looked beautiful; but, alas! she longed for a hat and feathers"; and in spite of anything that Byron could say or do, in spite of his burning her hats as soon as she bought them, she insisted on attempting to play the lady. "Then she would have her gowns with a *tail* . . . nothing would serve her but *"l'abito colla 'coua'* . . . and as her cursed pronunciation of the word made me laugh, there was an end of all controversy, and she dragged this diabolical train after her everywhere."

Naturally, there were outrageous scenes, as when on the last night of the Carnival she had snatched the mask from the face of the distinguished and high-born Madame Contarini, who happened at the moment to have accepted Byron's arm.[4] He

---

[4] ". . . I omitted to tell you her answer when I reproached her for snatching Madame Contarini's mask. . . . I represented to her that she was a lady of high birth, 'una dama,' etc. She answered, 'Se Elle è dama, mi [io] son Veneziana— If she is a lady, I am a Venetian.' This would have been fine a hundred years ago . . . but, alas! Venice, and her people, and her nobles, are alike returning fast to the Ocean." Byron to John Murray, August 9, 1819.

could daunt her, her lover found, if he was really angry; but more often he would dissolve into good-natured laughter because her slang and impudence and buffooneries were so disarming. At her most passionate she was invested with a kind of splendour; and among other impressions of the wonderful virago that he recalled at a later period was the picture of the Fornarina, one stormy night, awaiting him on the steps of the Palazzo Mocenigo. He had been overtaken as he returned from the Lido by a heavy squall; "the Gondola put in peril—hats blown away, boat filling, oar lost, tumbling sea, thunder, rain in torrents, night coming, and wind increasing. On our return, after a tight struggle, I found her on the open steps . . . with her great black eyes flashing through her tears, and the long dark hair, which was streaming drenched with rain over her brows and breast. . . . The wind blowing her hair and dress about her tall thin figure, and the lightning flashing round her, with the waves rolling at her feet, made her look like Medea alighted from her chariot, or the Sibyl of the tempest. . . . On seeing me safe, she did not wait to greet me . . . but calling out to me—*Ah! can'della Madonna, xe esto il tempo per andar' al'Lido* (Ah! Dog of the Virgin, is this a time to go to the Lido?), ran into the house, and solaced herself with scolding the boatmen. . . . I was told by the servants that she had only been prevented from coming in a boat to look after me, by the refusal of all the Gondoliers of the Canal to put out into the harbour . . . and that then she sate down on the steps in all the thickest of the Squall, and would neither be removed nor comforted. Her joy at seeing me again was moderately mixed with ferocity, and gave me the idea of a tigress over her recovered Cubs."

To these qualities she added a smattering of the more domestic virtues; and when, following a quarrel with the baker her husband (whom she stigmatized as that *becco etico* or consumptive cuckold), she finally established herself at the Palazzo Mocenigo in the role of housekeper or *donna di governo*, "the expences were reduced to less than half, and everybody did their duty better . . ." even the English valet whom she had terrified into complete submission. Byron appreciated a chance of economizing. Almost for the first time his expenditure did not exceed his income; the rent of his palace on the Grand Canal, which he had taken fully furnished from its Venetian owner, amounted to only two hundred pounds a year; and, although he had spent five thousand since his arrival in Venice, at least two-thirds of that amount had been devoted to women. But with security developed a recognition of the value of money. The writer who had once declined to accept his royalties (which he preferred should become the perquisite of his old friend Dallas) had now a very different attitude toward literary money-making, drove a hard bargain with his London publisher, and was insistent in his demands for a punctual settlement. Independence had begun to bring out a vein of stubbornness; and the egotism of a man who had always been lazy was now complicated by the habits that are bred of solitude, the self-sufficiency of an egotist who had been much alone. His freedom of action and peace of spirit he was determined to safeguard. Claire had continued to write to him after the birth of Allegra; and her pleas, which he continued to leave unanswered—he could not forgive her for initial shamelessness: there were still traces of the Scottish puritan in Byron's temperament—more often accompanied by letters from Shelley. Something must be done about Allegra's future. And, whereas Byron's intentions were generous, his plans were vague. On one point, however, he was extremely definite; and when his comfort seemed in danger he was often brutal. He would not permit Claire Clairmont to enter his life again.

If she liked to give up the child, he would gladly adopt her. "I shall acknowledge and breed her myself," he had written to Kinnaird, "giving her the name of Biron (to distinguish her from little Legitimacy). . . ." But there could be no place for Claire in any arrangement he made; and Shelley, assuming that curiously diplomatic style which he assumed when it became necessary to write to Byron, needed all his tact to prepare the way for a working compromise. Claire, he admitted, was exacting and tiresome—he had himself suffered from her moodiness and fits of temper—but if Byron sought to violate a mother's claims, "the opinion of the world might indeed be fixed on you, with such blame as your friends could not justify . . . wholly unlike those ridiculous and unfounded tales which . . . make your friends so many in England, at the expense of those who fabricated them." At last, after some bickering and, on the part of Claire, much misery and anxious hesitation, it was decided that the child should be handed over to her father. The Shelleys were now legally man and wife, for they had been married with Godwin's blessing on December 13, 1816; and during March 1818, accompanied by Claire and Allegra and their own two children, they left England, reaching Milan on the fourth of April. Hence Allegra, under the charge of a Swiss nursemaid, Elise Foggi, was dispatched on the twenty-eighth to join her father's household at the Palazzo Mocenigo. Byron admired the little girl's beauty and liked her spirit. He was determined that she should be provided for in a proper manner; but he was scarcely qualified to superintend her upbringing, which devolved on her nurse and the Italian servants, with occasional help from Margarita Cogni, who was inclined to spoil her and upset her stomach by gifts of sweetmeats. But Mrs. Hoppner, the wife of the British consul, like Elise "a Swissesse," pronounced by Shelley to be "mild and beautiful, and unprejudiced in the best sense of the word," was there to keep an eye on the child's development and safeguard her against the more mischievous effects of her Italian background.

Wild stories of Byron's life in Italy had already been circulated. Much might be forgiven to an Englishman who was young and rich; but even in Venice he was considered a somewhat extravagant personage; and he himself had never been reluctant to improve a scandal. Otherwise what need to keep John Murray posted on the details of his love-affairs and escapades? He knew that his letters would be handed around in Murray's parlour; and that literary gatherings at decorous Albemarle Street, in a setting of mahogany and damask and Turkey carpet, beneath the solemn classic busts that adorned the bookcase, would be stirred and enlivened by his account of some passing passion—the Carnival acquaintance, "a little Bacchante," whom he had made an appointment to meet that evening at her milliner's or the peasant girl he had picked up on his daily ride. In scandal as in everything else he liked effrontery. But, although his reputation, which by that time was beyond repair, suffered perhaps very little extra damage, and though the faculties of mind and imagination did not deteriorate, there were presently hints that his nerves were rattled and his health disordered. Solitude was beginning to make him touchy and petulant. True, he enjoyed the society of his social inferiors, but he missed his equals; and it infuriated him that his London friends, absorbed in their world of pleasure and politics—Kinnaird getting rid of his mistress, John Cam angling for election to Parliament—should be inattentive to his requests and unpunctual in the replies they sent to his letters. Might they not have guessed that he was sometimes lonely? The commissions he gave them were seldom executed; and, when he wrote for magnesia, hair-oil, tooth powder, the wrong articles were often procured or the books and medicaments he required were delayed in transit. Hobhouse, Kinnaird, Murray had all annoyed him. His lawyer, John Hanson, nicknamed "Spooney," had the impertinence to suggest that he should leave Venice and meet him half-way beside the Lake of Geneva merely to sign papers connected with the sale of Newstead. He would do nothing of the kind, he wrote to Hobhouse. Hanson must pack his bags and set out for Venice. He was unwell, he announced in April, and he could not move. The origins of his indisposition he did not specify.

It depressed him, moreover, to learn of the death of Lady Melbourne.[5] The time had gone by when he "could feel for the dead . . ." and such events left only "a numbness worse than pain," comparable in terms of the body to the effect of a violent blow on the elbow; but he remembered and regretted her as "the best, and kindest, and ablest female I ever knew—old or young." She had been his "greatest *friend*," he remarked elsewhere, "of the feminine gender:—when I say 'friend' I mean *not* mistress, for that's the antipode." There is reason to suspect that it was merely the difference of ages—the fact that, at the time of their first intimacy, Lady Melbourne was sixty-two and her admirer not yet twenty-five—that saved a delightful friendship from collapsing into a conventional love-affair. Had "dear Lady M." been a few years younger, what a fool she might have made of him, he once reflected! Luckily, although young in spirit and fresh in mind, she had been past the time of life

[5] Lady Melbourne died at Melbourne House, Whitehall, on April 6, 1818.

when a "scrape" was feasible; and their association had had some of the charms of love yet lacked its difficulties. The voice with which she spoke to him had the authority of an earlier period, an epoch that, although it accepted passion and cherished romantic vagaries, still subordinated both passion and romanticism to the dictates of common sense, and was rational and reflecting first and impulsive afterward. She had no use for the extravagances and tantrums of Lady Caroline Lamb. Not that—even to her own favourite second son—she would have expected any wife to be entirely faithful; what had disgusted her was the romantic parade of unbridled feeling, the perverse enjoyment of emotion for emotion's sake. Byron shared her prejudices and admired her worldly wisdom. In theory, at all events, he was the least romantic—indeed, the least Byronic—of human beings; and, had it been his way to live more by reflection and less by instinct, with Lady Melbourne's help, theory and practice might perhaps have been reconciled. As it was, though he had learned much from Lady Melbourne, had sought her advice during his miserable affair with her daughter-in-law and made her the confidante of his perplexities over Lady Frances Webster, "the white rose" whose virginal innocence had been so nearly sullied, "ma tante" was herself indebted to him for many strange discoveries —that there were situations in which common sense might be unable to shed its light, dark corners of the human spirit she had not yet penetrated, depths of moral indecorum beyond her guessing. In the end, it was Lady Melbourne who had been shocked and flustered, and she had weakly encouraged him to pay his court to her brother's daughter: marriage *à la mode* would calm and steady him. The collapse of her protégé's marriage, and the tremendous hubbub that had centred upon the separation, had quite jolted Lady Melbourne out of the remains of her *savoir vivre*. And from that point she had declined any further part in the Byronic drama.

For Byron her death meant the disappearance of yet another tie between himself and England. He valued friendship as he had never valued love—there were both elements in his passionate feeling for Augusta. And the loss of Lady Melbourne helped to increase that sense of solitude—of isolation, moral, physical, and intellectual—which had been growing on him since he had said good-bye to Hobhouse and had given himself up to the bohemian pleasures of the Palazzo Mocenigo. The only English acquaintance he met regularly was Richard Hoppner; for the consul had taken the place of Hobhouse as his companion in daily rides along the Lido, and Byron occasionally attended Mrs. Hoppner's evening parties. Then Shelley wrote, announcing that he would like to see him. This was during August 1818. The rumours that Shelley had at first tactfully discounted were growing more and more persistent. They were accompanied by complaints from Allegra's nursemaid, who spoke of herself and her charge as lost in a wilderness of foreign servants, mostly Italian menservants of indifferent morals. Claire announced vehemently that she must see Allegra. It was obvious that, if she travelled to Venice unaccompanied, Byron would regard her visit as an attempt on his privacy, and Shelley therefore promised to act as escort. After an exhausting journey they arrived in a violent rainstorm; as they crouched in the damp shelter of the gondola's cabin with the rain thrashing down upon the roof and blurred lights sliding past them along dark canals, the talkative gondolier (who knew nothing of their destination) related long stories of the English nobleman who had made his home in Venice—a fantastically extravagant and eccentric personage whose luxuries and prodigalities were common knowledge. At the hotel, a waiter took up the story—evidently it was a popular one in Venice—adding further details for the edification of the English tourists. That morning, soon after breakfast, they visited the consul. Mrs. Hoppner had immediately sent for the little girl, who looked pale and appeared to have "lost a good deal of her liveliness" but, to Shelley's eyes at least, was still extremely pretty. The account that the Hoppners gave of Byron "unfortunately corresponded too justly with most of what" the travellers had already heard, "though doubtless [added Shelley] with some exaggeration. We discussed a long time the mode in which I had better proceed with him, and at length determined that Claire's being there should be concealed, as Mr. Hoppner says he often expresses his extreme horror of her arrival, and the necessity it would impose on him of instantly quitting Venice."

The same day, at three o'clock in the afternoon, followed Shelley's cautious visit to the Palazzo Mocenigo. But Byron's attitude had never been easy to forecast; and (as Shelley noted with surprise) "he was delighted to see me . . . and the anxiety he shows to satisfy us and Claire, is very unexpected." True, he did not wish that Claire should take the child to Florence, "because the Venetians will think that he has grown tired of her and dismissed her; and he has already the reputation of caprice." Besides, very naturally, it had occurred to him that, should Claire once regain Allegra, she would be unwilling to give her up, "and there will be a second renewal of affliction and a second parting." However, he agreed to a week's reunion, and added that, after all, he had no right over the child. "If Claire likes to take it, let her take it. I do not say what most people would in that situation, that I will refuse to provide for it, or abandon it . . . but she must surely be aware herself how very imprudent such a measure would be."

In fact, the whole conversation passed off far more mildly than Shelley had anticipated; and, though he was anxious to rejoin Claire at Mrs. Hoppner's, it was difficult (since Claire's presence was yet unknown) to refuse to accompany Byron on his afternoon's exercise. Very unwillingly, therefore, he entered the gondola and was rowed out "to a long sandy island which defends Venice from the Adriatic. When we disembarked, we found his horses waiting . . . and we rode along the sands of the sea." Their talk (Shelley told Mary) "consisted in histories of his wounded feelings, and questions of my affairs, and great professions of friendship and regard for me." The impressions of that ride and of the splendid sunset that greeted them as they returned to Venice, with the distant Alps hovering upon the northern skyline and the Euganean Hills vaguely shadowed upon the west, formed the substance of *Julian and Maddalo*. Next morning rose "rainy, cold and dim." Shelley called at the Palazzo Mocenigo before Byron had finished dressing; and, while he waited, he played with Allegra in the deserted billiard room and amused her by trundling billiard balls across the floor. Then Byron entered, again affectionate, calm, and equable. Shelley's conviction of his greatness was not revised. "Count Maddalo [he was to write, in a prose foreword to the somewhat lame verses he composed that autumn] is a person of the most consummate genius, and capable, if he would direct his energies to such an end, of becoming the redeemer of his degraded country. But it is his weakness to be proud. . . . His passions and his powers are incomparably greater than those of other men; and, instead of the latter having been employed in curbing the former, they have mutually lent each other strength. . . . I say that Maddalo is proud, because I can find no other word to express the concentred and impatient feelings which consume him; but it is on his own hopes and affections only that he seems to trample, for in social life no human being can be more gentle, patient, and unassuming. . . . His serious conversation is a sort of intoxication. . . . There is an inexpressible charm in his relation of his adventures in different countries."

If Byron encouraged Shelley's inclination toward hero-worship, Shelley in Byron would seem to have evoked a kind of coquetry. For Byron enjoyed shocking his friend but was delighted to please him. And, simultaneously on his best and his worst behaviour, he was now caustic, disparaging, and misanthropic, now benevolent, accommodating, the creature of generous impulses. It was in the last mood that he proposed that the Shelleys and their household should take possession of a villa which he had rented from the Hoppners but had himself never occupied, near Este among the Euganean Hills.[6] Shelley accepted the invitation; but no sooner had Mary arrived at Este than Clara, their second child, fell ill with dysentery and they were obliged to hurry on to Venice, where the baby died. Both parents were deeply distressed; neither of them proved ultimately inconsolable. Clara had expired on Thursday, September 24; on Saturday, "an idle day," Mary went to the Lido and encountered Byron; on Sunday, after reading the Fourth Canto of *Childe Harold,* she visited "the Doge's palace, Ponte dei Sospiri, etc.," the Accademia with Mr. and Mrs. Hoppner, and the Palazzo Mocenigo, in which she caught sight of the Fornarina. From Venice the Shelleys turned back to the villa at Este, a romantic place, its garden

[6] "Allegra is well, but her mother (whom the Devil confound) came prancing the other day over the Apennines—to see her *shild;* which threw my Venetian loves (who are none of the quietest) into great combustion; and I was in a pucker till I got her to the Euganean hills, where she & the child are now. . . ." Byron to Mrs. Leigh, September 21, 1818.

divided only by a narrow ravine from a hill which bore on its summit a ruined castle. Below them stretched the vast extent of the Lombard lowlands; ". . . there was something infinitely gratifying to the eye [wrote Mary] in the wide range of prospect commanded by our new abode"; but the restlessness that devoured Shelley was not easily dissipated and mid-October found them again in Venice with the Hoppners and Byron, preparing for an expedition to the south of Italy. By the end of October Allegra had been committed to the care of Mrs. Hoppner (who Byron had now agreed should take charge of her upbringing, since conditions of life at the Palazzo Mocenigo became every day more and more irregular) and the Shelleys flitted south toward Rome and Naples.

Meanwhile Shelley had spent further hours in Byron's company. And Byron (one imagines), now tired of charming, had exhibited other aspects of his personality and had been more prodigal of hints and confidences than his companion cared for. The intoxication of his conversation was at length an irritant. Profound as was Shelley's reverence for Byron's poetic gift, he was disconcerted by the mood that informed *Childe Harold* and by the positive malevolence that he seemed to detect in its concluding canto. The spirit in which it was written (he remarked to Peacock) "is, if insane, the most wicked and mischievous insanity that ever was given forth. It is a kind of obstinate and self-willed folly, in which he hardens himself." He had remonstrated with the author (he added), but to very little purpose, "on the tone of mind from which such a view of things alone arises. For its real root is very different from its apparent one." The fact was that the Italian women among whom Byron spent his time were "perhaps the most contemptible of all who exist under the moon—the most ignorant, the most disgusting, the most bigoted; Countesses smell so strongly of garlic that an ordinary Englishman cannot approach them. Well, L.B. is familiar with the lowest sort of these women, the people his gondolieri pick up in the streets." But there was worse to come—a suggestion that Byron may for a time have reverted to the habits and prepossessions of his Levantine period. Venice was a cosmopolitan, half-Eastern city; and included in the list of his nefarious boon companions were "wretches [observed Shelley with chill disdain] who seem almost to have lost the gait and physiognomy of man, and who do not scruple to avow practices, which are not only not named, but I believe even conceived in England." Byron's attitude appeared to be one of splenetic lassitude. "He says he disapproves, but he endures. He is heartily and deeply discontented with himself; and contemplating in the distorted mirror of his own thoughts the nature and the habits of man, what can he behold but objects of contempt and despair?"

He did not doubt (Shelley concluded), and, indeed, for Byron's sake he ought to hope, that "his present career must end soon in some violent circumstance." Yet so remarkable are the defensive powers of human nature, and so diverse the materials on which genius feeds, that there was no dramatic or scandalous finale to Byron's existence at the Palazzo Mocenigo. It seems to have been true, nevertheless, that he was disgusted and discontented. From dissipation he had toppled over into flat satiety; and, although he was convinced that he had said good-bye to England and was out of patience with the majority of his English friends—he could not forgive Hobhouse, he wrote, "(or anybody) the atrocity of their late neglect and silence"—the present was still overshadowed by thoughts of his past life. Nervous exhaustion had begun to make him acutely sensitive. After many remonstrances and as many delays, his lawyer and his lawyer's son—"Spooney" and "Young

Spooney"—arrived in Venice with the Newstead papers on November 12. Unfortunately, they had brought only one of the three large packages entrusted by Murray to their care; and the package Hanson happened to have selected contained not a single book but "a few different-sized kaleidoscopes, tooth brushes, tooth powder, etc. etc." Byron's indignation and disappointment were extreme. For some hours he would not be pacified. Then his gondola drew up at the steps of the hotel and, at seven o'clock in the evening, John and Charles Hanson were conducted with ceremony to their employer's presence.

As in most Venetian residences of the more pretentious kind, the ground floor of the Palazzo Mocenigo was neither furnished nor inhabited. Damp, sea-smelling, obscure, it served as a repository for Byron's carriages, stranded there with raised shafts and tarnished armorial trimmings, and as a home for the various animals he had collected. To Mütz, the Swiss mastiff (who, ferocious as he appeared, was once put to flight by a pig during a drive through the Apennines), Byron had recently added a fox and a wolf, besides a heterogeneous assemblage of "dogs, birds, monkeys. . . . As his lordship passed to his gondola, he used to stop and amuse himself with watching their antics, or would feed them himself occasionally." It pleased him to live surrounded by dependent creatures; and to this trait rather than to any genuine love of animals (though he had valued the companionship of several enormous and devoted dogs) may perhaps be attributed that weakness for forming menageries which added so much to the discomfort and confusion of his domestic background. Having threaded their way between coaches and animal-pens, father and son now ascended a massive marble staircase which gave access to the master's apartments on the *piano nobile*. They were ushered through a vast and empty billiard room, next through a bedchamber, finally to the threshold of an inner room where Byron welcomed them. He seemed almost painfully nervous, Charles Hanson noticed. The lawyer belonged to his youth—to Newstead and Nottingham; he had been associated with the long-drawn crisis of 1816; and Byron, suddenly confronted by his staid and prosaic figure, for some moments could not speak, while his eyes were tear-fogged. At length, with an effort, he was able to break the silence. "Well, Hanson!" he brought out. "I never thought you would have ventured so far. I rather expected you would have sent Charles."

Other details of that first visit remain unrecorded. Much legal business was gone through; on November 17 Byron signed a new codicil to his will, which Fletcher witnessed. Then, learning from the Hansons that Mr. Townsend, who had accompanied them from England as the representative of Colonel Wildman, had been at Harrow, he sent his valet with an invitation to the Hôtel d'Angleterre. As soon as Townsend arrived, they moved to the billiard room; and during the two hours that the game lasted, Byron's spirits soared to the topmost level. "His questions about Harrow and the Drurys were incessant"; and as he talked he perpetually bit his finger-nails, a nervous habit to which all his life he had been addicted. In other respects, the impression he made was singular. What the younger man had expected we do not know—what disdainful poetic apparition, compact of fashionable arrogance and literary elegance, with pure lofty brow and classic profile. If he remembered Byron distinctly, it was as young and slender. But twenty-four months of Venetian excesses and the Venetian climate had altered his physical entity as much as it had changed his moral being. Already, during the course of the previous year, he had written to inform his sister that he had "got large, ruddy, & rubustious to a degree which would please you—& shock me"; and since that time the inroads of middle age had grown more and more manifest. ". . . He looked 40. His face had become pale, bloated, and sallow." There could be no longer any doubt that he was decidedly corpulent. Whereas he had once been muscular, alert, and upright, the outline of his shoulders was now heavy and stooping; and "the knuckles of his hands were lost in fat." [7] With his long, greying curls, his rings and brooches, the outmoded clothes he wore, he suggested less the eminent poet than the declining dandy—an expatriate of dubious propensities but distinguished origins, the somewhat spoiled and superannuated man of pleasure.

[7] "Of our poor dear B. I have received 2 letters within this last year:—the last dated Septr. This is all I can tell you *from* him, and that he wrote (*as usual to me*) on the old subject very uncomfortably, and on his present pursuits, which are what one would dread and expect; a string of low attachments. *Of* him,—I hear he looks *very well*, but *fat*, immensely large, and his hair long." Mrs. Leigh to Hodgson, December 30, 1818.

Chapter Four

Y ET there would have been no truth in any imputation of
literary decadence. However his Venetian career had
affected his health and spirits, it had not dulled the edge
of his creative faculty or at all hindered the execution of his
poetic plans. Though during the latter part of 1818 very often
he is said to have been so disturbed by the confusion of his
household that he would leave the palazzo and spend the night
in his gondola out on the lagoon, and though the complication
of his intrigues was labyrinthine, seldom had he been more
busily occupied or to better purpose. Erratic hours and irregular methods had always suited him. He preferred to write
when his imagination was inflamed, with the cumulative excitement of the day coursing through his system; and, since
frequently he did not leave his bed till late in the afternoon
and (like Brummell) passed several hours in bathing and
dressing, after which he needed exercise and congenial company, he could rarely sit down to his writing table till night
had descended. Then he wrote rapidly, feverishly, with few
erasures. During recent months he had given much thought to
the condition of poetry and, in solitude, had formed a definite

scheme of his tastes and prejudices. The moderns he abhorred, though an exception was made for Crabbe and his old acquaint- ance, the banking poetaster Samuel Rogers; but "I am con- vinced, the more I think of it [he had written to Murray] that . . . *all* of us—Scott, Southey, Wordsworth, Moore, Camp- bell, I—are . . . in the wrong, one as much as another; that we are upon a wrong revolutionary poetical system, or sys- tems, not worth a damn in itself, and from which none but Rogers and Crabbe are free; and that the present and next generations will finally be of this opinion. I am the more con- firmed in this by having lately gone over some of our classics, particularly Pope. . . . I took Moore's poems and my own and some others, and went over them side by side with Pope's, and I was really astonished . . . and mortified at the ineffable distance in point of sense, harmony, effect, and even *Imagina- tion*, passion and *Invention*, between the little Queen Anne's man, and us of the Lower Empire. Depend upon it, it is all Horace then, and Claudian now . . . and if I had to begin again, I would model myself accordingly.

"Crabbe's the man [he continued], but he has got a coarse and impracticable subject, and Rogers, the grandfather of living Poetry, is retired upon half pay. . . ." Odd as it may strike the contemporary reader that the weak finicking elegance of Rogers's verses, and the bareness and grimness of Crabbe's rustic narrative (from which occasional beauties spring like flowers of heath and foreshore, struggling with effort through a harsh and sandy soil), should be thus admired by the more exuberant and fertile poet, there is no reason to doubt the sincerity of Byron's criticism. His own influence in modern literature he had always depreciated. If not ashamed of *Childe Harold*, he was certainly tired of him—tired of the imitation and uncomprehending adulation which the antics of that prodigious personage still aroused; and he had determined that his new poem should reflect a completely different mood— one far closer to the spirit of his Venetian holiday. Naturally, since he was above all things a creature of paradox and since, both in question of poetry and the problems of personal life, instinct proved invariably stronger than considered judgment, the work as it took shape was by no means classical and had little in common with the concision and correctitude of the English Augustan poets. On the contrary, its scheme was loose and its detail slipshod. As before, the quality that redeemed the work was an abounding gusto.

Few poems seem to have been produced with more enjoyment than the First and Second Cantos of *Don Juan. Beppo*, written soon after his arrival in Venice, a dashing verse anecdote of ninety-nine stanzas, was a *ballon d'essai* for the longer poem; and, having grown accustomed to a divagatory expansive strain and abandoned his original idea of attempting a prose story, he set about the creation of a non-romantic hero. At last he would be as honest in literature as the conventions allowed him. Into the character of *Don Juan* he would pour all his own youthful experience—as much of it, at any rate, as he could convey with propriety—and the considered cynical judgment of his adult years. The tone was to be lightly astringent, mildly scathing—like youth itself, buoyant and yet bitter, carelessly cheerful and pessimistic in the same degree. It was meant (he wrote to Moore on September 19, 1818, announcing the completion of Canto I) "to be a little quietly facetious upon everything." He doubted whether it were not "too free" for his modest public, who would tolerate libertinism only if it were sentimental. "However, I shall try the experiment anonymously; and if it don't take, it will be discontinued."

On November 12, under the somewhat incongruous chaper-
onage of Lord Lauderdale, a stolid Scottish nobleman who
happened to pass through Venice, the First Canto of *Don Juan*
was sent back to London. By way of preface, there was a "good,
simple, savage" apostrophe to the Poet Laureate, Bob Southey,
whom Byron had admired at Holland House—chiefly on account of his magnificent head—but for whom his feelings had
now turned to violent hatred, since Southey had thrown in his
lot with the government party and had circulated a malicious
rumour regarding Byron's adventures in Switzerland.[1] The
renegade Pantisocrat and his fellow Lake poets were soundly
battered—Coleridge and his metaphysical incomprehensibili-
ties:

> . . . Like a hawk encumber'd with his hood,—
> Explaining metaphysics to the nation—
> I wish he would explain his Explanation

—Wordsworth and the ponderous products of his conservative
middle age:

> . . . Wordsworth, in a rather long "Excursion"
> (I think the quarto holds five hundred pages)
> Has given a sample from the vasty version
> Of his new system to perplex the sages;
> 'Tis poetry—at least by his assertion,
> And may appear so when the dog-star rages . . .

—Southey himself, the lick-spittle laureate of a Tory minister,
who had prostituted the language of Milton to the service of
tyranny:

> Think'st thou, could he—the blind Old Man—arise,
> Like Samuel from the grave, to freeze once more

[1] "I have given it to Master Southey. . . . I understand the scoundrel said,
on his return from Switzerland two years ago, that 'Shelley and I were in a
league of Incest,' etc., etc. He is a burning liar! . . ." Byron to Murray, November 24, 1818.

The blood of monarchs with his prophecies,
　　Or be alive again—again all hoar
With time and trials, and those helpless eyes,
And heartless daughters—worn—and pale—and poor;
Would *he* adore a sultan? *he* obey
The intellectual eunuch Castlereagh?

Equally downright was the spirit that informed his narrative poem; and no sooner had he introduced his Spanish hero than in the portrait of Don Juan's mother, Donna Inez, he began—perhaps at first not quite intentionally—to reproduce the features of Lady Byron, blue-stocking, mathematician, prude, and moralist, the only woman from whom he had received as much pain as he had himself inflicted. After the complicated and agonizing emotions of the last two years, the regrets, the recriminations, the baffled fury, it was a relief to descend to light-hearted ridicule:

His mother was a learned lady, famed
For every branch of every science known—
In every Christian language ever named,
With virtues equalled by her wit alone:
She made the cleverest people quite ashamed
And even the good with inward envy groan,
Finding themselves so very much exceeded
In their own way by all the things that she did . . .

Her favourite science was the mathematical,
Her noblest virtue was her magnanimity;
Her wit (she sometimes tried at wit) was Attic all,
Her serious sayings darken'd to sublimity . . .

Some women use their tongues—she *look'd* a lecture,
Each eye a sermon, and her brow a homily,
An all-in-all sufficient self-director,
Like the lamented late Sir Samuel Romilly,
The Law's expounder, and the state's corrector,
Whose suicide was almost an anomaly—

One sad example more, that "All is vanity,"—
(The jury brought their verdict in "Insanity.")

In short, she was a walking calculation,
Miss Edgeworth's novels stepping from their covers,
Or Mrs. Trimmer's books on education,
Or "Cælebs' Wife" set out in quest of lovers,
Morality's prim personification,
In which not Envy's self a flaw discovers;
To others' share let "female errors fall,"
For she had not even one—the worst of all.

The reference to Sir Samuel Romilly was a later addition, written in during the period of the Hansons' visit. Against that distinguished reformer and famous advocate the poet had long cherished a bitter grudge because, having accepted a retaining fee from Byron at the time of the separation proceedings, he had subsequently acted in Lady Byron's interest.[2] During the first week of November 1818, the whole Liberal world was horrified to learn that Romilly had committed suicide by cutting his throat. It was said that the loss of his wife had unhinged his mind. The news reached Byron on November 25. Taking his gondola, he had himself carried to the Hansons' hotel; and "How strange . . . [he remarked when he had told the story] that one man will die for the loss of his partner, while another would die if they were compelled to live together!" This remark, added Charles Hanson, was made "so pointedly that my father never again referred to the delicate subject of his domestic affairs. . . ."

Yet that same week Byron once more gave way to the temptation of apostrophizing Annabella. His excuse was Romilly's death; his theme, the feeling of cold uncanny satisfaction with which it had inspired him. "Sir Samuel Romilly has

[2] Romilly, however, declared that the retaining fee had been received by a clerk without his knowledge.

cut his throat for the loss of his wife. It is now nearly three years since he became, in the face of his compact . . . the advocate of the measures and the Approver of the proceedings, which deprived me of mine." Little (he continued with venomous emphasis) could Romilly have supposed, "while he was poisoning my life at its sources . . . that in less than thirty-six moons . . . in the fulness of his professional career—in the greenness of a healthy old age—in the radiance of fame, and the complacency of self-earned riches . . . a domestic affliction would lay him in the earth, with the meanest of malefactors, in a cross-road with the stake in his body, if the verdict of insanity did not redeem his ashes from the sentence of the laws he had lived upon by interpreting or misinterpreting, and died in violating." To complete the impression, he added a touch of outrageous rhetoric—the sort of rodomontade that in others he found supremely ridiculous but that he himself could seldom resist when the context prompted: "it was not in vain that I invoked Nemesis in the midnight of Rome from the awfullest of her ruins"—and wound up with a curt but significant: "Fare you well."

Such was the intensity of exasperation to which thoughts of his wife's "unfeeling" and "inhuman" conduct could still occasionally arouse him! And it is characteristic of Byron's two-sided temperament—and the disingenuousness of his whole attitude toward his marriage—that in the portrait of Donna Inez already quoted he should have put forward his own case with the utmost restraint and humour, and exhibited his wife's absurdity with a quiet satirical cunning:

> Now Donna Inez had, with all her merit,
> A great opinion of her own good qualities . . .
> But then she had a devil of a spirit,
> And sometimes mix'd up fancies with realities,

> And let few opportunities escape
> Of getting her liege lord into a scrape . . .
>
> For Inez call'd some druggists and physicians,
> And tried to prove her loving lord was *mad*,
> But as he had some lucid intermissions,
> She next decided he was only *bad*;
> Yet when they ask'd her for her depositions,
> No sort of explanation could be had,
> Save that her duty both to man and god
> Required this conduct—which seem'd very odd.

Was this the aggrieved husband who had invoked Nemesis among the ruins of Rome—a conjuration also boasted of in one of his letters to Murray [3]—and who talked of the workings of Fate like a romantic Avenger, fresh from some fantastic story by Walpole or Radcliffe? In fact, though his literary gifts were at their highest pitch, his control over his private feelings had begun to weaken. Gradually he grew more moody, restless, and irritable. During the day that followed his successful meeting with Mr. Townsend at the Palazzo Mocenigo, when Byron's spirits had appeared so good as to be almost boisterous, "Fletcher hinted to us [wrote Charles Hanson] that his lordship was becoming fidgety for our departure"; and the legal party thereupon announced that they were leaving Venice, a decision "which his lordship seemed readily to acquiesce in." Now and then he might suffer from the pangs of loneliness; he was still subject to excruciating attacks of ennui, and yawned as deeply and dismally as once in England when he had stood at his Bennet Street window and stared out at the London fog; but solitude was a condition he had come to terms with. Youth had deserted him; health threatened to

---

[3] "So Sir Samuel Romilly has cut his throat. . . . You see that Nemesis is not yet extinct, for I had not forgot Sir S. in my imprecation, which invoked many." Byron to Murray, November 24, 1818. See *Childe Harold*, Canto IV, stanzas CXXXII–CXXXVII.

follow in the steps of youth; but he had taken the measure of his own sympathies and tastes and genius.

Don Juan is the product of a completely adult mind. It is the most mature of all Byron's poems; for, notwithstanding the irregularity or redundancy of some passages, the vulgarity of others, it gives the impression of a writer who has at length arrived at that balance which every writer aims at—between the style he handles and the subject he deals with, between the world on the one hand and himself on the other, between the inward and the outward view, the claims of observation and the charms of introspection. Simultaneously, he had been at work on a second manuscript—this time the narrative was in prose—but it seems possible that the two works were interdependent and that the clarification he achieved by writing his Memoirs was of use to him when he came to compose *Don Juan*, which received, so to speak, only an essential residue. The exact nature of his autobiography will always remain mysterious. It consisted, we know, of a sketch of his existence up to the year 1816 and terminated presumably with the story of the separation; but many important circumstances—indeed, he afterward confessed, some of the most important—had been omitted from a regard for the feelings or reputation of living persons; with the result (he informed Murray) "that I have written with too much detail of that which interested me least" and there was a danger "that my autobiographical Essay would resemble the tragedy of Hamlet at the country theatre, recited 'with the part of Hamlet left out by particular desire.' " [4] Concerning the manner of the narration, witnesses

[4] "Mr. Murray is in possession of an MSS. Memoir of mine (not to be published till I am in my grave) which, strange as it may seem, I never read over since it was written. . . . In it I have told what, as far as I know, is the *truth*— not the *whole* truth—for if I had done so I must have involved much private and dissipated history. . . . I do not know whether you have seen those MSS.;

vary. According to Lord Rancliffe, neither a trustworthy nor an unprejudiced critic, the Memoirs were of such "a low pot-house description" as thoroughly to have deserved the doom that overtook them in Mr. Murray's fireplace; while the sensitive and puritanical Lord John Russell considered that only two or three passages were in the least improper and that, apart from those passages, the autobiography might well have been printed. . . .

Today, in the possession of Byron's original publisher, there exists a notebook from which more than half the pages have been removed. Attached is a line to the effect that this notebook once contained a transcript of a part of Lord Byron's Memoirs, burned at the same time as the master copy. Otherwise the autobiography must be accounted a total loss. No doubt the style adopted resembled the prose of his letters—slightly more formal but distinguished by an equal liveliness in the choice of epithets, as characteristic in its turns of imagery and as sweeping in its enunciation of private prejudice. At the end of August 1818, he had already covered "above forty-four sheets of very large, long paper" and expected the work to extend to fifty or sixty. His intention, he explained to Murray, was to preserve the completed narrative among his papers, where it would serve as "a kind of Guide-post in case of death," forestalling some lies and helping to "destroy some which have been told already." Meanwhile the Second Canto of *Don Juan* was making extremely rapid progress. Begun on December 13, it was finished by January 20 of the following year. Juan, the precocious sixteen-year-old son of Donna Inez, having enjoyed an illicit passage with a married woman, is shipped from Spain in the hope that he will improve his conduct. The

but as you are curious in such things as relate to the human mind, I should feel gratified if you had." Byron to Isaac Disraeli, June 10, 1822.

vessel is wrecked and he is cast up on a Grecian island. Here
the destiny to which he has been born once again overwhelms
him; for he awakes from an exhausted swoon between the
arms of Haidée, a kind of nineteenth-century Miranda in Turkish costume, and without premeditation slips into a second
love-affair, as innocent, animal, and confiding as youth can
make it. To Byron, Greece and youth were almost synonymous;
and, with a delicacy not found in earlier or later poems, he
sets the scene and evokes the spirit of the time and place—
the vast glittering emptiness of a summer sea, the enormous
hush that descends at the advance of nightfall, the unperceived
isolation of the embracing lovers:

> They were alone, but not alone as they
> Who shut in chambers think it loneliness;
> The silent ocean, and the starlight bay,
> The twilight glow, which momently grew less,
> The voiceless sands, and dropping caves, that lay
> Around them, made them to each other press,
> As if there were no life beneath the sky
> Save theirs, and that their life could never die.

To credit the poem with a morality or "message" would
be, of course, absurd. Few works are more amoral in intention
or attitude. But beneath the advocacy of feeling for feeling's
sake, of sensation as an end in itself or an escape from world
despair—

> Man, being reasonable, must get drunk;
> The best of life is but intoxication:
> Glory, the grape, love, gold, in these are sunk
> The hopes of all men, and of every nation;
> Without their sap, how branchless were the trunk
> Of life's strange tree, so fruitful on occasion!

—runs a fatalism not to be confused with pagan stoicism,
which owed something perhaps to the influence of Byron's

Calvinist childhood. Caught in the weary cycle of emotional cause-and-effect (to which he is condemned by his "terrible gift of intimacy," the fatal domination that he exerts over the feelings of others), Don Juan must take the consequence of the emotions he rouses. Both the pleasure he gives and the pain he inflicts demand atonement. Both will recoil upon him through the ineluctable workings of fate. Retribution is implicit in every conquest of happiness:

> Alas! they were so young, so beautiful,
> So lonely, loving, helpless, and the hour
> Was that in which the heart is always full,
> And, having o'er itself no further power,
> Prompts deeds eternity cannot annul,
>   But pays off moments in an endless shower
> Of hell-fire—all prepared for people giving
> Pleasure or pain to one another living.

It is the troubled background from which the point of view of the poem emerges, together with the original conception of the work itself—a modern epic poem purposely stripped of all heroic trimmings—that makes *Don Juan* one of the great typical achievements of the European nineteenth century. Here (notwithstanding the author's preferences) is no attempt at symmetry or pretension to dignity. Far from wishing to attune his mind to the height of literature, the poet scales down literature to suit experience, and confers on his literary form the idiosyncrasies of his heart and temperament. An Augustan poet could address a society that shared his standards; Byron was consciously at variance with the world he spoke to; and that world, already profoundly disordered and deeply divided, still suffering from the aftermath of 1789 and from the disillusionment that followed Napoleon's downfall, showed little cohesion either in the sphere of art or in the field of politics. Such a society invites attack by the creative writer (who suffers among his contemporaries and resents the state of critical solitude in which he is obliged to exist); and *Don Juan* is deliberately provocative from start to finish. The product of an often angry but only half-embittered man, sufficiently close to the experiences of his own youth to remember its ardours, but advanced far enough in middle age to have begun to acquire detachment, the poem was likely to puzzle the young as much as it annoyed the old. For the writer treated of youth with sympathy yet in the spirit of levity, and of age and its moral judgments with youthful cynicism.

The greatest works of literature are independent of the conditions among which they were conceived: it is as an afterthought that we inquire into the facts of their genesis. To *Don Juan*, on the other hand, our response is personal; and, as we read, we are reminded at once of the Palazzo Mocenigo and of the studious nights, following idle and self-indulgent days, when Byron, usually fortified by gin-and-water, would sit up over his manuscript till dawn had broken. He seems to *talk* in verse, with the same flashes of eloquence and explosions of wit, the same light-hearted digressions and irregular expansive flow (now rising to the level of poetry, now declining to facetiousness), that we might have expected had we been listening to his conversation, though his actual conversation according to most accounts was far less brilliant. A vast number of topics are briefly covered, from the inevitable injustice of a woman's lot to a passage of expert advice concerning the treatment of hangovers. But most characteristic of all and, indeed, most moving, since it reflects alike the gaiety and the despair of the writer's mood, is the detached stanza found scribbled on the back of Canto I:

> I would to heaven that I were so much clay,
> As I am blood, bone, marrow, passion, feeling—
> Because at least the past were pass'd away—
> And for the future—(but I write this reeling,
> Having got drunk exceedingly today,
> So that I seem to stand upon the ceiling)
> I say—the future is a serious matter—
> And so—for God's sake—hock and soda water!

Byron hoped that *Don Juan* would irk his enemies: he had expected that it would be the cause of some consternation among members of his enthusiatic and gullible public: he had not imagined that it would plunge his supporters into alarm and perplexity. Yet such was the effect of its appearance at Albemarle Street. During December he was amazed to learn that Hobhouse, Kinnaird, Scrope Davies, Moore—all the friends whom John Murray had consulted—were "unanimous in advising its suppression." Many objections were alleged by these prudent men of the world: "the inexpediency of renewing his domestic troubles by sarcasms upon his wife . . . the indecency of parts . . . the attacks on religion . . . the abuse of other writers . . . "No doubt their advice was well meant; it was none the less infuriating. To Hobhouse and Kinnaird jointly he wrote back that, although the stanzas on Castlereagh might be omitted (since he was not in England to face the Minister's personal challenge), he would have no "cutting and slashing" of the body of the poem. If the composition had poetic merit, then it would stand; but he declined to give way to "all the cant of Christendom. I have been cloyed with applause, and sickened with abuse; at present I care for little but the copyright; I have imbibed a great love of money, let me have it; if Murray loses this time, he won't the next. . . . But in no case will I submit to have the poem mutilated."

At last, on Hobhouse's insistence, he decided—a decision

soon afterward revoked [5]—that *Don Juan* should be printed in an edition of fifty copies for private circulation only. The whole affair left him considerably vexed and ruffled. It was yet another proof of the slackness and cowardice of his English friends; it helped to exaggerate the condition of nervous irritability—of fidgetiness and sensitiveness, combined with spleen and lassitude—into which for the last twelve months he had been slowly sinking. This year the south wind and the Carnival arrived together. Again, as during 1817 and 1818, he devoted whole nights to the pursuit of pleasure, and wrote to Murray "in a passion and a Sirocco," having stayed up till six o'clock among Carnival gaieties. By the end of January his health was causing him serious trouble. It was his stomach, he supposed, or perhaps his liver. At least, he was unable "to eat of anything with relish but a kind of Adriatic fish called *Scampi*, which happens to be the most indigestible of marine viands." Plainly the time had come when he must reform his mode of existence: to the warnings sounded by his own constitution—which threatened complete collapse or premature decrepitude—was added the headshaking of his Venetian doctors. As a preliminary measure they recommended that he should purge his household—advice that Byron accepted with uncommon mildness. There ensued a general exodus of his more outrageous favourites; and comparative quiet settled down upon the inner apartments of the Palazzo Mocenigo.

The Fornarina, however—expelled about this period, partly, no doubt, because the physical demands she made upon him grew more and more exacting, partly because (as he told Murray) she had recently become "quite ungovernable" and

---

[5] "Tell Hobhouse that *Don Juan* must be published—the loss of the copyright would break my heart." Byron to Kinnaird, February 22, 1819.

other members of the household complained of her conduct—did not take her departure till she had put up a struggle. He had told her quietly and firmly that she must leave the palazzo —"she had acquired a sufficient provision for herself and mother, etc., in my service"—and she had gone, "threatening knives and revenge." Next day, in she stalked again with her usual effrontery, "having broke open a glass door that led from the hall below to the staircase, by way of prologue." Byron was at dinner; she snatched a knife from his hand, "cutting me slightly in the thumb in the operation," but was immediately disarmed by the valet and led down to a gondola, whence she immediately plunged head over heels into the Grand Canal. Byron, again disturbed at the dinner table, to see her carried limp and dripping up the marble stairs, superintended her resuscitation with a calm efficiency that was bred of long experience—he was no great believer in feminine suicides. His terrified servants urged him to apply for police protection —"they had always been frightened at her, and were now paralysed . . ."; but he laughed at their apprehensions and refused their pleas. "I had her sent home quietly after her recovery, and never saw her since, except twice at the opera, at a distance amongst the audience. She made many attempts to return, but no more violent ones."

With the expulsion of the Fornarina and the reformation of life at the Palazzo Mocenigo closes a whole period of Byron's development. It had marked the decisive pause between youth and middle age, when—accompanied very often by an abrupt recrudescence of physical energy—there occurs a final precipitation of tastes and talents (crystallized at length in their adult form), and a writer looks around and begins to know himself. To youth the spectacle of its own enormities is always fascinating. Middle age, though a sensitive mind may never lose its capacity for admiration, in the end forgoes its tendency to feel surprise. Not that Byron, even at this stage, had achieved self-knowledge, but he was glad now to leave his temperament the enigma he found it, and no longer harboured romantic delusions as to the enigma's import. Unluckily such discoveries are largely negative. There remained the problem how he should dispose of the years that remained to him—whether in authorship (a calling he still somewhat despised: he had always considered it a poor substitute for the life of action) or in action. But what action could he nowadays contemplate—a luxurious exile, the helpless victim of his own celebrity, his every movement watched and noted by the Austrian secret police, who gladly condoned his vices but would certainly not excuse any pretensions to heroic virtue? Besides, he was by temperament an exceedingly slothful person. He loved his comfort; he was becoming infected with the love of money.

During his adult life Byron had confronted many complex problems. Almost without exception, the outlet that he discovered was amatory or sentimental. In love he found a refuge from the pains of life, and in the experience of making love a shadowy substitute for some other more satisfying, more substantial experience—as to its precise nature he had never been definite. Once again he had notions of settling down. He was eminently suited, at least in his own opinion, to the domestic state and asked little enough of the women he lived with—merely that they should laugh with him and make him laugh, keep clear of him in his dark moods, and respect his privacy. It was too late, he feared, for an exuberant youthful passion—

No more—no more—Oh! never more on me
The freshness of the heart can fall like dew . . .

—but there was still time, and he had still the energy, to form a new attachment in which he would stabilize the vagrant emotions of the last few years and give his heart and his senses the rest they needed. The Carnival had gone by; the agitating south wind had dropped when the spring came. Sobriety had improved his health. But recovered health (as not infrequently happens in such a case as Byron's) brought with it a hollow feeling of anti-climax.

True, the temptations of promiscuity were not altogether abandoned; and to this winter belongs the story of a young Venetian girl, "unmarried and the daughter of one of their nobles," at whose window he was espied late at night by "an infernal German," a certain Countess Vorsperg, the occupant of a neighbouring palazzo, with the result that the girl was shut up on a diet of "prayers and bread and water," while a priest and a commissary of police were dispatched to Byron. He received the ambassadors civilly and gave them coffee; and afterward, when the nights grew darker at midnight and the brother had retired to Milan and the father was laid up, it proved possible to return to Angelina's bedroom or balcony. He was dismayed, however, to learn that she was determined to marry him and "proposed to me to divorce my mathematical wife. . . ." Byron replied by attempting to explain the English divorce laws, and concluded with the observation that he supposed Angelina did not wish Annabella *poisoned!* "Would you believe it? She made me *no answer.* Is not that a true and odd national trait? It spoke more than a thousand words, and yet this is a little, pretty, sweet-tempered, quiet feminine being as ever you saw. . . . I am not sure that my pretty paramour was herself fully aware of the inference to be drawn from her dead silence, but even the unconsciousness of the latent idea was striking to an observer of the Passions; and I never strike out a thought of another's or of my own without trying to trace it to its Source."

Byron's first mention of Angelina occurs in a letter to Douglas Kinnaird of March 6, 1819, where reference to "a business about a Venetian girl" who had wanted to marry him during the previous month shares the postscript with a description of a runaway elephant, "a prodigious fellow," which had terrorized Venice till slain by a cannon-shot. The second is dated May 18 and embellished with an exceedingly characteristic account of how, that same night, setting out to a rendezvous, his foot had slipped on the weedy palace-step as he entered his gondola, "and in I flounced like a Carp, and went dripping like a Triton to my Sea nymph and had to scramble up to a grated window," at which for an hour and a half he had been obliged to cling without a change of garments. The chronology of the episode is worth remarking; for, although during mid-May he was still on terms of surreptitious acquaintanceship with Angelina, at the beginning of April he had embarked on a far more serious intimacy which, in spite of himself, was to absorb him and at length subdue him, gradually robbing him of the independence he had always prized but in return bringing the emotional security he had often hankered after. While he whispered through the bars of Angelina's casement, he was already the *cavaliere servente* of a married woman.

Chapter Five

IT WAS Byron's first experience of that peculiarly Italian institution—the triangular relationship of husband and wife and lover, founded on self-interest but trimmed with sentiment. At a social distance, such households had often amused him and he had observed how smoothly and decorously they appeared to work—the husband, as soon as jealousy had gone the way of passion, politely resigning his functions to some acceptable lover (on the understanding that the lover was to maintain his dignity and do nothing to lower his wife's credit in their friends' esteem), the lover submitting to a voluntary servitude, carrying the fan, calling the carriage, and embellishing the opera-box, in return for privileges from which the regular consort preferred to abdicate. These arrangements might last a season or endure a lifetime; and pointed out both in their own circles and the whole of the Italian world were certain couples who had established a record in adulterous constancy—the grizzled *cicisbeo* still offering his arm to the decrepit mistress, year in and year out continuing to support her salon, as permanent a part of its furniture as tables or fire-screen.

Since his arrival in Italy, Byron had been careful to keep clear of sentiment; and it is the more surprising, then, that the adventures of a very few weeks or days—an assignation proposed at an evening party, followed next day by a secret rendezvous—should have been sufficient to revolutionize his line of conduct. He was himself somewhat taken aback by this change of attitude. But the origins of any love-affair are hard to analyse; for, besides the immediate physical or sentimental sympathy that may be assumed to spring up between two human beings (an element that in the majority of love-affairs is often exaggerated), we must recognize the period of preparation that precedes acquaintanceship and the various factors that have produced a determination to fall in love. On Byron's side, the existence of preparatory factors was fairly obvious. After two years of dissipation he was sick of debauchery; mentally and physically he was a little tired; while to be out of love was a condition that had always irked him —it was as if his temperament were cut off from a drug it needed. Equally plain to distinguish were the motives of the other party. Teresa Guiccioli was between nineteen and twenty and had been married a year. The third wife of a rich Romagnol landowner, she had taken over a family of grown-up step-children, and the time had come when, by all the conventions, she might demand her liberty. Nor was Guiccioli the kind of husband to dispute her wishes—sixty years old, wealthy, and good-natured, absorbed in local politics, a cultivated man of the world, with his life behind him. He was prepared for infidelity though he would demur at scandal. Things might take their course according to the accepted usages of the Venetian moral code.

Byron was neither by birth a Venetian nor by taste a moralist, and it remains astonishing that a naïve and sentimental Italian

married woman—not very different from the married women
he had known in England, no more disinterested though perhaps more downright—should have succeeded where her predecessors had so often failed. But Teresa had the strength of
mind that goes with insensitiveness. And since Frances Webster, whom in some ways she slightly resembled—both were
young, both ardent, and both unhappily married—has been
compared by Byron's biographers to an English wild rose,
with petals that have already begun to brown and curl, Teresa
Guiccioli might be likened to some Mediterranean blossom
whose relative permanence depends upon its leathery texture.
There could be no question of the ascendancy that she soon
established. Byron had first met her in the house of the Countess
Albrizzi; but he was not presented till April 1819 at a party
which was given by the Countess Benzoni. "This introduction
[she professed to remember in after years] . . . took place
contrary to our wishes, and had been permitted by us only
from courtesy. For myself, more fatigued than usual that evening on account of the late hours they keep at Venice, I went
with great reluctance to this party, and purely in obedience to
Count Guiccioli. Lord Byron, too, was averse from forming
new acquaintances, alleging that he had entirely renounced
all attachments, and was unwilling any more to expose himself to their consequences. . . ." But he was unlike any man
she had yet encountered. "His noble and exquisitely beautiful
countenance [wrote Teresa Guiccioli], the tone of his voice,
his manners, the thousand enchantments that surrounded him,
rendered him so different and so superior a being to any whom
I had hitherto seen, that it was impossible he should not have
left the most profound impression upon me." In fact, Byron
advanced a proposal that was promptly snapped up. It was
no more and no less than he had done on other occasions.

"From that evening [adds Teresa], during the whole of my subsequent stay at Venice, we met every day"; and when at last she deserted the city he prepared to follow. The summons reached him during the early summer months of 1819. Byron's carriages were made ready and he set out for the mainland.

It was only to be expected that, once launched, he should begin to feel shy of the venture. Never fond of rapid movements or of abrupt decisions, from Padua, which he reached on the second of June, he looked back toward the safety of Venice with slightly regretful eyes and forward to his goal at Ravenna with a very moderate eagerness.[1] In Venice, the development of the episode had been less incalculable; but even there Teresa's imprudences had sometimes alarmed him; for, though pretty, she had exceedingly little tact, "talked aloud" when convention suggested she ought to whisper and had recently—at a time while she was still resisting—horrified a correct assemblage at the Countess Benzoni's "by calling out to me 'mio Byron' in an audible key, during a dead silence of pause in the other prattlers, who stared and whispered their respective serventi." Well, she had capitulated, as most women did; but that was not the end of the matter, since she declined to be "content with what she had done, unless it was to be turned to the advantage of the public. . . ." In other words, she was "a sort of Italian Caroline Lamb," much prettier, it was true, but with "the same red-hot head, the same noble disdain of public opinion. . . ." Amid the dust and glare of Padua, Byron grew increasingly hesitant. Were he not a paragon of constancy, he complained to Hoppner, he might now be swimming from the beach at the Lido. Besides, there was a before and an after in every love-story; and with the second stage

[1] According to Hoppner, at a much later period, it "depended on the toss-up of a halfpenny" whether Byron followed the Guicciolis to Ravenna or returned to England.

came a diminution of the desire to move, when it meant exposing oneself to the discomforts of the Italian summer season. He would travel as far as Bologna but not a step beyond—certainly not to her home in Ravenna, as she now suggested. "To go to cuckold a Papal Count . . . in his own house" seemed (as he told Hoppner) a somewhat foolhardly enterprise; there were "several other places at least as good for the purpose."

On the road to Bologna, he paused at Ferrara; and as he wandered in the Carthusian burial place outside the city, he caught sight of a pair of Italian epitaphs that touched his imagination.

Martini Luigi
Implora pace

read one; and the other:

Lucrezia Picini
Implora eterna quiete

The modesty of the requests he found deeply moving: "the dead had had enough of life; all they wanted was rest, and this they '*implore*.' " He hoped (he added, after transcribing the inscriptions for the benefit first of Hoppner, then of John Murray) that, were he to die, he would be buried at the Lido and "those two words, and no more" put over his tomb. Meanwhile he continued his journey toward Bologna; and it was here, some three days after his arrival, that he received a letter from Teresa Guiccioli which caused him to change his mind and break the firm resolution he had expressed to Hoppner. Teresa wrote that she was ill and her life despaired of, Within a few hours he had left for Ravenna and his mistress's bedside.

Naturally his arrival in that obscure provincial town, amid all the pomp and circumstance of the Byronic travelling equipage—the vehicles, the carriage dogs, the numerous servants—produced the stir to which Teresa had been looking forward. Ill though she was, after a serious miscarriage, of which the effects were further complicated by a consumptive tendency, she was well enough to note that the appearance of so distinguished a foreign traveller "gave rise to a good deal of conversation. His motives for such a visit became the subject of discussion, and these he himself afterward involuntarily divulged; for having made some inquiries with a view to paying me a visit, and being told that it was unlikely he would ever see me again, as I was on the point of death, he replied, if such were the case, he hoped that he should die also; which circumstance being repeated, revealed the object of his journey." Teresa's husband immediately called on Byron and begged that they might have the pleasure of seeing him at the family palazzo; for Count Guiccioli's sense of decorum was always faultless, and he hoped (wrote his wife) that Lord Byron's presence "might amuse, and be of some use to me in the state in which I then found myself. . . ." Next day, Byron accepted the invitation. It was impossible (declared Teresa) to describe "the anxiety that he showed, the delicate attentions that he paid me"; and, since he felt no confidence in the local doctors, he obtained permission from the much gratified and flattered nobleman to call in at his own expense the celebrated Professor Aglietti.

Such a concentration of solicitude—the anxious attentions of husband and lover, with the sympathetic interest of the whole community—could not fail to be productive of the results desired. In a few weeks (although Byron was still occasionally doubtful and wrote to Hoppner that he feared "that the Guiccioli is going into a consumption. Thus it is with every-thing and everybody for whom I feel anything like real attach-ment . . . I never even could keep alive a dog that I liked or that liked me") the cough and the spitting of blood had quite subsided and "something else," he informed the consul, "has recommenced." The Countess bore up "most *gallantly* in every sense of the word"; and "by the aid of a Priest, a Chambermaid, a young Negro-boy, and a female friend" the lovers were able to renew their meetings, though their relation-ship was still attended with danger and difficulty. Byron, at least, would not have been surprised to receive a stiletto be-tween his shoulder-blades one dark evening; but it is possible that his view of Count Guiccioli was somewhat too romantic; for the latter, having first invited him to visit the Countess, continued to treat him to disarming displays of courtesy, till Byron had to admit that he was completely baffled. *Savoir vivre* so accomplished became at length an embarrassment. The Count (he complained) was "a very polite personage, but I wish he would not carry me out in his Coach and Six, like Whittington and his Cat." A pleasant contrast to these parades in the husband's carriage, under the eyes of all the "good society" of a decaying provincial town, were rides through the sandy avenues of the famous pine-forest, scene of Boccaccio's tale and Dryden's fable. Teresa was now sufficiently recovered to bear him company, mounted on a pony that belonged to her husband, and arrayed in "a sky-blue tiffany riding-habit" and a hat "like Punch's." He had ceased to regret Venice or the life he led there. The habit of dependence, which is the habit of fidelity, was slowly forming.

Thus, when the Guicciolis left for Bologna, Byron followed them. The two months at Ravenna had "passed viciously and agreeably"; he had "effeminated and enervated" himself "with love and the summer"; but the bond that held him to Teresa Guiccioli had not yet weakened. This affair, he had already decided, was to be his *"last* love." But it is in Byron rather than in Byron's mistress—in the preceding years, and the whole drift of his emotional temperament, rather than in any immediate change effected by Teresa—that we have to look for the explanation of this unusual constancy. Perhaps Teresa's greatest virtue was to be largely negative. Neither hopelessly, if lovably, plastic as had been Augusta, nor wild and irresponsible as had been Caroline Lamb and many others, she gratified his sensuality and pleased his sentimentality, but did not encroach upon his independence in the more individual sphere. "A nice, pretty girl [as Mary Shelley was to describe her at their first meeting], without pretensions, good-hearted, and amiable," she had regular features, statuesque but a little heavy, abundant yellow hair which she was fond of wearing in loose tresses about her shoulders, a white skin, and gracefully modelled neck and bosom. Her expression was engaging and her smile attractive. But one defect made an immediate impression on those who met her—her head and bust were out of all proportion to the rest of her body; her legs, in fact, were far too short for the weight they carried. An enthusiast, a reader of poetry, and an easy talker, she had that bloom of intelligence which gives a heightened quality to youth and freshness.

That Byron did not intend—or originally, at least, had not intended—to play the part of full-fledged *cavaliere servente*, or that the devotion he professed was other than eternal, were ideas that it would seem she had never harboured. And what Byron knew was expected of him he often did. Besides, in the lax mood induced by his Venetian life, complicated by a growing sense of personal solitude, he was grateful for the

readiness with which she had returned his passion, the eagerness with which she was prepared to sacrifice her husband
and prospects, for the warmth and candour of her youth, the
simplicity and the sincerity that she brought to a love-affair.
Nor had he any excuse for defection in her husband's attitude. The Count still gave no signs of annoyance or jealousy;
and, while sheer good nature and a certain pride in his wife's
accomplishments may no doubt have had something to do
with the line he took, it soon became evident that he had a
secondary motive. After many flattering attentions and drives
in his coach-and-six, he tendered a request that had long been
near to his heart. Like most foreigners, he underestimated
the extreme complexity of the English political and social
system. Count Guiccioli was known to the police as a secret
liberal; the political game he played in the Romagna was
somewhat risky; and he wished to have "British protection,
in case of changes." Would not his friend, therefore, arrange,
through the numerous influential connexions he, of course,
possessed in England, that he should be appointed honorary
consul or vice-consul at Ravenna? The suggestion was made
during August and immediately passed on by Byron to his
London publisher, who had valuable connexions with the Tory
party. Could not Croker do something, or Peel, or Canning?
The candidate was "a man of large property—and noble, too.
. . . Will you get this done? It will be the greatest favour to
me. If you do, I will then send his name and condition. . . ."

So Byron wrote from Bologna on August 12; for thither he
had followed the Guicciolis during the previous day. The same
letter contains an account of a theatre-party to see "the representation of Alfieri's *Mirra*. . . ." Byron (one may infer)
did not know the subject of that famous tragedy, which con-
cerns the misadventures of a Princess of Cyprus about to be

married to Pereo, the Prince of Epirus. When the play opens, Mirra is discovering a mysterious reluctance to wed the man for whom she is intended by her father. She reaches the altar but falls into a demoniac frenzy. Pereo commits suicide; and her father eventually begs Mirra to tell him the name of the man she loves, promising that he will not oppose her wishes. Mirra then confesses that it is her father himself. The old theme! Byron had watched the unfolding of the drama with fascinated attention. It was clear (his mistress saw) that he was "deeply affected. At length there came a point at which he could no longer restrain his emotions." He had been *convulsed*, he told Murray; "I do not mean by that word a lady's hysterics, but the agony of reluctant tears, and the choking shudder, which I do not often undergo for fiction. . . . The worst was, that the '*dama*,' in whose box I was, went off in the same way, I really believe more from fright than any other sympathy. . . . But she has been ill, and I have been ill, and all are languid and pathetic this morning, with great expenditure of Sal Volatile."

Some days later, the Guicciolis left for the country on a short visit; and Byron felt so disconsolate and so deserted that he sent to Venice for Allegra to relieve his tedium. By way of additional solace, he made friends with a peasant family and every day rode out to a neighbouring garden, where "I . . . walk . . . under a purple canopy of grapes, and sit by a fountain, and talk with the gardener of his toils, which seem greater than Adam's, and with his wife, and with his Son's wife, who is the youngest of the party, and, I think, talks best of the three." At other times, he re-visited the Campo Santo. His old friend, the sexton, had "the prettiest daughter imaginable; and I amuse myself with contrasting her beautiful and innocent face of fifteen with the skulls with which he has peopled several cells. . . . When I look at these, and at this girl . . . why, then, my dear Murray, I won't shock you by saying what I think. It is little matter what becomes of us 'bearded men,' but I don't like the notion of a beautiful woman's lasting less than a beautiful tree—than her own picture, her own shadow, which won't change so to the Sun as her face to the mirror. I must leave off, for my head aches consumedly: I have never been quite well since the night of the representation of Alfieri's *Mirra*, a fortnight ago.''

Soon afterward the Guicciolis returned to join him; and the Count, still complaisant or unsuspicious, presently moved on to his estates near Ravenna, leaving the Countess in her lover's charge. So far an open scandal had been avoided. Then, much to the dismay of Teresa's friends and to the stupefaction of the Austrian police spy who watched their movements, the pair left Bologna and returned to Venice, where they established themselves at Byron's house on the Brenta. Just why they should have thus affronted convention remains mysterious. Teresa (we know) had a taste for melodrama, and Byron, tired of travel and makeshift and subterfuge, no doubt hankered after the comforts of his Venetian household. Their acquaintances in Venice, including the Countess Benzoni, were greatly scandalized. Only Teresa's husband retained his sang-froid; and they had not been at La Mira many weeks before they received a letter from Count Guiccioli in which he requested that Byron would oblige him with a loan of a thousand pounds. Some years earlier Byron had received the same request from another deluded husband; but whereas he had assisted Wedderburn Webster—an old friend, hopelessly improvident and chronically hard up, whose matrimonial misadventures inspired him with a certain rueful generosity—he declined to come to Count Guiccioli's help, whatever the circumstances.

From this snub, and from the Count's failure to obtain a consulship, dated a gradual worsening of the relations between wife and husband.

Outwardly at least, Byron did not repent of his bargain. He was prepared to shoulder the responsibility for Teresa's well-being—in his feelings toward her there was a touch of paternal tenderness; and at Bologna on the last page of a romantic novel he had written during her absence a declaration of undying love, more convincing perhaps because less declamatory than he had yet made to any woman except Mrs. Leigh. Teresa (he wrote), should she chance to find it, would not understand the language in which it was composed; "but you will recognize the handwriting of him who passionately loved you. . . . My destiny rests with you." He would never leave her (he promised) unless she wished it. At the same time, inward misgivings did not cease to trouble him. In the very plenitude of love there are the seeds of discontent; the more voluptuous the surroundings among which he passed his days, the more insistent became the prompting of that other nature, the puritan who had survived the inroads of his life at Venice, the man of action who still persisted after years of idleness. Suddenly an idea occurred to him that he might leave for the New World. In a newspaper his eye alighted upon a paragraph which spoke of a scheme of colonization "submitted to the Government of Venezuela by a few patriotic gentlemen"; and he wrote off to Hobhouse asking further details. What was there in his present existence that could hold him back? Hobhouse, he announced, must not talk to him of England. The country he believed was on the brink of revolution, and revolutions he knew were "not to be made with rosewater"; he had no affection for a society that had decreed his exile, "but I do not hate it enough to wish to take part in its calamities, as on either side harm must be done before good can accrue. . . ." As to Italy—he was not yet tired of his adopted home; "but a man must be a Cicisbeo and a Singer in duets, and a connoisseur of Operas—or nothing here—I have made some progress in all these accomplishments, but I can't say that I don't feel the degradation." In South America, he believed, he might begin anew; and vaguely he envisaged a land of congenial, courageous natives—"those fellows are fresh as their world, and fierce as their earthquakes"—where he might build himself a house and establish a dynasty and turn out in the end an ordinary "decent Citizen." Anything was preferable to the life he led. "Better be an unskilful Planter, an awkward settler . . . than a flatterer of fiddlers, and fan-carrier of a woman. I like women—God he knows—but the more their system here develops upon me, the worse it seems. . . . I have been an intriguer, a husband, a whore-monger, and now I am a Cavaliere Servente—by the holy! it is a strange sensation."

During the course of the autumn, however, he frequently changed his mind. Hearing further reports of a Jacobin movement in England, he pictured himself, in a half-serious and half-facetious spirit, leading a revolutionary commission into Leicestershire and rendering an exact account of his mother-in-law's "cattle, corn, and coach-horses, etc., etc., etc." The South American project was still under consideration; and when Tom Moore, who had recently crossed the Alps for the purpose of sight-seeing, arrived on October 7 at the house by the Brenta, Byron admitted over the dinner table that he might say good-bye to Europe. Meanwhile they talked and drank and laughed immoderately. Rosy, curly-headed, brisk, and sanguine, a talented, good-humoured Irish opportunist, Moore was a friend of long standing and of proved devotion.

Together they could look back upon Byron's years of success, remembering, for example, 1814 and that celebrated "Summer of the Sovereigns," the exciting crowded weeks of masquerades and balls and parties given in honour of the Tsar Alexander and the attendant Allied monarchs, or the Year of the Waltz by which it had been preceded—in Byron's life an even more important epoch, since it was then that he had awoken to fame and love and become the fashionable hero of the same society that had at length expelled him. Moore had been a literary supporter, a personal confidant. Byron must sneer at him sometimes and deride his snobism, remarking that it was Tom's weakness that he "always loved a lord"; but he had a deep respect both for his poetic capacities and for his domestic virtues.

Thoroughly pleasurable were the days that they passed in Venice. It was during the early afternoon that Moore alighted at La Mira; Byron, who had just risen, was still in his bath. He made haste, nevertheless, and soon descended; but whereas Byron noted of Moore that, although nine years his senior, he looked "quite fresh and poetical . . . this comes of marriage and being settled in the country," Moore observed of Byron that he was growing corpulent and that corpulence had spoiled "the picturesqueness of his head." "In high spirits and full of his usual frolicsome gaiety," Byron immediately insisted that Moore should take up his quarters at the Palazzo Mocenigo. Together they drove to Fusina in Moore's carriage, embarked in a gondola, and were rowed to the Grand Canal. The evening was splendid; ". . . the view of Venice and the distant Alps (some of which had snow on them, reddening with the last light) was magnificent"; but his companion's conversation, Moore recorded, "though highly ludicrous and amusing, was anything but romantic. . . ." Such was the devotion exacted of him by the Countess Guiccioli that Byron announced that he could not absent himself from La Mira overnight; but he remained to dine with Moore before returning and talked with his usual energy of many subjects—his own Memoirs, South America and the Duke of Wellington, *Don Juan* (of which he was composing a third canto), together with "much curious conversation about his wife." Next day, Moore was introduced to Madame Albrizzi's salon; and the old lady, who proved exceedingly gay and garrulous, bade him scold Byron for the scrape he had now got into, adding, rather surprisingly: "Till this, *il se conduisait si bien*"*!* To the heroine of the scrape Tom Moore had already been presented. At first sight she struck him as "not very pretty," though when they met again his judgment was a little more favourable. With these impressions and the manuscript of Byron's Memoirs, which had been handed over to him to dispose of as he pleased, Moore departed for Rome and Southern Italy.

A visit much less agreeable marked the month that followed. For during November who should arrive but Count Guiccioli, suddenly insistent on his matrimonial rights. Teresa must choose between himself and Byron; and, the Countess having at once elected to retain her lover, there ensued a succession of deplorable and distressing scenes, in which the Count alternately threatened and pleaded, and Byron, while his mistress enjoyed the supreme pleasures of romantic renunciation, sought to damp down the excitement with some drops of common sense. The Count (Byron recorded) "actually came to *me*, crying about it. . . ." Teresa's friends and relatives were in despair, since "an *elopement* in Italy is the devil; worse even than with *us*, because it is *supererogation*, and shows a headlong character." With the happiness of his mistress and the honour of her family both at stake, Byron's decision could scarcely have been more difficult. On the one hand, he must sacrifice "a woman whom I loved, for life; leaving her destitute and divided from all ties in case of my death"; on the other, "give up an *'amicizia'* which had been my pleasure, my pride, and my passion." At twenty, of course, he would have acted differently; but at thirty, "with the experience of *ten such years!"*—he reviewed the backward vista of tears and grievances and recriminations, scandals and disappointments and hopeless bitterness—he decided that he must play safe and act in the spirit of middle age. "With the greatest difficulty" he persuaded Teresa to rejoin her husband and go back to Ravenna and her home and family. For himself he did not "absolutely deny" that he might at length rejoin her. Otherwise she had declared that she would not obey him.

It was a loophole. But he was determined that he would not take it. He had groaned now and then under the gentle servitude imposed by Teresa's passion, complaining to Hobhouse that it was not to be expected that a man should "consume his life at the side and on the bosom of a woman, and a stranger," but once she had gone and he had begun to consider his solitude—"in a gloomy Venetian palace, never *more* alone than when alone—unhappy in the retrospect, and at least as much so in the prospect"—he felt so wretched, so cut off from any domestic comfort, that after all, he determined, he must return to England. There, at least, he would have the consolation of executing a long-cherished plan of revenge and calling out Henry Brougham, another legal villain of the drama of 1816. Perhaps he would settle down modestly and obscurely with Mrs. Leigh. . . . Preparations were already far advanced, and the dreaded business of "packing and parting" had already begun, when from Dr. Aglietti, the family physician, he learned that Allegra had fallen ill of the tertian fever that was then ravaging Venice. He must wait; and delay induced reflection, and accompanying reflection came indecision. By the time Allegra was recovered he had changed his plans. There was a moment, nevertheless, during the winter of 1819, at which (according to a story told by one of Teresa's confidantes) he had stood ready dressed for an immediate journey, "his gloves and cap on, and even his little cane in his hand." His luggage had been stowed away aboard the gondola; only his travelling armoury had not yet been packed. At this juncture, "milord, by way of pretext, declares that if it should strike one o'clock before everything was in order . . . he would not go that day." The clock struck the hour, and Byron remained in Venice.

With remarkable promptitude from Ravenna arrived the expected summons. Since their parting, Teresa's health had again deteriorated; and so terrified was her father, Count Ruggiero Gamba, that, although up till now he had opposed the relationship, he obtained Count Guiccioli's leave to send for Byron. Back in Ravenna, whither he had hurried as in duty bound, Byron discovered that there was to be no escape. The husband acquiesced; the father welcomed him; and Teresa, rising as by a miracle from her bed of sickness, was proud to appear on his arm among her friends and relatives. To walk into a trap with eyes wide open is a course that for some temperaments possesses a certain perverse appeal; and (though Byron, writing to Hoppner apropos of a report that he had abducted a girl from a convent at Ferrara, had recently complained that he would "like to know *who* has been carried off —except poor dear *me*. I have been more ravished myself than anybody since the Trojan war") he now submitted with perfect good grace to the role allotted him. Good-bye, then, to the projects he had formed in the autumn months! There was to be no more talk of South America, its volcanoes, gigantic prospects, savage freedom-loving people; no further question of a defiant return to England, where he would restore his fallen credit by fighting Brougham and perhaps plunge into the turmoil of revolutionary politics. Instead, as the accepted *cavaliere servente* of an Italian married woman, neither very pretty nor intellectually distinguished, he crossed the threshold of the Marchese Cavalli's drawing-room—the Marquess was Teresa's uncle and a pillar of local "good society"—and took his place among the other *serventi* attending their mistresses, made conversation, listened to chamber music, and manipulated the shawl and fan.

That it was a distinctly humdrum mode of existence he did not disguise—either from himself or from the friends with whom he corresponded; since, although the Italians visited the theatre to intrigue and gossip, they went "into company to hold their tongues." Their *conversazioni*, he commented, were "not Society at all. . . . The *women* sit in a circle, and the men gather into groups, or they play at dreary *Faro* or *'Lotto Reale,'* for small sums." The obligations of *serventismo* were many and complicated: "their system has its rules, and its fitnesses, and decorums, so as to be reduced to a kind of discipline or game at hearts, which admits few deviations unless you wish to lose it." The motives of Teresa's conduct were still incompletely clear, but "it seems [he told Hoppner] as if the G. had been presumed to be *planted*, and was determined to show that she was not—*plantation*, in this hemisphere, being the greatest moral misfortune." That, however, was only guesswork; "for I know nothing about it—except that everybody are very kind to her, and not discourteous to me." Her father and all her other relatives were "quite agreeable"; even the Papal representative, the Cardinal Vice-

Legate, had been exceedingly polite at the Marchese Cavalli's party; while Count Guiccioli had relapsed into his habitual quietude. Evidently Byron could not break away without creating a further scandal. He had arrived in Ravenna before the new year and, on January 20, wrote to Hoppner that he had as yet "not decided anything about remaining. . . . I may stay a day, a week, a year, all my life"; the decision depended on circumstances that he could "neither see nor foresee." He had come because he had been called; he would go if he considered his departure proper. But Teresa Guiccioli had no thoughts of dismissing Byron—she was devoted to him as deeply and genuinely as her nature allowed her—and on Byron himself the effects of habit were always cumulative. The snows fell and the snows melted; he had begun to enjoy his servitude. Venice, that "Sea-Sodom," that "empty oyster-shell," was now relegated to regions of the remote past, among detested and disgraceful memories.

Yet more remote, yet more unalluring, were reminders of the English scene. On January 29, 1820, expired George III. "Old, blind, mad, despised, and dying," a ghostly shape who wandered at large through the darkened, silent rooms of Windsor; now pausing at the organ to play fragments of an oratorio by Handel, now living again the recollections of a previous century, he had long been lost to the real world of men and politics. But the closing years of his existence had been not unhappy.[2] The ingratitude of his children, and the hatred of his subjects, the failure of ministers, the loss of possessions, the triumph of his foes—all had disappeared beneath the filmy curtains of madness; and there remained a dream life of

---

[2] "There is something poetic in the picture of this old, blind king wandering about in his castle among shadows, talking with them; for he lived his life among the dead—playing on his organ and never losing his serenity and his illusions." Princess Lieven to Metternich, February 9, 1820.

imagination and of affection. In death, said the Duke of York, the least unamiable of his many ill-starred offspring, he resembled with his flowing snow-white beard a venerable rabbi. Behind him he left a kingdom torn by discontent. His eldest son, a disreputable and discredited figure—distrusted alike by friends and enemies, by the Whigs he had abandoned and the Tory party whose principles he had adopted—succeeded to a throne of which he had been in fact the occupant, though with little distinction to himself or advantage to the Commonwealth, since the King's reason had collapsed finally during 1813. For the government of Castlereagh and Liverpool and the order it symbolized, Byron felt the detestation of every English liberal; he had a warm though vague sympathy for the plight of the labouring classes, particularly the population of the industrial North, whose cause he had championed in his maiden speech; but the reports he heard of the reformers themselves alarmed and shocked him—a set of "low, designing, dirty levellers, who would pioneer their way to a democratical tyranny"—and he was disgusted to learn that even the fastidious Hobhouse had come to terms with those two "ruffians," Henry Hunt and William Cobbett. Thus, when he received news of the Peterloo Massacre, at which lives had been lost owing to a hasty and mismanaged attempt to disperse one of Hunt's open-air meetings, he wrote that he thought he might say that he had "neither been an illiberal man, nor an unsteady man upon politics," but he also thought "that if the yeomanry had cut down *Hunt only*, they would have done their duty"; while, as it was, they had "committed murder, both in what they did, and what they did *not* do . . . punishing the poor starving populace instead of that pampered and dinnered blackguard," whom he had likened already to Wat Tyler or Jack Cade.

At the end of February, Thistlewood's plot to dispose of the entire English Cabinet, and to follow up their mass execution by proclaiming a republic, came to light through the offices of a London police spy. What a gang of "desperate fools," exclaimed Byron, were "these Utican conspirators!" As if in London a secret could have been kept among thirty or forty persons! And, supposing they had accounted for his old friend Harrowby—"in whose house I have been five hundred times, at dinners and parties," and whose wife he remembered as one of "the Exquisites"—would the bloodshed have been of any advantage to the cause of freedom? It was amusing, then—though, of course, it was also saddening—to hear that Hobhouse's association with the extremist radicals should have led him, if not to Tyburn, at least to Newgate. For, in December 1819, certain passages in a recent political pamphlet of which he admitted the authorship having been voted by the House of Commons a breach of privilege, John Cam was committed to Newgate Gaol, where he remained in nominal confinement till the following February. Byron made the occurrence an excuse for facetious rhyming; and John Cam, who had always a solemn sense of his own importance and after his release had been again chosen as candidate by the liberals of Westminster,[3] was much annoyed by the levity of the doggerel verses. His "dearest Byron" would have been less lovable had he been less incalculable. Yet at such a moment one hardly expected he would side with one's persecutors!

During March arrived news of the extinction—at least as far as London was concerned—of another English boon companion, the easy-going, irresponsible, perpetually effervescent Scrope Davies, who had at length ruined himself by gambling

[3] Hobhouse was elected for Westminster on March 25, 1820.

and had fled to Bruges. Thus poor Scrope (whom Byron recollected having deserted hopelessly drunk at a gambling hell where he appeared to be losing heavily and discovered next morning fast asleep, a chamber-pot brimming with banknotes beside his bed) had followed in the footsteps of his acquaintance Brummell. At Bruges, he would be condemned to drink Dutch beer, and, no doubt, "shoot himself the first foggy morning!" With a sigh Byron considered his fellow-exiles, writing from an Italian palace to Hobhouse immersed in a London jail—"Brummell at Calais; Scrope at Bruges, Buonaparte at St. Helena, you in your new apartments, and I at Ravenna, only think! so many great men! There has been nothing like it since Themistocles at Magnesia, and Marius at Carthage." But times changed, he added; "and they are luckiest who get over their first rounds at the beginning of the battle." His own seclusion might be monotonous; it was by no means painful. And, once he had accustomed himself to the initial indignities of *serventismo*, he soon settled down to the peaceful regimen of love and small talk. At due times, he visited the theatre or drove on the Corso. Besides, he was "drilling very hard to learn how to double a shawl" and reported that he would succeed to admiration had he not often folded it inside out or brought away two shawls instead of one, much to the confusion of the other *serventi*. By the end of March, nothing had happened to disturb his peace of mind, except that now and then Teresa had been a little jealous. Ravenna was a "dreadfully moral" city: ". . . you must not look at anybody's wife except your neighbour's."

Meanwhile he had taken a set of rooms in the Palazzo Guiccioli. It was an arrangement that suited Byron, pleased Teresa, and recommended itself to her husband's sense of pecuniary fitness. For more than a year the Palazzo Guiccioli was to be his home; and as much a part of his life as the Palazzo Mocenigo or the dusty Palladian house beside the Brenta became his rooms in this sombre provincial mansion in one of the obscurest and least visited of Italian cities. Venice might be dilapidated, but it had still the ocean. From Ravenna even the sea had at length retreated. In Byzantine times the wooden Venice of the Western Empire, approached and defended by a network of shallow waterways (notorious in the Roman period for their cloacal scum), it was now cut off from the seashore by miles of waste land and lay stranded and almost forgotten among its marshes and pine-forest. The capital of Honorius and Placidia, of Valentinian and Majorian, where little Romulus Augustulus had assumed the purple and Odoacer had fallen in the Palace of the Laurel Grove to Theodoric the Ostrogoth, which Justinian had reconquered and Charlemagne pillaged, during Byron's residence Ravenna was the dull headquarters of a Papal Vice-Legate. Only the gaunt basilicas of San Vitale and Sant' Apollinare, the Baptistery and the Tomb of Galla Placidia, lined with the triumphs of Byzantine mosaicists, blue, gold, and iridescent as a tapestry of peacocks' feathers, and the mausoleum of Theodoric beyond the city, still hinted at the noisy metropolis of monks and exarchs. Byron appreciated Ravenna's historical background; but, if he visited these monuments, he did not write of them.

His chief interests and his real pleasures were both at home. Vast, ancient, dignified, and somewhat gloomy, the Palazzo Guiccioli, like other Italian palaces, looked out onto a deep, sunless, cobbled street, commanded by high blank walls and thick-barred windows. Its massive frontage was divided by cavernous *porte-cochère;* over the arch projected a wrought-iron balcony; otherwise its external aspect was severely plain, pierced by large shuttered windows on the first and second floors, flush with the solid masonry of which the house was built. Such palaces are to be found in every Italian city. Seldom are the double leaves of the main door opened; but through the wicket-gate one catches a glimpse of the garden courtyard, an external staircase, and evergreen bushes flowering in pots or tubs. A number of different families may inhabit the house itself, leading separate lives and maintaining separate households, only communicating through their servants as the need arises. And Byron, when he had moved into the Palazzo Guiccioli, accompanied by a menagerie that always followed him, by the lackadaisical, complaining, devoted Fletcher and Tita,[4] the gigantic gondolier he had brought from Venice, was on visiting rather than on domestic terms with his host and hostess. The mornings were passed in sleep; he rode out during the afternoon; toward dusk he became the *cicisbeo*, either in the public or in the private aspect.

---

[4] Giovanni Battista Falcieri, who afterward sat for his portrait to Maclise, became a Foreign Office messenger and a protégé of Lord Beaconsfield.

Chapter Six

EVEN for our virtues we must pay a price. From the moment that he took up his quarters at the Palazzo Guiccioli, Byron gained in respectability and composure and well-being. The price that his fate exacted of him was paid in boredom. But it was not boredom of a virulent or particularly destructive kind—rather the acquiescent half-contented ennui of a man who has outlived his capacity for violent feeling and is glad to believe that the stormier emotions can no longer touch his heart. His passion for Teresa might have lost its freshness, but he liked the sense of security her devotion gave him; while as a man who had suffered often from the pangs of solitude—and had been never lonelier or more miserable than during his stay in Venice—he enjoyed the idea that here in Ravenna he had a home and a family. The Gambas, father and son, were gallant and well bred. In common with the majority of their neighbours, they were ardent patriots; and Byron, conscious perhaps of his own imprisonment, a condition he might not fret against but was bound to recognize, shared with them their enthusiasm for the cause of Italian freedom. 1820 had proved a fateful and an exciting year. Throughout Italy secret

societies were meeting and conspirators were arming. In every
large city there were groups of liberals; the Austrian service
itself sheltered liberal sympathizers. The whole country, though
pinned down by foreign garrisons, bewildered and disorgan-
ized by a decade of servitude, awaited the gesture of release
and redemption that would explode its energies.

In the meantime Metternich and the Austrian system were
still omnipotent. Directly, Vienna governed Venetia and Lombardy. By indirect but powerful means, through Austrian
princes, Metternich controlled Tuscany, Parma, and Modena.
Piacenza, Ferrara, Comacchio were garrisoned by the imperial
troops; and Ferdinand of Naples, an insensate Bourbon who
owed the recovery of his kingdom to Austrian bayonets, had
concluded a secret pact which left the Two Sicilies an Austrian
apanage. Even from the Papal States Metternich's influence
was not excluded; and he was confident of being able to secure
the choice of an Austrian candidate at any future Papal election. But, although the effects of his system were pervasive,
they were hardly uniform; and, of the three duchies presided
over by Habsburg princelings, whereas Modena endured the
bigoted rule of the tyrannous Duke Francis, Parma continued
to enjoy the comparatively enlightened code that had been
introduced during the period of French dominion, and in
Tuscany Duke Ferdinand and his minister Fossombroni had
established a form of government which, described by some
critics as "enervating and demoralizing," was also generally
acknowledged to be "mild and benevolent." Nor did the one
native dynasty then in power set a good example. At Turin
Victor Emmanuel of Sardinia conformed to the accepted pattern of reactionary potentate and oppressed his liberal subjects with as much thoroughness as any Austrian archduke.
For the "impure"—the subversive patriots, the poets, and the

liberals—was reserved "every form of intellectual and moral torment."

As confused as the situation of the peninsula were the aims of the revolutionaries. Carbonari, Adelfi, and Bersaglieri d'America—all had their secrets and passwords, their lodges and ceremonies, and hatched desperate plots relieved and decorated by a touch of play-acting. Unlike the English radicals and revolutionaries whom Byron distrusted, these Italian conspirators were with few exceptions men of the upper and upper-middle classes. Particularly in the south, the lower classes were often reactionary; and the Sanfedisti of Naples (reminiscent of the Black Hundreds of Tsarist Russia) were recruited from the Neapolitan slums to hunt down patriots. Liberalism went with education and a love of literature; and it was natural then that, while it partook of the literary virtues, it should also have its full share of literary shortcomings. Much time was wasted in talk, and much in sentiment. Generous emotions were accompanied by an inability to combine and organize. There were many heroes but few real leaders and rarely a general plan. The great revolt anticipated by liberals in 1820 —for which Byron and the Gambas listened among the Romagnol marshes—was to die out crackling and sputtering like a string of firecrackers.

The exact extent of Byron's commitments is still a trifle vague. We know, nevertheless, that, incited by Teresa's father, a fine white-headed old gentleman of noble manners, and her brother, the impulsive and charming Pietro Gamba, he joined the secret society of the Carbonari and attended their clandestine meetings in the depths of the pine-forest. No one, they hoped, would suspect an Englishman. Before long his rooms in the Palazzo Guiccioli were full of conspirational gear and mysterious documents, besides serving as a place of rendezvous for the numerous local liberals. Not surprisingly, his landlord grew at length impatient. Count Guicciolo was apprehensive of the position he occupied; and, although he was both an indulgent husband and himself a liberal, it did not suit him that his house should become a nest of plotters. Such, at least, seems to be the most probable explanation of the sudden change in his attitude toward Teresa's escapade. Abruptly, during the spring of 1820, while the walls of the Palazzo Guiccioli and adjacent houses were scrawled with inscriptions exalting the republic and prophesying death to popes and monarchs, and the Papal carabiniers were trying in vain to unearth the culprits, Count Guiccioli announced that his patience was ended. Once again he demanded that Teresa should give up her lover; and once again, caught in the turmoil of two furious families, Byron advised his mistress that she should obey her husband. Teresa retorted with romantic vehemence. She would stay with Guiccioli, she declared, if the Count would allow her to remain with Byron. It was hard that she should be "the only woman in Romagna who is not to have her *amico*." Were Guiccioli to refuse her request, she would not live with him; " 'and as for the consequences, love, etc., etc., etc.'—you know how females reason on such occasions." The Count thereupon threatened to divorce his wife; but when the Gambas, who were now thoroughly incensed against him, proposed a separation (which involved the return of the Countess's dowry), the Count's avarice proved to carry more weight than his offended honour. The whole tangled affair, through the Papal Vice-Legate, was finally referred to the Pope's arbitrament; and his answer did not reach Ravenna till the twelfth of July. The Guicciolis were pronounced by Papal decree formally separated: Teresa was to leave her husband, with alimony amounting to two hundred pounds a year, but there was also a stipulation that she should retire to her father's house.

It was an admirable example of Papal tact. In obedience to the command of the Holy Father, Teresa removed to Count Gamba's villa outside the city; but Byron kept his apartments at the Palazzo Guiccioli and continued to visit Teresa by her father's leave. In essentials, the situation remained unaltered. Warned to look out for an ambush in the surrounding forest— Count Guiccioli according to local rumour had already contrived or connived at two assassinations—Byron did not discontinue his evening rides but took the precaution of increasing his usual array of weapons. Like other neurasthenics, he possessed his full share of nervous courage; and it was with an elation not by any means unpleasant that he looked forward to the prospect of a dramatic "row"—whether with Guiccioli's hired bravoes or the hirelings of the Austrian tyrant. But, week after week, then month after month, Byron's sanguine prognostications were disappointed. No thicket or pine-bole concealed an ambush; there was no attempt at a "stilletation" as he traversed the forest glades; and the only blood shed in Ravenna was that of certain local functionaries, victims of private spite or public vengeance, shot at from street corners or knifed in stabbing affairs. Nor, though the whole countryside was seething with excitement and Byron's Carbonari friends were extremely active, were there any definite signs that a general revolt might soon materialize. When it did so, he expected to give a good account of himself; but, whereas he was patient and resolute under the threat of danger, his natural irritability was not proof against minor annoyances—the supposed defalcations of his former Venetian servants and a long wrangle over the tenancy of the Palazzo Mocenigo. Worse—among the letters he received during April were two characteristic flippant but nagging effusions from that most detestable of discarded mistresses, the mother of Allegra.

From Pisa, where she was now domiciled with the Shelleys, Claire wrote, suggesting that, for the summer at any rate, which they expected to spend at the baths of Lucca, the child should be returned to her maternal care. Otherwise she threatened to come to Venice or Ravenna—"*bada a voi* in that case. The French nurses used to still their crying charges with 'Marlborough's a-coming.' If you are not good the Fornaria [*sic*] will get hold of my name to frighten you into order." Only Claire could have turned so sound a cause to so little purpose, or given her pleas a tone at once so whining and so provocative. Byron was susceptible to Shelley's charm when he saw him daily and raised no objection to his friend's adopting the role of mediator; but at a distance his attitude was far more critical, and the Shelleys' bohemianism struck him as what in some aspects no doubt it was—a mixture of loose thinking and slipshod living, flavoured, in spite of the poet's goodness, by a touch of self-conscious intellectual superiority. Who was Claire, the girl who had thrown herself into his unwilling arms and begged for seduction as for an act of grace, that she should presume to deliver lectures on the theme of paternal duty? Had the Shelleys any qualifications to be considered successful parents? Both children born to them were already dead, for William Shelley had expired in Rome the previous summer— a catastrophe that Byron attributed, perhaps not without reason, to the effect of a vegetarian diet on youthful stomachs; and, having received the second of Claire's imploring letters, he wrote crossly to Hoppner that he would say only this: ". . . I so totally disapprove of children's treatment in their family that I should look upon the Child as going into a hospital. . . .

Have they *reared* one?" Allegra's health had hitherto been excellent and her disposition not bad. Though now and then vain and obstinate, she was also clean and cheerful; "and as, in a year or two, I shall either send her to England" (where he intended that she should live with Augusta's offspring), "or put her in a Convent for education, these defects will be remedied as far as they can in human nature. But the Child shall not quit me again to perish of starvation, and green fruit, or be taught to believe that there is no Deity."

As it happened, conditions in the Shelley household were such as to lend an added point to Byron's strictures. The horrors of a persecution part real and part imaginary,[1] the perpetual conflict between the claims of the real and ideal, which even in his relationship with Mary was now becoming more and more apparent, the miseries of hypochondria and the agonies of disordered nerves—all had contrived to make 1818 and 1819 a period for Shelley of growing creative strength but of increasing personal gloom. Again he was haunted by the twin images of the sea and death; and thoughts of extinction stole sleepily over his fevered consciousness, like the undertone of waters rustling on a southern beach, whenever the beauty and tragedy of actual life seemed most intolerable:

> Yet now despair itself is mild,
> Even as the winds and waters are;
> I could lie down like a tired child,
> And weep away the life of care
> Which I have borne and yet must bear,
> Till death like sleep might steal on me,
> And I might feel in the warm air

[1] Savage as were the newspaper attacks made on Shelley at this and other periods, it must be remembered that attacks of equal ferocity were made by both sides, and that very few writers of the early nineteenth century escaped such invective. The story of the assault on Shelley by an unknown Englishman in the post-office at Leghorn was told by Shelley himself and unauthenticated by any other witness.

My cheek grow cold, and hear the sea
Breathe through my dying brain its last monotony.

Those lines had been written in the autumn of 1818. During the spring that followed, wandering through the "mountainous ruins of the Baths of Caracalla, among the flowery glades, and thickets of odoriferous blossoming trees, which are extended in ever-winding labyrinths upon its immense platforms and dizzy arches," canopied by the "bright blue sky of Rome," Shelley embarked on the continuation of *Prometheus Unbound*, a drama as fragmentary and fantastic, but in certain isolated passages at least as oddly beautiful, as the wilderness of stones and flowers amid which it was composed. In Rome died William Shelley, to be buried under the pyramid of Caius Sestius; and the household moved gloomily on to Florence, where Mary gave birth to her third and last child, christened by the rites of the English Church Percy Florence, who grew up to be a baronet, an affectionate son and husband, and a diligent devotee of amateur theatricals.

From Florence, where Shelley in his impulsive haphazard way engaged in a flirtation that seems to have been something more than strictly platonic with a family connexion, Sophia Stacey, they pursued their restless course to lodgings in Pisa. Here they formed the congenial acquaintance of a certain Lady Mountcashell, "a singular character," described by Godwin as "a democrat and a republican in all their sternness . . . uncommonly tall and brawny, with bad teeth, and a handsome countenance," who had eloped with a Mr. Tighe and lived with him at Pisa under the style of "Mr. and Mrs. Mason." Here, too, the Shelleys bade good-bye to the Gisbornes, thus further postponing, and, as it turned out, at length being obliged finally to abandon, Shelley's airy dreams of constructing a monster steamboat in which he had already invested much time and money. The entire household was meanwhile disturbed by reports of Allegra. From Venice in 1819 the not altogether good-natured Mrs. Hoppner had written that, whereas her own child was in brilliant health and spirits, *"Allegra, par contre, est devenue tranquille et sérieuse comme une petite vieille, ce qui nous peine beaucoup."* Byron's life (she added) was *"une débauche affreuse."* Such replies as they managed to elicit from him were curt and uncommunicative; and for six months they were without news of the child or its parent. Eventually they learned that he had deserted Venice and received information of his establishment at the Palazzo Guiccioli.

Naturally they supposed that his existence at Ravenna would be a repetition of the life he had led at Venice; but, in fact, beside their harassed and uneasy household, distracted by the bitter quarrels that frequently broke out between Claire and Mary, and disturbed by the electric fluctuations of Shelley's genius, Byron's way of life had now an almost humdrum respectability. Its pivot was the relationship, no longer very passionate but sober and semi-domestic, that he had established with Teresa; his pursuits were as regular as those of a country gentleman; literature and local politics divided his hopes and interests. Always further into the distance floated the idea of England. During the early months of 1820 Byron was half amused, half disgusted by what he read of the Queen's Trial on connected charges of adultery and high treason. A masterpiece of mismanagement from start to finish, this strange and squalid affair, which filled London with riotous indignant mobs and brought the kingdom once again to the verge of revolution, had its origins in the unscrupulous machination of Byron's old enemy Henry Brougham, who had persuaded his client to return to England, having given an assurance to the

Government that she would remain abroad. Neither Brougham nor any other of her influential Whig supporters imagined that the Queen was completely innocent; they regarded her as a useful weapon with which to attack the Tories. But the commercial and lower classes were more uncritical—for them the Queen was the helpless victim of monarchic despotism: her grievances represented the woes of centuries. Castlereagh found it impossible to leave the Foreign Office; fear of his subjects confined the timorous King to Carlton House; vast processions marched with bands and placards from the City to Westminster.

Between detachment and disenchantment Byron was only remotely interested. During 1820 the letters that he wrote to England are brief by comparison with the correspondence of his earlier Italian years; and the tone that distinguishes a great many of them is harsh and irritable. Solitude has seldom a softening effect on the recluse's character. In Byron it exaggerated his natural petulance; and when Hoppner, in a letter written that autumn, repeated a scandal concerning the Shelleys which was being circulated by Allegra's former nurse-maid Elise Foggi and her recently acquired husband, a dishonest courier whom they had once employed,[2] Byron's response was neither discriminating nor very generous. The origins of the story—for it had no doubt some basis—are no longer ascertainable. It is established, however, that during their stay in the South of Italy Claire had fallen ill and that, at the same time, Shelley had occupied himself with the welfare of an unknown protégée, afterwards referred to as "my poor Neapolitan." A child was somehow involved in the latter

[2] On discovering that the maid was pregnant by the courier, the Shelleys—rather surprisingly for people of their principles—had insisted that the pair must at once be married. Hence the dislike with which they were now regarded by Elise and her husband.

episode; and Elise now announced that Claire was Shelley's
mistress, that both of them had treated Mary with the utmost
brutality, that Claire had become pregnant and, in spite of her
lover's attempts to procure an abortion, had given birth; at
which Shelley had consigned his bastard to the Foundlings'
Hospital. All this was repeated to Byron by Hoppner, and by
the poet immediately accepted without a word of disbelief.
Claire's pleas in the last few months had been consistently exasperating; Shelley's tactful interpositions had done nothing
to improve his temper. He wanted only to be left alone, to the
life that suited him.

Thus he was prepared—even eager—to swallow Hoppner's evidence. Elise, he admitted, was an unreliable witness;
"Shiloh" (or Shelley) had "talent and honour," crazily incensed though he was "against religion and morality"; "of
the facts, however," he added on October 1, "there can be little
doubt; it is just like them." A story more *unlike* Shelley—at
least in the majority of its details—could scarcely be conceived. But Byron was too feminine to be quite consistent or
attempt to achieve a spiritual harmony between mood and
mood—too lazy, too corrupt perhaps, to resist an easy cynicism. It was a simple method of dismissing Claire's pleas, of
breaking Shelley's spell, of settling back again into the placid
life their existence threatened. And across a letter from Claire
Clairmont which he sent for Hoppner's inspection, "the moral
part . . . [he scribbled] comes with an excellent grace from
the writer now living with a *man* and his *wife*—and having
planted a child in the Fl— Foundling, etc."

If only patriots and oppressors would decide to come to
blows! But, although during the previous spring and winter
months the authorities had seemed thoroughly perturbed, the
Cardinal had "glared pale through all his purple" and offered

public prayers for the salvation of the city, while Byron and his friends had lived in momentary expectation of being called on to take up arms in the cause of liberty, the general rising, postponed till the autumn, when the autumn came was stifled unborn by the defection of Bologna, which suddenly withdrew its assistance from the patriot league. At the moment both sides displayed a partiality that Byron could not but deplore for "shooting around a corner"; and on the evening of December 9 at eight o'clock, just as he was donning his overcoat to visit Teresa, musket shots reverberated through the lane below. All the servants, he found, were clustered on the balcony, excitedly exclaiming that a man had been murdered; but only Tita would follow him as he ran downstairs. Not far from his door lay the Military Commandant of Ravenna, a brave but unpopular man, stretched on his back, pierced by five shot wounds. His adjutant bent over him, weeping like a child. Near by were a surgeon who, cautiously, "said nothing of his profession," a priest "sobbing a frightened prayer," some bewildered soldiers, who attempted to prevent the Englishman from passing, and "one or two of the boldest of the mob." The street was "dark as pitch, with people flying in all directions." Since none of the onlookers would do anything but "shake and stare," Byron, brushing aside remonstrances and disregarding the soldiers, ordered that the dying man should be carried into the shelter of the Palazzo Guiccioli. There, with no word save for murmured ejaculations of *O Dio* and *O Jesu*, the Commandant expired on Fletcher's bed. Ravenna was thrown into complete confusion. The identity of the criminal was not discovered; and it remained doubtful whether the crime was the work of a private assassin or the Commandant had fallen because he was suspected of liberal sympathies. Then suddenly and inexplicably the excitement subsided. Byron was considerably dis-

appointed if not much astonished. More and more he was
driven back upon his own resources; and more and more often,
during his empty nights and his indolent afternoons, when a
dead summer silence filled the street outside, or winter showers
pricked at the windowpanes or splashed on the cobblestones,
he took refuge among the pleasures and pains of memory.

After all, the early days had been the best days. Even at the
age of nineteen he was an addict of memory, obsessed by recollections of his career at school and gnawed by regrets for his
vanished happiness; and at thirty-two the past, like the base
of an iceberg, gigantically outmeasured the present's value.
The autumn and winter of 1820 produced no change. During
the first frozen week of the new year he embarked on a journal,
which he continued till he had "filled one paper-book (thin-
nish), and two sheets or so of another," from January 4 to
February 27, 1821. The result was detailed survey of his
thoughts and feelings. Vile weather made it almost impossible
to leave the palace, for a deep snowfall had half melted beneath the clammy south wind, and his usual ride through the
pine-woods was completely out of the question. At home he
stared at the fire and awaited the post bag. It arrived late and
brought six copies of Galignani's *Messenger*, "a letter from
Faenza, but none from England." More neglect! "Very sulky
in consequence," he sat down to devour a copious meal—with
Byron a hearty appetite was often a sign of wretchedness—
from which he rose, restive and thoughtful, to absorb the news-
papers. At eight, the carriage was announced—he now made
love, he once observed bitterly, by the stroke of the clock—and
he paid his regular evening visit to the Countess Guiccioli,
whom he found "playing on the pianoforte" and with whom
he "talked till ten, when the Count, her father, and the no less
Count, her brother, came in from the theatre. Play, they said,

Alfieri's *Fileppo*—well received." At eleven, or a little before, he returned to his own rooms, ruminated, wrote up his journal, and retired to bed.

Such, as long as the snows lasted, was the pattern of his daily life. "Weather dripping and dense" was followed by "mist— thaw—slop—rain," and, next morning, by a further snowfall with fog and drizzle "and all the incalculable combinations of a climate where heat and cold struggle for mastery." Byron's mood was one of resigned impatience and reflective lassitude. Reading Swift, finishing a cross letter to his English publisher, who demurred at *Don Juan* and disliked his tragedies, feeding or playing with his domestic animals—the hawk, the tame crow, the monkeys, the mastiff—he dawdled his way dully but quietly through the hours of daylight. He was bored, of course, but not so bored as he had been in London; for, though it was true that all his life he had been "more or less *ennuyé*," he was "rather less so now" than ten years earlier. What was the explanation, he wondered, of this habitual spleen? It was constitutional, he supposed, "—as well as the waking in low spirits, which I have invariably done for many years." Temperance and vigorous exercise brought **no** improvement; but tumultuous passions, if they agitated, at least enlivened him. "A dose of salts has the effect of a temporary inebriation, like light champagne, upon me. But wine and spirits make me sullen and savage to ferocity—silent, however, and retiring, and not quarrelsome, if not spoken to. Swimming also raises my spirits, but in general they are low, and get daily lower."

Still he contemplated some escape into a life of action. But an excuse failed to materialize in spite of numerous false alarms. Thus, on January 7, after an idle day passed reading Spence's *Anecdotes*, the fourth volume of the second series of *Tales of My Landlord*, and the *Lugano Gazette*, Byron was drawn aside at an evening party by Pietro Gamba, who reported he had secret information that the Papal Legate had received orders to make several arrests, and that as a precautionary measure the patriots were arming and bodies of Carbonari had been posted in the city's streets. What should be done? asked Gamba. To which Byron replied that they must fight for it rather than be taken in detail, and offered, if any of the Carbonari were in immediate danger, to harbour and defend them in the Palazzo Guiccioli. Gamba accepted the advice, but declined to borrow his pistols; and Byron hurried home through a tempest of rain and wind.

At home, he replenished the fire and sat up to await events, turning over a score of books in search of a quotation that continued to elude him, and straining his ears for the roll of drums or the crackle of musketry. All that he heard was "the plash of the rain and the gusts of the wind at intervals"; and next day he learned that the scare was groundless; "the Government [said Gamba] had not issued orders for the arrests apprehended . . . the attack in Forli had not taken place . . . and that, as yet, they are still in apprehension only." Gamba asked "for some arms of a better sort," which Byron gave, settling meanwhile that, "in case of a row, the Liberals are to assemble *here* (with me), and that he had given the word to Vicenzo G. and others of the *Chiefs* for that purpose." Meanwhile both Gambas, father and son, had elected to go hunting. Dismayed by this odd suspension of warlike activities, the Englishman tried on a new coat, read Bacon's *Apothegms*, wrote a letter to Murray, and visited Teresa, in whose rooms he went through the usual regimen of love and small talk. Luckily, the weather had begun to change. He was soon able to ride out again over the muddy roads, occupied with reflection upon his past life and Italian liberty.

"How odd are my thoughts," he recorded on January 12. His eyes had alighted on the words of the song from *Comus:*

> Sabrina fair,
> Listen where thou art sitting
> Under the glassy, cool, translucent wave,
> In twisted braids of lilies knitting
> The loose train of thy amber-dropping hair . . .

and, in an instant, fifteen wearisome years had rolled away from him and he had recaptured the poetic essence of that delightful period when, accompanied by Edward Noel Long, one of the dearest of his Harrow and Cambridge intimates, he had practised diving in the Cam's not very translucent waters for "plates, eggs, and even shillings." He remembered the landscape of the murky water-world, and a tree-stump in the bed of the river round which he used to cling, pleased with the strangeness of his sensations in the wavering half-light. Long had joined the Guards and had been drowned on the passage to Lisbon; and Byron had attempted, but not had the heart to complete, his epitaph.

Three weeks later, his memories again attacked him—but from a completely different quarter. "What I feel most growing upon me [he wrote] are laziness, and a disrelish more powerful than indifference." He presumed he would end, like Swift, in madness, and was going on to observe that he did not "contemplate this with so much horror as he apparently did for some years before it happened" (though it was true at his present age "Swift had hardly *begun life"),* when he was interrupted by the music of a strolling barrel organ. ". . . A waltz, too [he exclaimed]; I must leave off to listen." For that very waltz he had "heard ten thousand times at the balls in London, between 1812 and 1815." Up rose the buried years of fame and fashion. In Byron's life the waltz had special historic value, since the same year that brought the waltz to London dance-floors, and saw the great world go gliding off to its lascivious measure, had introduced the wild beginnings of the Byron craze, that period of celebrity so intense and unparalleled that the poet's name formed the murmured background of every dinner party—Byron—Byron—Byron—in an incessant monotonous rhythm.

"Music is a strange thing," he remarked concisely. Almost a decade had passed; on January 22, 1821, he had composed a mock epitaph to celebrate the extinction of his thirty-third year; yet certain undertones of feeling were still persistent, running through pleasure and satiety, the triumphs and failures, haunting his middle age as they had haunted his youth itself. Between the mind and experience stood always a mysterious barrier. "Why [he wrote], at the very height of desire and human pleasure—worldly, social, amorous, ambitious, or even avaricious—does there mingle a certain sense of doubt and sorrow—a fear of what is to come—a doubt of what *is*—a retrospect to the past, leading to a prognostication of the future?" The greater the elevation the mind achieved, the more vertiginous that "sentiment of the gulf" by which it was attended. "I feel most things [he concluded] but I know nothing, except—" and here with the point of his hurried and careless pen Byron broke into three long rows of impatient dashes, as if to symbolize the final hopelessness of the quest embarked on, from which the forces of the imagination fell back in disarray. He took up and threw down again a volume by Friedrich von Schlegel. For all his wealth of words, the German metaphysician could tell him nothing.[3]

It was Byron's virtue, in the face of mystery, to remain un-

[3] "I dislike him the worse . . . because he always seems upon the verge of meaning; and, so, he goes down like sunset, or melts like a rainbow, leaving a rather rich confusion. . . "

usually clear-headed. Self-deception he might indulge in with regard to his private problems; but, confronted by the large enigma of human destiny, his intellect was clear and honest, if his view was limited. To attempt to force an explanation, or to wring the confirmation of a theory from the facts of experience, was antipathetic to the nature of his instinctive genius. To systematize the material of life is to lose half its value; to concentrate on the destination to which we may or may not be bound entails inevitably some loss of the journey's interest. We are travellers and, in the condition of travellers, we must feel and speculate. Meanwhile the world of appearances is beautiful, varied, inexhaustibly surprising; and, interspersed with the doubts and cogitations, the regrets and memories, occur passages in Byron's journal of extraordinary descriptive brilliance that reveal the sharpness of his eye and the strength and skill with which he sometimes handled the English language.

Came home *solus* [he wrote of Ravenna by moonlight]—very high wind—lightning—moonshine—solitary stragglers muffled in cloaks —women in masks—white houses—clouds hurrying over the sky, like spilt milk blown out of the pail—altogether very poetical. It is still blowing hard—the tiles flying, and the house rocking—rain splashing—lightning flashing—quite a fine Swiss Alpine evening, and the sea roaring in the distance.

Through these scenes he made his way to a *conversazione*. The women (he noted) were all frightened by the tempest and "*won't* go to the masquerade because it lightens! . . ." He heard the customary talk of revolution and approaching war; but, as the weeks went by, the prospects of a revolt seemed more and more unhopeful, and the behaviour of his fellow-conspirators seemed less encouraging. "I always had an idea [wrote Byron on February 24] that it would be *bungled*; but was willing to hope, and am so still." Even the Gambas' conduct was so indecisive as to appear almost pusillanimous; and on February 16, without a syllable of warning, Count Pietro Gamba, having taken fright at a recent order prohibiting the concealment of arms, sent his servant to Byron's house carrying "a bag full of bayonets, some muskets, and some hundreds of cartridges" which the poet had purchased at the request of his Carbonari friends. Luckily, Zambelli, his Italian steward, was there to receive them; for if they had been delivered to any other member of his household, except the steward, Tita the gondolier, or William Fletcher, he would immediately have been denounced to the Papal police. Yet there was no bitterness or tendency to recrimination in Byron's attitude; and meanwhile he was delighted to learn of the success of the insurrectionary movement in the kingdom of the Two Sicilies, where the Neapolitans were reported to be "full of energy," to "have broken a bridge, and slain four pontifical carabiniers." Unfortunately the sovereign of Naples appealed to Metternich; the constitution granted during the previous July was at once repealed; and in March the armies of Austria met the patriot forces. At the battle of Rieti and on the field of Novara (where a rising among the Piedmontese was promptly stifled) the monarchical system gained a crushing advantage over the liberal vanguard.

Within a few weeks the plans of years had been reduced to chaos. There ensued throughout Italy a period of savage repression and methodical proscription; Byron's Milanese acquaintance, the poet Silvio Pellico, and a number of his associates had been condemned to the dreadful fortress of the Spielberg (where Pellico was to remain for several years); and the high tide of persecution swept through the Romagna. Naturally the Gambas were not excepted; and, during February, both father and son, "in common with thirty or more of all ranks" known to have been attached to the patriot cause, received an order of immediate expulsion from the Papal domains. They were "hurried from their home without process —without hearing—without accusation." As to the exact circumstances surrounding their departure we are a little vague (since Byron knew that his post bag was carefully scrutinized and did not wish to incriminate them when he wrote to England), but no doubt it was as dramatic and moving as befitted the Italian temperament and accompanied by tears and vows and protests of eternal loyalty. From Ravenna, the Gambas and Teresa moved to Florence. But Byron, though his reasons for remaining in the Romagna were no longer operative and presumably he had given some promise that he would rejoin his mistress, did not at once leave his comfortable quarters in the Palazzo Guiccioli. Whether from a determination to annoy the local authorities, who had struck at the rich and powerful Englishman through his unfortunate Italian friends, from a willingness (which an English visitor [4] had already noted) to give Teresa the slip if ever an occasion offered, or indeed from his habitual dread of change and movement, complicated by the indolence of an exceedingly selfish man, he treated the authorities' wishes and his mistress's feelings with equal disregard. The Gambas had been expelled at the beginning of February; it was the end of October 1821 before Byron (amid "all the sweat, and dust, and blasphemy of an universal packing. . . . It is awful work, this love," he was to write to Moore) braced himself to take a further turn on the romantic treadmill.

[4] Sir Humphry Davy writing to Tom Moore.

Chapter Seven

D URING the previous months he was neither particularly unhappy nor by any means inactive. The Fifth Canto of *Don Juan* was triumphantly concluded; and, in addition to his English rendering of the Paolo and Francesca episode from Dante's *Inferno* and a translation of a part of Pulci's mock epic poem, *Morgante Maggiore*, he produced during the period of his stay at Ravenna no less than three tragedies, *Marino Faliero, Sardanapalus, The Two Foscari* (works of which he himself was extremely proud but which Murray's "back-shop synod" persisted in condemning), *Cain, Heaven and Earth*, a couple of trifling satires, *The Blues* and *The Irish Avatar*, and—best of all perhaps—the admirable *Vision of Judgment*, a brilliant and concentrated essay in poetic diatribe. It seemed that he had reached the topmost curve of his strength and genius. Shelley, who visited him at his invitation during the month of August to discuss the awkward question of Allegra's future, was again overwhelmed by a generous conviction of Byron's greatness. "I despair of rivalling Lord Byron [he wrote from the Palazzo Guiccioli], as well I may . . ."; and, though he distrusted the critical system that Byron advocated and thought that he recognized its "pernicious effects" in *Marino Faliero*, he was enchanted by the Fifth Canto of *Don Juan*, which fulfilled, he admitted regretfully, "in a certain degree, what I have long preached of producing—something wholly new and relative to the age, and yet surpassingly beautiful."

Once again, Shelley lost confidence in his own abilities. He wrote nothing, he informed Peacock, and probably would write no more. "It offends me to see my name classed among those who have no name. . . . The cup is justly given to one only of an age; indeed, participation would make it worthless. . . ." Shelley reached Ravenna on the seventh of August; and that night and the small hours of the day that followed went by in incessant absorbing conversation which revolved around the problems of verse and politics. Byron talked easily, boldly, gaily, with the worldly bias to which he was always inclined in earnest company; Shelley with his habitual enthusiasm and fevered brilliance. But beneath the radiant surface of their renewed intimacy there were dangerous depths still. Shelley noticed that the influence of Teresa Guiccioli had been soothing and steadying: Byron was "greatly improved in every respect—in genius, in temper, in moral issues, in health, in happiness"; but the "canker of aristocracy" had not yet been eradicated; while "between two persons in our situation" (he wrote to Mary) lurked always "the demons of mistrust and pride." Nevertheless, the slight *malaise*, moral or intellectual, from which he found that in Byron's company there was no escape did not prevent him from enjoying his stay at the Palazzo Guiccioli or appreciating the odder aspects of its master's life there. Byron's household appealed to his love of fantasy. Besides Fletcher, Lega Zambelli the steward and man of business, and Tita the gondolier—"a fine fellow with a prodigious black beard"—it consisted at the time of "ten horses, eight enormous dogs, three monkeys, five cats, an eagle, a crow, and a falcon; and all these, except the horses, walk about the house, which every now and then resounds with their unarbitrated quarrels. . . ." Having compiled this list for Mary's benefit, he opened his letter again to add that his "enumeration of the animals in this Circaean palace" turned out to be defective: on the grand staircase he had just encountered "five peacocks, two guinea-hens, and an Egyptian crane. I wonder who all these animals were, before they were changed into these shapes."

Byron, like a true enchanter, preferred night to day. He did not rise till the afternoon, when he met Shelley (who got up at twelve) for a belated breakfast; after which they sat in conversation till the hour of sunset and then galloped, from six to eight, through the surrounding pine-forest. Sometimes they would dismount and, using a pumpkin as a target, try their hands at pistol-practice, an exercise in which Shelley was almost Byron's equal. Returned home, they would dine together and sit up talking throughout the night. In the antiquities of Ravenna, apart from the Tomb of Dante and the Mausoleum of Theodoric, Shelley showed singularly little interest. Though his education was far more complete than that of Byron and his æsthetic susceptibilities on the whole more acutely developed, he regarded the monuments of Byzantine civilization as debased relics of a degrading and degraded dogma, and observed that it seemed to have been "one of the first efforts of the Christian religion to destroy the power of producing beauty in art." This generalization is not easy to reconcile with his worship of Dante, but neither in his loyalties nor in his antipathies had he ever been consistent; for to the rational and generous indignation that he felt against society

Shelley added a strain of irrational prejudice which caused him to divide the whole world into persecutors and persecuted, with parents, monarchs, and priests upon the one hand and himself, devoted and forlorn, invariably in the opposite camp. For such a view of the universe, as soon as it has been firmly established, circumstances have a knack of providing a constant supply of fresh material; and the comparative tranquillity of his stay with Byron was presently overclouded by a fresh exposure of human baseness. Around him, as had happened so often during the course of his wanderings, opened infernal perspectives of guilt and infamy.

The fault was Byron's. Exposed to the strange charm of Shelley's character, his distrust of Shelleyan principles rapidly melted away. There might be times when he was stiff and silent and would surround himself with the attributes of mysterious melancholy; but at other times—not always well chosen—he was recklessly talkative. And no doubt it was in such a mood, obeying some vagrant impulse of friendship and affection, that, with complete disregard of the promise he had given Hoppner, he informed his companion of the scandal disseminated by Elise Foggi. Naturally, he did not add that he himself, on first hearing of it, had concluded that it was "just like" his former friends. Shelley's immediate response was one of disgust and horror—not so much, however, at the suggestion that Claire might have been his mistress as at the imputation that he had ill-treated Mary and exposed the child. Writing off to Mary on the seventh of August, he explained that Byron had acquainted him with a circumstance that shocked him exceedingly "because it exhibits a degree of desperate and wicked malice for which I am at a loss to account." His patience and philosophy (he declared) had been "put to a severe proof" and it was with difficulty that he refrained "from seeking out some obscure hiding-place, where the countenance of man may never meet me more." He thereupon proceeded to repeat the story. "Imagine my despair of good! imagine how it is possible that one of so weak and sensitive a nature as mine can run further the gauntlet through this hellish society of man!" But the remedy he proposed was typically practical. Mary must at once write to Mrs. Hoppner, contradicting the whole monstrous fabrication, and forward her denial to him, to be sent on to Venice. His letter reached Mary at Pisa on the twentieth of August and she sat down, shaken and miserable, to compose a counterblast.

Of the depth and genuineness of her distress there could be not the slightest question—or of the honesty of the devotion that bound her to her husband. Having declared that the story was generally false and in certain minor details (such as the circumstances supposed to have surrounded Claire's confinement) palpably inaccurate, she wrote that she was forwarding the letter to Shelley at Ravenna and wished that Lord Byron might read it also, since "though he gave no credit to the tale . . . it is as well that he should see how entirely fabulous it is." By Shelley, Mary's communication was promptly handed on to Byron, who "engaged to send it with his own comments to the Hoppners." Byron's position (Shelley admitted) was a trifle awkward, "for the Hoppners [he told Mary] had extracted from Lord Byron that these accusations should be concealed from *me*. Lord Byron is not a man to keep a secret, good or bad; but in openly confessing that he has not done so, he must observe some delicacy, and therefore wishes to send the letter himself. . . ." Whether Byron posted the letter or quietly suppressed it, preferring to save himself the embarrassment of further complications, is a problem on which the controversy may never end.

We know, at least, that Mary's letter was found after his death, with seal broken, among Byron's private papers. Are we to assume that it did not leave him, or that, having been read by the Hoppners, it was returned to Byron? And, if returned, for what reason did the Hoppners send it back? A rather naïve suggestion has been advanced that Byron may have requested they should return the document because he was eager to have safely within his hands the refutation of a scandal that concerned the mother of Allegra. Were that hypothesis correct, it is odd that he himself, in his letters to the consul, should have assented so enthusiastically to the Hoppners' attack on Claire. It is not impossible that Hoppner may have sent back the missive, accompanied by a note that Byron did not preserve (though he was an inveterate hoarder of the smallest written trifle); but it seems more probable that Mary's protest was never dispatched to Venice—certainly from Mrs. Hoppner Mary never received a reply.[1] Byron was annoyed at being "caught out"; he was bored and lazy. Shelley's magnanimity irked him: he was exasperated by what he considered Shelley's humbug.

Yet Shelley's good nature was, as usual, utilized. Would he not write to the Countess Guiccioli (whom he had never met), proposing that, instead of going to Switzerland with her father and brother as she was at present eager to do, they should fix their place of exile, more conveniently, in Tuscany or Lucca? Shelley wrote; Teresa agreed—but wound up with a further commission for the unknown Mr. Shelley: *Non partire da Ravenna senza Milord*. Next, there was the question of Byron's establishment. Supposing that he should at length

[1] In later years, Mary Shelley cut Mrs. Hoppner on meeting her with her daughter in the street. Reasons for supposing that Byron may possibly have forwarded Mary's letter are ably set forth by the editor of *Lord Byron's Correspondence*, I.i.

decide to leave Ravenna, Byron would need an unfurnished house, of opulent proportions. Poor Claire must not be in the immediate neighbourhood; and Shelley, therefore, was disinclined to think of Florence but favoured Pisa, where English tourists were much less numerous and a society might be established which would include his friends the Masons, and his newer and even dearer friends Jane and Edward Williams. But Shelley's first object had been to discuss Allegra. The little girl was no longer at her father's house; for on her fifth birthday, January 12, 1822, Byron had at length done what he had often announced that he intended to do, and put her in charge of the sisters of a neighbouring convent.

The institution selected was the Capucine Convent of Bagnacavallo, twelve miles beyond Ravenna. On learning of Allegra's fate, Claire had again begun to bombard Byron with petitions and remonstrances; and it was in his usual role of mediator or friend-of-all-work that Shelley had agreed to visit the Palazzo Guiccioli. Having discussed the question, he was obliged to admit that, grave as might be the disadvantages of a Catholic upbringing for the child, Byron's intentions were good and the motives that influenced him not injudicious. Byron's house would be no place for a child in times of revolution. Besides, while Byron declared that she was growing beautiful, he indicated that she had her full share of the Byronic temperament and was too vain, obstinate, and imperious for any servant to manage. Nor did his own household, composed as it was "entirely of dissolute menservants," provide the domestic background that Allegra needed; and, when Shelley had ridden over to see her at the convent, he reported that, although she had become "tall and slight for her age" and was "much paler, probably from the effect of improper food," she appeared happy enough if quieter and more obedient.

"She yet retains [he wrote to Mary] the beauty of her deep blue eyes and of her mouth"; but she had acquired in the last year "a contemplative seriousness" which, combined with her "excessive vivacity," was strange and touching. The rule of the place was strict but not tyrannical; and Allegra, "prettily dressed in white muslin, and an apron of black silk, with trousers," among the other children "seemed a thing of a finer and higher order." At first she had been shy; but, reassured by Shelley's gift of a gold chain he had bought in Ravenna and a basket of sweets, she had conducted him at breakneck speed all over the garden and convent, and had shown him her bed and her playthings and her chair at the dinner table. "I asked her what I should say from her to her mamma, and she said—

> *'Che mi manda un bacio e un bel vestituro.'*
> *'E come vuoi il vestituro sia fatto?'*
> *'Tutto di seta e d'oro.'*

Her predominant foible seems the love of distinction and vanity. . . . Before I went away, she made me run all over the convent like a mad thing. The nuns, who were half in bed, were ordered to hide themselves, and on returning Allegra began ringing the bell which calls the nuns to assemble. . . . It required all the efforts of the prioress to prevent the spouses of God to render themselves, dressed or undressed, to the accustomed signal. Nobody scolded her for these *scappature*, so I suppose that she is well treated as far as temper is concerned. Her intellect is not much cultivated. She knows certain *orazioni* by heart, and talks and *dreams* of Paradise and angels and all sorts of things, and has a prodigious list of saints, and is always talking of the Bambino. This will do her no harm, but the idea of bringing up so sweet a creature in the midst of such trash till sixteen!"

With these misgivings and this report, Shelley returned home toward the end of August. In spite of his imperfect sympathy with Shelleyan principles, Byron had been anxious that he should prolong his stay, and Shelley, notwithstanding his distrust of Byron, felt that his visit to Ravenna had done him good. He returned, nevertheless, *"senza Milord."* But it had been agreed that, as soon as Byron could prevail upon himself to leave Ravenna, he should come to Pisa, and that he should be joined there by Teresa Guiccioli and her father and brother. Teresa and the two Counts Gamba reached Pisa during the latter days of August. Mary, who had expected perhaps a second Fornarina, was agreeably surprised; for Teresa, she discovered, was neither bold nor dissolute, but pretty, pleasant, sentimental, and unassuming. Together they sat down to expect the poet; and within seven or eight weeks, in lordly travelling style—accompanied by servants, saddle-horses, and domestic animals, basketed birds, caged monkeys, and dusty enormous dogs—he swept out of Ravenna and took the road to Bologna. At one point Byron's equipage crowded off the highway the public coach in which Miss Clairmont was travelling to Florence; and at Bologna by previous arrangement he met Samuel Rogers, the parchment-faced, bald-headed banking poetaster, with whom he passed a day at Bologna and crossed the Apennines. They had been friends once in London; they were strangers in Italy. Rogers was notorious for his savage tongue; and Byron, who had not seen him since 1816 and feared perhaps that Rogers must find him altered —he had been out of touch so long with the London great world, where the other in due course would repeat his story, among the Lambs and at Holland House, in the clubs and drawing-rooms—made a reserved and, it would appear, an unfriendly travelling companion. Rogers was devoted to the cult of the "picturesque"; Byron had no love of sight or scenery; and "if there was any scenery well worth seeing [lamented Rogers], he generally contrived that we should pass through it in the dark." On October 31 every window of the hotel in Florence was flung open to see Byron and his attendants leave for Pisa. Rogers symbolized London at its worst and worldliest. Far more important to Byron and far more moving had been an earlier encounter—on the road between Imola and Bologna; and if Byron when he met Rogers seemed unusually overcast, it may well have been because his heart and his nerves were both disordered.

For a few minutes he had come face to face with the past he loved. Some weeks previously, in his journal of *Detached Thoughts*, the second of the two journals he had kept at Ravenna, Byron had included a note on his Harrow friendships —"with *me passions* (for I was always violent)"—adding that he did not know of "one which has endured (to be sure, some have been cut short by death). . . . That with Lord Clare began one of the earliest and lasted longest. . . ." It was the hazard of separation, not coldness, that had finally parted them: "I never hear the word '*Clare*' without a beating of the heart even *now*. . . ." Seven or eight years had gone by. Suddenly they met on an Italian highroad. "It was a new and inexplicable feeling, like rising from the grave, to me. Clare, too [Byron wrote], was much agitated—*more* in appearance than even myself; for I could feel his heart beat to his fingers' ends, unless, indeed, it was the pulse of my own which made me think so. He told me that I should find a note from him, left at Bologna." Their encounter was very brief— it lasted in all five minutes—and though what was said we cannot tell, probably it was little enough, for deep emotion made Byron shy and hesitating; but those five minutes left behind them an ineffaceable imprint— "I hardly recollect an hour of my existence which could be weighed against them." Clare was the past; Clare was youth; Byron's devotion to him had gone far deeper than his love of women, by whom his instinctive unreasoning puritanism was often offended; Clare represented the ideal amalgam of love and friendship. But Clare was bound south and Byron westward. They said good-bye and set out again upon their different journeys.[2]

Arrived in Pisa, Byron moved into the Palazzo Lanfranchi. A massive and dignified Renaissance building with a ghost on the floors above, a labyrinth of underground chambers beneath the water-level, in which it pleased Byron occasionally to spend the night, and a façade said to have been designed by Michelangelo, it looked across the yellow turbulent flood of the Arno to a smaller pile, the Tre Palazzo di Chiesa, where the Shelleys and the Williamses had taken separate flats. Byron's accommodation was suitably magnificent. Less to his taste, however, was the coterie he found expecting him. Of the second-rate, Shelley himself was always nobly tolerant: his personality was a lamp that attracted many curious insects which clustered, effusive and adoring, in the light of genius. Not so Byron, more snobbish and more irritable, with fewer enthusiasms and a smaller fund of emotional gullibility. It was hardly to be expected that Lady Mountcashell would much amuse him—middle-aged, raw-boned, and "democratical"—or Mr. Tighe, her retiring and bookish consort. In addition to the Masons and the Shelleys, there were also the Williamses— Edward Williams, a half-pay soldier of literary pretensions who was living with the deserted wife of a fellow-cavalry

[2] "My greatest friend, Lord Clare, is in Rome; we met on the road, and our meeting was quite sentimental—really pathetic on both sides. I have always loved him better than any *male* thing in the world." Byron to Moore, March 1, 1822.

officer, Jane, an unusually attractive woman with a pretty singing voice. Other intimates were "Count" Taafe,[3] an eccentric Irish wanderer, and Tom Medwin, Shelley's cousin, that "perplexing simpleton," who wrote verse tragedies which it fell to Shelley's lot to read and criticize. Then, in January, a new enthusiast joined the Shelley circle, a romantic, untrustworthy, mysterious personage, the former freebooter and professional adventurer Edward John Trelawny.

Few men have been privileged more completely to look the part. A fine hawk-like nose, dark eyes—perhaps a little too close together—cold, shining, and expressionless as those of a bird of prey, heavy bristling eyebrows and black moustaches, combined to make Trelawny the perfect realization of a romantic hero. Had he stepped straight from the dream world of *The Corsair* or *The Giaour?* As befitted his appearance, Trelawny's early life was enveloped in deep obscurity, and even today the cloud that covered it has not been dissipated. We know that he came of ancient Cornish stock; that he had hated his father, a ferocious despot; that he joined the navy as a boy, deserted at Bombay after thrashing a superior officer, and had shipped with a privateer in the French service named Sénouf or de Witt; and that in 1813 he had returned to England and contracted an unhappy marriage. So much at least it seems permissible to deduce from that strange mixture of distorted or magnified fact and melodramatic fantasy later published as *The Adventures of a Younger Son.* Though not an accurate record of the author's life, Trelawny's autobiography is a faithful impression of his personal temperament.

[3] John Taafe, described by Byron as "a very good man, with a great desire to see himself in print," was the author of a voluminous *Commentary on Dante,* which the poet endeavoured to persuade Murray to publish. "It will make the man so exuberantly happy. . . . He is such a good-natured, heavy . . . Christian, that we must give him a shove through the press. . . . Besides, he has had another fall from his horse into a ditch the other day. . . ."

Of such stuff are made soldiers of fortune, patriot guerrilla leaders, sometimes great criminals. Trelawny was a man of passionate enthusiasms, strong appetites, fierce and lasting hatreds. He was also an inveterate, if not always a deliberate, liar.

Engaging he might be; reliable or strictly honest at no time could Trelawny have ever seemed. In one respect, however, his mind was constant. For Shelley he had a jealous and protective love, compounded of a certain pity for Shelley's weakness, real attraction toward the central integrity of Shelley's nature, and a naïve confused appreciation of the poet's genius. In Switzerland he had been captivated by a chance reading of *Queen Mab* and, when he reached Pisa on his way to shoot wild fowl in the marshes of the Maremma, he made haste to visit his friends the Williamses. That they were Shelley's housemates he already knew; but he was not prepared for the juvenile oddity of Shelley's looks. Across the threshold from the shadows of the door where he had been lurking, till he was lured forth by Jane Williams with the reassuring exclamation: "Come in, Shelley, it's only our friend Tre . . . !" glided a tall slight adolescent figure, "habited like a boy, in a black jacket and trowsers," both garments shrunken and far too small for him. Blushing and embarrassed, he held out his hand. Only when Jane Williams, to relieve the awkwardness, asked the name and nature of the book he carried, his face cleared and his utterance grew bold and lively, as he talked of the play by Calderón of which he was translating fragments. There followed a silence. Trelawny raised his eyes. The poet was gone again. "Where is he?" Trelawny asked. "Who? Shelley?" said Mrs. Williams. "Oh, he comes and goes like a spirit, no one knows when or where."

It was not Trelawny's habit to lose the chance of improving

an anecdote. No doubt the celebrated accounts of his meeting with Shelley, and of his call next day on Byron at the Palazzo Lanfranchi, were touched up in many details by the writer's dramatic sense; but they are too close to other existing records to be entirely fabulous. In both stories the bias is fairly evident. Almost from the first moment, Shelley's apparition was inspiriting and delightful; from the beginning his relations with Byron were far less easy. Shelley might disappear and appear at pleasure; Byron must be approached—and approached with circumspection. Escorted by Shelley, he ascended a gigantic staircase, passed through a spacious apartment above the hall, and entered a smaller room containing books and a billiard table. Here they were welcomed by the growls of Moretto the bulldog, which Byron posted to warn him of intruders' presence; and almost immediately its master joined them. His lameness was perceptible but his step was quick; and though he was exceedingly pale—with the "moonlight pallor" so much admired by women—his whole appearance was "fresh, vigorous, and animated." As an athlete, Trelawny admired his broad shoulders, compact well-proportioned body, "small highly finished head, and curly hair." In person, his life at Ravenna had much improved him; the grossness of his Venetian period had dropped away; and there was not "a stain or furrow" on his transparent skin. As for his dress— that struck Trelawny as by no means singular: a blue velvet cap with a gold band, a braided tartan jacket ("he said it was the Gordon pattern," explaining that on his mother's side he was of the Gordon family), and loose nankeen trousers carefully strapped down to conceal his feet. His manners, on the other hand, were decidedly disconcerting; for it was obvious that the great poet was extremely shy and did his best to conceal his embarrassment beneath an air of flippancy, the devil-may-care detachment of a Regency man of the world. In a light off-handed fashion, he asked for Shelley's advice on "the versicles I was delivered of last night, or rather this morning," and suggested that he and Trelawny should try a game of billiards.

Having once regained his composure he began to talk; and his mode of talk was as unexpected as his former shyness. On and on, while he limped briskly around the table, flowed the stream of gossip and anecdote and chit-chat: "Old Bathurst" in whose frigate he had sailed to Greece; wigs and what he meant to do when he was obliged to wear one; the already hackneyed tale of how he had swum the Hellespont. Shelley's reappearance brought a different atmosphere: "He never laid aside his book and magic mantle; he waved his wand, and Byron, after a faint show of defiance, stood mute; his quick perception of the truth of Shelley's comments on his poem transfixed him. . . ." Trelawny was impressed, at the same time, by "Byron's mental vivacity and wonderful memory; he defended himself with a wealth of illustrations, precedents, and apt quotations from modern authorities, disputing Shelley's propositions, not by denying their truth as a whole, but in parts, and the subtle questions he put would have puzzled a less acute reasoner than the one he had to contend with." Toward his companion Byron's attitude was gay and friendly, respectful and even deferential in questions of literary judgment, on worldly subjects provocative and slightly teasing. His nickname for Shelley (Trelawny discovered) was now "The Snake": Shelley reminded him (he said) of a serpent that walked on the tip of its tail—so strange and rapid were his movements, so remote his habits—glistening, ubiquitous, and hard to capture. "I go on [Shelley declared] till I am stopped; and I never am stopped." To Byron's passivity and earth-bound fatalism there could have been no sharper contrast.

Those characteristics were soon to appear under their most disastrous guise. The Shelleys had expected that, if he left Ravenna, his daughter would accompany him; and when he arrived alone they felt that Allegra had been deserted. Byron, however, was reluctant to change his plans; and it is easy to understand, if not to excuse, his obstinacy. On the whole, he felt that his behaviour had done him credit. Again and again, to the Shelleys and to his friends in England, he had expressed his intention of providing handsomely for his natural daughter. He would see that she married well and was properly educated —in the Catholic religion,[4] since it was the faith he liked best —and now, when he had placed her in a decent convent where some of the first families of the Romagna were content to board their children, it was intolerable that he should thus be beleaguered and reproved and bothered. Claire's tears and pleas and imprecations merely increased his stubbornness; while the knowledge that the entire Pisan circle was unanimous in its disapproval—Mr. Tighe had made a personal visit to the convent of Bagnacavallo and reported it unhealthy and damp and chilly; Claire wished Shelley to challenge Byron and implored her friends to rescue Allegra by force of arms —merely helped to confirm him in the cynical and careless line that he had at first adopted. To Shelley's remonstrances he smiled and shrugged, till Shelley said that he had been strongly tempted to knock him down. But Shelley held his hand; and nothing was done and nothing decided. Allegra remained at her cold and unhealthy convent. Then an epidemic

[4] "I am no enemy to religion, but the contrary. As a proof I am educating my natural daughter a strict Catholic in a convent of Romagna; for I think people can never have *enough* of religion, if they are to have any." Byron to Moore, March 4, 1822.

rose from the Romagnol marshes and approached the convent walls. The good sisters took no steps to warn Allegra's guardians. Fever broke out, and on April 20, 1822, Allegra died.

Thus, at the age of five years and three months, expired the second (or possibly the third) of Byron's daughters, a queer self-willed vain impressionable nervous child, Mrs. Hoppner's difficult charge, the spoiled plaything of the Fornarina and Teresa Guiccioli. Byron had been carelessly and casually fond of her—never more so than when in her beauty and natural obstinacy he thought he recognized a resemblance to himself—but news of her death struck him a violent and numbing blow. Once again death was abroad in his immediate circle. All Byrons were ill-fated; most were short-lived. His first response, then, was acquiescent and even apathetic. "I do not know [he wrote to Shelley on April 23] that I have anything to reproach in my conduct, and certainly nothing in my feelings and intentions towards the dead. But it is a moment when we are apt to think that, if this or that had been done, such event might have been prevented—though every day and hour shows us that they are the most natural and inevitable. I suppose that Time will do his usual work. . . ." "A long letter from Lord Byron today [recorded Tom Moore in his diary, under June 21]: he has lost his little natural daughter . . . and seems to feel it a good deal. When I was at Venice, he said, in showing me this child, 'I suppose you have some notion of what they call the parental feeling, but I confess I have not; this little thing amuses me, but that's all.' . . . Evidently . . . he feels much more naturally than he will allow."

Other troubles had preceded the news of Allegra's sickness. Already, after two or three months at Pisa, Byron's household was in bad odour with the ducal police, and the threat of banishment was again hovering over Teresa's family. Here as at Ravenna Metternich's spy-system was omnipresent; and it was hardly to be wondered at that the arrival of a famous modern poet, reputed to be mad, rich, revolutionary, and atheistical, who was accompanied by a train of carriages and a horde of servants and carried on a regular and voluminous correspondence with foreign countries, should have been regarded with some suspicion by the established Government. From Florence the local police received a reassuring report that the authorities were "well aware that Byron goes to Pisa solely for the beautiful daughter of Count Gamba," whose permit to reside at Pisa was in due course to be renewed. But Byron's own behaviour was more disturbing. Soon after his arrival he made through Lega Zambelli a request that he should be given leave to practise pistol-shooting in the gardens of the Palazzo Lanfranchi—a request that, since it was forbidden to carry arms, the governor of the town, the Marchese Niccolò Viviani, was obliged to decline in a categorical though courteous fashion. Secondly—an example of the faculty that certain characters have always possessed of incurring publicity while appearing to shun it—Byron commissioned Mr. Taafe to wait on the Grand Duke and beg His Highness to excuse him from paying his respects, his reason being that, as he had not yet been presented to any other of the reigning princes of Italy, it would be improper to make an exception for the Grand Duke Ferdinand. Finally, Byron's Italian servants were wild and quarrelsome. When they swaggered about the streets they had all the appearance of a private bodyguard.

For a time, however, the police, though they watched Byron carefully, could find little to complain of in his mode of conduct. But "at length [wrote the Cavaliere Torelli, a secret agent who reported directly to the Austrian Chancellor] Lord Byron with his company of assassins, gave us a taste of the temper he had shown in other places." On the evening of March 22, a certain Sergeant Major Masi, who had been dining in the country, was riding back toward Pisa where some duties awaited him. Not far from the gates of the city, he found that the road was blocked. Byron, accompanied by Pietro Gamba, Shelley, Trelawny, John Taafe, and a Captain Hay, their servants, and Teresa in her carriage, was riding in the same direction just ahead. As they did not make way Masi endeavoured to push through. Taafe was a timid and incompetent rider. His horse shied and he lost his hat, whereupon, no doubt to cover his confusion, he called out to the others that he had been insulted. Immediately the English party rode forward, overtook Masi, and demanded an apology; while Byron, who thought that he was an officer, pulled out his card. As the procession rolled on through the dust toward the city gates, tempers grew more explosive and voices higher; and, when the gates were reached, an attempt was made to arrest the Englishmen. Shelley tumbled from his saddle, struck by the flat of a sword; Captain Hay was wounded in the nose, endeavouring to parry a blow; Byron put spurs to his mount and gained the palace.

At once the Lung'Arno resounded with shouts and hoofbeats. Dismounting at the door of the Palazzo Lanfranchi, Byron hastened upstairs to call his steward, then descended and was returning toward the gates when he encountered again the now thoroughly distracted soldier. Tita, who had the post of doorman, rushed from the palace and seized Masi's bridle. Byron ordered him to desist; but in the shindy that followed the sergeant major was stabbed by one of the Gambas' servants. His helmet off, pale as a corpse, "his terrible face made more fearful by a mass of flaming red hair" which (according to an

onlooker who described the incident many years afterward)
stood upright upon his head, Masi collapsed at the threshold
of "Don Beppe's Caffè." Luckily, his wound, though serious,
proved not fatal; and the governor took an indulgent view
of the whole absurd affair. But Tita was arrested and ordered
to shave off his beard,[5] since beards and whiskers were an
indication of revolutionary sympathies, and a Gamba footman, suspected of delivering the blow, was also apprehended.
The subsequent proceedings were long-drawn and inconclusive;
but it was meanwhile signified to the Gambas that they would
do well to leave the city.

During April, therefore, Byron took a villa belonging to
the banker Dupuy at Monte Nero near Leghorn; and thither
the two unfortunate Counts presently departed. Himself, he
was in no hurry to say good-bye to Pisa. He liked his life there.
More important, it had become a habit; and habit was a drug
he had always relied on. Every day he would emerge from
his bedchamber at one or two o'clock, breakfasting usually
off "a cup of strong green tea, without milk or sugar," and
an egg of which he devoured the yolk raw. Medwin, Trelawny,
or Shelley was often in attendance, and when Medwin admired
the abstemiousness of his meal, Byron would explain that his
digestion was weak, that he was too bilious to eat more than
once a day, and that just now he was living on claret and soda
water. Next he petted his monkey or proposed a game of billiards, which continued till the horses or the carriage were
ready. They were "very ordinary-looking horses," observed
Trelawny, who, among his accomplishments, considered himself a judge of horse flesh; but "they had holsters on the

---

[5] Tita was imprisoned for a time in Florence. "There [writes the police spy]
he was ordered to shave off his long Asiatic beard. At first he thought it was
to be given to his master, Lord Byron. But when he found that this was not
the case, he wrapped up the hair very carefully in a sheet of paper."

saddles, and many other superfluous trappings, such as the Italians delight in, and Englishmen eschew." Byron did not mount till they had cleared the city—to avoid, he said, being stared at by the damned British tourists; and "after an hour or two of slow riding and lively talk—for he was generally in good spirits when on horseback—we stopped at a small *podere* on the roadside, and dismounting went into the house, in which we found wine and cakes. From thence we proceeded into the vineyard at the back. . . ." Pistols were produced and a five-part piece, the size of a half-crown, was fixed as a mark in a split cane at a distance of fifteen paces. Byron's hand trembled but he was a practised shot. Each fired five or six bullets. Byron "pocketed the battered money and sauntered about the grounds." Evening fell; and they trotted slowly home down the road to Pisa.

At that distance, the prospect was unreal and enchanting. "With its hanging tower and Sophia-like dome," Pisa reminded Byron of an Eastern city; and through the heavy smoke that drifted away from its roofs and ramparts appeared the massive configuration of golden evening clouds. Fine, said Byron, though not so fine as Venetian sunsets. "Ask Shelley." But Shelley, in his shrill discordant ecstatic voice, spoke with enthusiasm of the view from the Ponte Vecchio, when the river seemed on fire with the rays of the declining sun and "the graceful curve of the palaces" along its banks came to a full stop with the so-called dungeon-tower of Ugolino, which stood up solid and dark against the western sky. At the door of the Palazzo Lanfranchi, the party would disband. "It is impossible [declared Medwin] to conceive a more unvaried life than Lord Byron led at this period." His conversation, if not monotonous, was by no means various; and to an observer, who, like Trelawny, came fresh from England, it was clear that he lived on the memories of a preceding age. His talk was anything but literary except when Shelley was near him "but seasoned with anecdotes of the great actors on and off the stage, boxers, gamblers, duellists, drunkards, etc., etc.," and embellished with slang and scandal that he alone remembered. Now and then he would become conscious of his years of exile, and recognize that slang may alter and conventions change; and at such times he was particularly reluctant to join an English gathering and would fall back, even on the unpolished Trelawny, for social guidance. "Does rank lead the way [he was anxious to learn], or does the ambassadress pair us off into the dining-room? Do they ask people to wine? Do we exit with the women, or stick to our claret?"

Even worse was the recognition that he might be losing his public. At Pisa as at Ravenna, his days were desultory, and his evenings generally devoted to love and small talk; but the hours of darkness were busily occupied, often till the dawn appeared. More and more he was possessed by a rage for writing. But there was no corresponding increase in his critical faculty; and much of the work that he produced at Pisa is weak and slipshod. The blank-verse dramas, for instance, are scarcely readable. Yet it was on these dramas, Byron repeated again and again, that his celebrity, he was convinced, would ultimately come to rest. John Murray, a cautious bookseller, did not agree. There arrived a moment when suddenly and horribly it occurred to Byron, noting in Murray an unmistakable reluctance to send his manuscripts to the printing press as soon as they were delivered, that perhaps his publisher was beginning to regard him as an increasingly doubtful asset. But the row over *Cain* was at least encouraging; and Byron was glad to see that ponderous Biblical concoction become the focus of a violent literary controversy on which many different intelligences were brought to bear, from Anglican clergymen who trumpeted against it all over Europe, in pulpits as widely sundered as Kentish Town and Pisa, to Lady Granville, an old acquaintance and Caroline Lamb's cousin, who informed a correspondent that she found it "most wicked" but admitted that hearing her husband read it aloud had reduced her to a paroxysm of helpless weeping and that she had "roared" until she could "neither hear nor see." Shelley and the aged Goethe both praised it warmly. Yet Murray still refused to admire its companion works; and Byron's mood grew more petulant as the year proceeded. If Mr. Murray was not appreciative, he would take his poems elsewhere. To vilification he was accustomed; neglect and indifference were irritants he had not yet sampled.

They did not suit him; and his judgment became more unsure. Already, during the autumn of 1821, he had allowed his critical sense to be overridden by the claims of sentiment and given a promise to Teresa that he would drop *Don Juan*. None of his poems had been composed with greater gusto; none of them had unfolded to his own more intense delight; but the majority of the feminine readers thought the work "abominable." The resentment it aroused had at first diverted him. In these protests Teresa Guiccioli was not alone; and soon after the appearance of the opening cantos, he had received, while he was still established at Ravenna, a long scrawl signed by the notorious courtesan Harriette Wilson, whom he had once met at the zenith of her fame and fortune:

Dear *Adorable* Lord Byron [wrote Harriette at "exactly 20 minutes past 12 o'clock at night," from 64 Rue Neuve-des-Petits-Champs, whither she had retired since the failure of her attempt to marry Lord Worcester], *don't* make a mere coarse old Libertine of yourself. . . . When you don't feel quite up to a spirit of benevolence . . . in *gratitude* for the talent which after all must have caused you exquisite moments in your life, throw away your pen my love & take a little *calomel. . . . Ecoutez mon Ange.* It is not in my power or in my nature to forget any kindness shown me [6] (supposing I had not half loved you before) but I would not even to *you*, who in a wrong-headed moment wrote it, lie under the imputation of such bad taste as to admire what in your cool moments you must feel to be *vulgar* at least and half destroys the effect of the most delicious beautiful poetry you ever wrote in your life. . . .

More sentimentally, Teresa expressed a similar prejudice— *Don Juan* was the literary antithesis of her private emotional creed; and Byron had been cajoled or blackmailed into complete surrender. In 1822, he obtained her permission to embark on the concluding cantos; but it was understood they were to be in a less immoral and a more romantic strain.

In Shelley's career such an influence was never operative. Painful and honest as were the feelings of diffidence that often overwhelmed him, wild and apparently haphazard as was the course he followed, he still rushed ahead obeying his own convictions and propelled by his own momentum. But, though faith was not yet extinct, of hope he had little enough. Trelawny, with the anxious eyes of a new admirer, noted how careless was his hold on life and how often and eagerly he was apt to revert to the idea of suicide. Thus, when Trelawny, after "performing a series of aquatic gymnastics" in a deep pool of the Arno, suggested that Shelley would find it easy to swim, the poet plunged from the bank but immediately sank to the bottom, where he lay on the riverbed extended "like a conger eel, not making the least effort or struggle to save himself. He would have been drowned if I had not instantly fished him out. When he recovered his breath, he said, 'I always find the bottom of the well, and they say Truth lies there. In another

[6] This letter—the last of several—had been preceded by a request for money, which Byron had gratified to the extent of a thousand francs.

minute I should have found it. . . . It is an easy way of getting rid of the body.'" It was "a great temptation," he added; but, "Don't tell Mary—not a word!" On a later occasion he begged Trelawny, who was visiting Leghorn, to procure him, if he should meet with any scientific person capable of preparing it, a small quantity of "the *Prussic Acid, or essential oil of bitter almonds* . . . I would give any price for this medicine; you remember we talked of it the other night, and we both expressed a wish to possess it; my wish was serious, and sprang from the desire of avoiding needless suffering. I need not tell you I have no intention of suicide at present, but I confess it would be a comfort to me to hold in my possession that golden key to the chamber of perpetual rest. . . . A single drop, even less, is a dose, and it acts by paralysis."

His habits were as solitary and elusive as Byron's were unvaried. Once Trelawny pursued him into the depths of the Cascine forest. Mary Shelley, who had started out on the expedition, was presently defeated—"the loose sand and hot sun soon knocked her up"—but Trelawny skirted the forest and reached the sea, then turned back into the thickest shades of the pine-woods, shouting the poet's name as he wandered among stagnant meres from which herons rose flapping away across the heavy silence. After a time he met an old peasant who was gathering pine-cones and who volunteered to show him that part of the accursed wood in which *l'inglese malinconico* was usually to be discovered. Beside a deep pool of dark glimmering water lay hat, books, and scattered leaves of manuscript. *"Eccolo!"* said the old man; and for a second Trelawny supposed that he meant to indicate that Shelley was even now beneath the surface; for "the careless, not to say, impatient way in which the Poet bore his burden of life caused a vague dread among his family and friends that he might lose or cast it away at any moment." But soon he caught sight of him under the lee of a fallen trunk. When he was called, he turned his head; and, Trelawny having explained that Mary awaited them, "Poor Mary!" he ejaculated as he started to his feet and bundled his books and manuscripts together into his hat and pockets. "Hers is a sad fate. Come along; she can't bear solitude, nor I society—the quick coupled with the dead."

According to Trelawny, whose word at this and at every other juncture can be accepted only with reservations, the manuscript that lay scattered among the pine needles, beside the edition of Æschylus and a volume of Shakespeare's plays, contained a rough draft, scrawled and corrected and irascibly finger-smudged, of the celebrated verses on a musical instrument:

> Ariel to Miranda:—Take
> This slave of Music, for the sake
> Of him who is the slave of thee . . .

Jane Williams was the Miranda to whom he addressed those lines, in his emotional firmament the star that had followed Emilia Viviani, the fascinating deceptive heroine of *Epipsychidion*, just as Emilia had followed Sophia Stacey, and Sophia herself had succeeded to a galaxy of earlier lights. Again, we meet the contrasted problems of Byron's and of Shelley's character. Was Byron demonic, and Shelley angelic? But, if Byron glowed with a dark destructive energy, hurtful to himself and sometimes fatal to others, it must be allowed that often angels make dangerous house companions. They are dangerous, that is to say, because, lacking the earthly virtues of common sense, they wave their wings and scatter their gifts a trifle indiscriminately, for the sheer joy of exercising their heavenly office. It is an angel's business to love, and love he must. He does not reflect always that the value of love depends to a very large extent upon the attention and delicacy with which it is placed, and that love seriously misplaced may be worse than hatred. Love can demoralize more quickly than loathing. It gives trivial objects an importance they cannot sustain, lifts weak spirits to an altitude from which they are bound to tumble, envelops a Harriet and throws her at last into the suicide's graveyard. Shelley believed in love with an abstract fervour. The sentiment provided its own nobility and its own excuse.

The passion of love may be abstract; its results are concrete. A Byronic rake, less concerned with theory than practice, is sometimes more merciful than a Shelleyan idealist—at least, the wounds he inflicts are more easily curable and he embarks on each new adventure with wide-open eyes. In the first delirious trance of a new enthusiasm, Shelley was incapable of distinguishing the features of the person he loved; but that enthusiastic obliquity could not last for ever. From repeated disillusionments he learned little or nothing; and the fact that the heroine of *Epipsychidion* might afterward turn out to be cold, conventional, and calculating merely strengthened his belief that he was the victim of tyranny, and that the personified forces of Custom and Prejudice still rose to frustrate and harry him at every turn. And then, regarding the nature of love itself, Shelley's point of view was frequently somewhat hazy. Like all idealists who have contracted the insidious habit of discussing philosophy late into the night with attractive and susceptible young women, long after their wives have gone exhausted to bed, Shelley seems not always to have been very clear when philosophy withdrew from the field and passion replaced it. He was passionate; one may surmise that he was normally sensual. Whatever the exact colouring of his relationship with Claire Clairmont (who certainly advocated a community of wives and husbands), there is no doubt of the quality of his feeling for Jane Williams and almost as little doubt that the heavenly love-affair reached an earthly conclusion. At times the enthusiast's wife grew restive and miserable. Even the daughter of Mary Wollstonecraft was not proof against jealousy.

A regular social position, she had begun to understand, might produce positive benefits. Brought up in the dismal bohemianism of Godwin's household, swept as a young girl into Shelley's orbit, and by him hurried through a succession of alien cities where sickness and weariness lay in wait for herself and death for her children, Mary was already wearying of the role allotted her. Shelley had insufficient cynicism to be an acute psychologist. Well might he, with raised voice and pathetically extended arms, exclaim on the strange perversity of Byron's principles: "I do believe, Mary"—pausing as if reluctant to expose a friend—"I do believe, Mary, that he is little better than a Christian!" Mary's own unorthodoxy was somewhat suspect; and the worst happened when she threatened to give a party. It was to be a musical gathering, her husband informed Jane Williams; "there are English singers here, the Sinclairs, and she will ask them, and every one she or you know—oh, the horror!" By much diplomacy, Mary was persuaded to curtail her project and limit the guests to a few of their most intimate friends and some of the Gamba family; but it was clear that her independence was being gradually worn down. "Mary [Shelley concluded] is under the dominion of the mythical monster 'Everybody.' I tell her I am one of the Nobodies." But the shadow of the mythical monster was lengthening across Mary's spirit.

Here was a limited mind and an inelastic nature. There

was a hint of primness in those grey eyes and that small but definite mouth; and it is a tribute to Mary's gift for devotion that she continued to bear with Shelley, even when his moods and vagaries were most exasperating. During the latter part of April, soon after Allegra's death, the Shelleys moved at a few days' notice from their lodgings in Pisa, where Mary had been making tentative advances to the conventional English colony, and bundled themselves with Jane and Edward into a desolate seaside house which Trelawny and Williams had discovered near Lerici on the Gulf of Spezia. Their reason for making this sudden move was the necessity of breaking the news of her daughter's death to Claire Clairmont at a place where there was no immediate likelihood of seeing Byron; but it was also in accordance with a long-established plan. Since early spring, Byron and Shelley had both been boat-owners, for, under Trelawny's influence, they had commissioned his friend Captain Roberts of the Royal Navy to construct them two craft in the shipyards of Genoa. By May, Shelley's boat, the *Ariel*, thirty foot in length and undecked, was delivered at Lerici; while Byron's yacht, the *Bolivar*, was ready a month later. Trelawny had been appointed captain of the *Bolivar*, which he pronounced to be fast and seaworthy and easy to handle; but regarding the other boat, constructed according to specifications Williams had brought out from England, he claimed afterward to have been much less optimistic. "Fast, strongly built, and Torbay rigged," she was reported to be "a ticklish boat to manage"; and it had required "two tons of iron ballast to bring her down to her bearing." But Williams, who believed that he was a judge of boats, would hear no ill of her; and Shelley looked for unlimited delight from this new and romantic plaything.

He was enchanted, moreover, with the house at Lerici.

Nearer to the waves than any house he had yet inhabited, it was a plain two-story building with an arcaded ground floor planted almost in the water. Above there was a room for the Shelleys and a room for the Williamses divided by a passage. Otherwise it had few comforts; and when the sirocco blew up, as it did soon after their arrival, sheets of foam were flung against the whitewashed house-front, the wind howled, and the breakers crashed; and its shivering inhabitants imagined themselves passengers in a ship at sea. Then suddenly the storm would fall; and at their feet stretched the waters of the bay, smooth, tideless, radiant, enclosed to the east by the old castle of Lerici, to the west by the distant shape of Porta Venere. Behind, the Casa Magni ran up a precipitious hillside fledged with young trees, planted by the eccentric owner of the estate who had destroyed the olive yards to make way for his plantations and built the unfinished and now half-ruined house that crowned the summit. A rough and winding footpath led to Lerici; but the country was trackless upon the other side, and the neighbouring peasants seemed as wild as the rocks they lived among. When the nights were hot they would frolic in the water, men, women, and children, dancing and singing the refrain of loud and discordant ballads. Housekeeping, complained Mary, was extremely difficult; they could not have been more isolated had they been shipwrecked sailors. But Shelley, with his passion for sea and solitude, and the passion for sympathy and beauty that fed on the sight of Jane, lived in a halcyon world of sensation and imagination, where Mary and the influence of her mythical monster could rarely penetrate.

This summer he would sail—and the extent of the voyages on which he intended to embark with Williams grew steadily more and more ambitious—but, before the summer was over, he expected Leigh Hunt and, with Byron's help, would strike a fresh blow in the cause of freedom. During the previous August, he had spoken to Byron of Leigh Hunt's plight, explaining that Hunt had been in poor health since his release from prison (where he had passed two years of not uncomfortable confinement after a particularly ferocious attack on the sovereign) and that he needed rest and sunshine and relief from financial cares. As a matter of course, Mrs. Hunt had invoked Shelley's assistance; and, during his stay at Ravenna, Shelley proposed that Hunt should be invited to Italy, and that the three of them should join forces in editing a liberal magazine. Byron liked the project and had promised to support the paper. With Hunt himself he had already some slight acquaintance; for he had visited him on several occasions at the Surrey Gaol and been received in the trellised, painted, and flower-filled sitting-room into which Hunt had metamorphosed his prison chamber. Subsequently, he had called on him at his suburban lodgings. With gratitude, Hunt remembered the brisk, well-built, curly-headed young man who would enter the room, carrying a couple of quartos that he hoped might provide hints for the *Story of Rimini*, or sit astride the children's rocking-horse as he talked of literature. During his later visits, Lady Byron would remain below in the carriage; and, although Byron's expression was "not unmixed with disquiet," an effect presumably of the domestic trials he was undergoing, "the turn of his head and countenance" was bold and spirited. "His dress, which was black, with white trowsers, and which he wore buttoned close over the body, completed the succinctness and gentlemanliness of his appearance."

He would find the democrat (Byron informed Trelawny), notwithstanding a taint of Cockneyism that he owed to his Hampstead circle, unmistakably "a gentleman in dress and address." The idea of assisting Hunt appealed to his good nature, though he knew that it might alarm Murray and infuriate Hobhouse; and he liked the idea that he would have a controlling voice on an important liberal journal. To wield such influence would be a substitute for a career of action. Meanwhile life at Pisa was calm and easy. Rogers reappeared, accompanied him when he rode out in the afternoons, and was amused to note, on the face of a peasant girl said to be Byron's favourite, a look of pleasure and dignity as they passed her by. Early in June the poet removed to Leghorn. Described by Trelawny as a "new, flimsy-built villa—not unlike the suburban verandaed Cockney boxes on the Thames—" Monte Nero proved "ten times hotter than the old solid palace he had left, with its cool marble halls, and arched and lofty floors. . . ." At this house he was delighted to be able to welcome Lord Clare, who paused briefly at Leghorn on his way back to England; and Teresa Guiccioli, in one of the more vivid passages of her otherwise unreadable memoirs, records the intense satisfaction with which Byron received his friend and the gloomy premonitions with which he saw him go.[7] For such companionship the society of the Gambas was an exceedingly poor exchange. He was attached to, but often exasperated by, Teresa's father and brother, that amiable, dignified, yet incurably ineffective pair, who now regarded him, almost too literally, as one of the family circle, with a relative's responsibility toward his helpless kinsmen. Either they would not or could not control their servants; and the tranquil course of existence at Monte Nero—in spite of Trelawny's

---

[7] "Lord Clare's visit also occasioned him extreme delight. . . . The day on which they separated was a melancholy one for Lord Byron. 'I have a presentiment that I shall never see him more,' he said, and his eyes filled with tears. The same melancholy came over him during the first weeks that succeeded to Lord Clare's departure whenever his conversation happened to fall upon this friend."

strictures, a pleasant enough seaside house, which looked out toward the islands of Elba and Corsica, across the dense or shimmering blue of the Mediterranean seascape—was presently interrupted by a succession of violent quarrels. Already suspicious of the household at Monte Nero, the authorities scored a further black mark against the Byron and Gamba names.

Very different was the atmosphere of the Casa Magni. Like some strange aquatic creature that had never learned to swim, Shelley passed his days in or near the water, either helping Williams to sail the *Ariel*, which he did in a manner equally brave and inexpert, or alone at the oars of the light flat-bottomed dinghy that Williams had constructed. This flimsy craft he would scull out to sea—"he felt independent [he said] and safe from land bores"—then let it drift with the current, till a rising breeze sent waves lapping over the gunwale and, slowly and regretfully, he was wafted to land again. As he disembarked, he would sometimes miss his footing and enter the house, leaving a puddle at every step, refreshed and radiant, his thick hair matted with sand and sea-salt. Once at least he distressed Mary by returning naked from a bathe and in that condition gliding swiftly through the common dining-room where the party, which included a literary visitor, were all assembled. Jane Williams was still the emotional pivot around which his life revolved; and at night he would listen to her while she sang and played, or submit to experiments in what he believed to be "animal magnetism." Her hands on his forehead he found deeply soothing; but the old nervous troubles and the familiar hallucinations did not grow less persistent. Between Shelley's nightmares and those of Byron there is a curious parallel; but whereas Byron's, from which he awoke sick and shaken and terrified, giving no hint of the experiences he had undergone, suggest the tormented dreams of an earth-bound giant, pinned under a rocky weight of abhorrent and fearful memories, Shelley's visitations seemed to explode from above like an Alpine thunderstorm. Late on a stormy night Jane Williams was aroused "by the weight . . . falling against her door and moaning." When the Williamses opened the door, "Mrs. Shelley, in her nightdress, tumbled into their room, helpless and tongue-tied by terror. The Poet, unconscious of everything, his eyes wide open . . . stood over her, upright and motionless, holding a lighted candle at arm's length. On Mrs. Shelley's recovering her senses she told Mrs. Williams she had been awakened by the glare of a light. . . . Opening her eyes she beheld Shelley. . . . She spoke but he did not answer. His eyes were wide open, but misty; he resembled a statue. . . . Williams watched the sleep-walker; he stalked to the door leading out to the veranda, seemingly listening to the crashing of the waves, then walked into his room, put the candle on the table, and stretched himself on his bed." According to another account, also written by Trelawny, Shelley, as soon as he had returned to consciousness, explained that an image of himself had appeared before him, had beckoned him into the hall, and there vanished with the exclamation: "Shelley, are you satisfied?"

His affections, like his aversions, worked by a process of synthesis; and it was inevitable that Shelley's love of the sea and his love of Jane, with that impulse toward self-destruction which the sea evoked, should be woven into the same strand of romantic feeling. One hot evening, as Jane sat with her children on the beach, Shelley emerged from the house, dragging his boat. In his vehement excited way, he invited her to join him and, as soon as she and the children were seated on the bottom, rowed them around a promontory into deep blue water. Here he rested on his oars and seemed to lose consciousness of his passengers' existence. They were alone: a single movement would have upset the boat. Suddenly his face brightened and he appeared to return to life, with the exclamation: "Now let us together solve the great mystery!" Managing to control her terror, Jane replied in a firm yet gentle voice, and little by little was able to persuade him to return inshore, but once in shallow water she plunged overboard with her children and scrambled to safety. That night, Shelley's expression was rapt and guileless as he glided into the living-room to snatch a haphazard meal which consisted as usual of grapes and a crust of bread. For the moment he was completely absorbed in the world of the Spanish drama.

It is not impossible that the entire incident had passed from his memory. Between his waking life and the life of dreams the distinction he made had always been indefinite; and earlier in the year, as they walked together on the terrace, observing the effect of the moonlight on the waters, Shelley had complained to Williams of being unusually nervous. ". . . Stopping short, he grasped me violently by the arm, and stared steadfastly on the white foam upon the beach under our feet. . . . I demanded of him if he were in pain. But he only answered by saying, 'There it is again—there!' He recovered after some time, and declared that he saw, as plainly as he then saw me, a naked child (Allegra) rise from the sea, and clap its hands as in joy, smiling at him. This was a trance that it required some reasoning and philosophy to awaken him from, so forcibly had the vision operated on his mind."

Yet his strong practical flair did not desert him. It was Shelley who had prepared the way for Leigh Hunt's visit, who had negotiated the loan from Byron when his own resources failed, and had arranged for his friend to occupy an apartment in the Palazzo Lanfranchi. On him, no doubt, would fall the main burden of preparing the magazine. What Shelley did not know, and Hunt did not explain till he had arrived in Italy, was that, some months since, he and his brother had ceased to own the *Examiner* (which the others had counted on to launch their project) and that he had left England penniless and empty-handed. In money matters, as in all else, Hunt's was a complex character; and it was his misfortune that, although his virtues did not at once emerge, his shortcomings, personal and intellectual, were all of the surface. Buried in the depths of his nature were many admirable qualities; but, wherever they grew upward and outward into his public life, they were apt to fritter themselves away in gush and artifice. Thus, for social purposes, his real devotion to a host of friends was transmuted into sentimentalism and vapid coterie talk, while his knowledge and intense love of art and literature tailed off in the attitudinizing of a suburban *petit-maître*. Such was the aspect of Leigh Hunt that had disgusted Keats, who, after many pleasant evenings passed in the Vale of Health, in an atmosphere of puns and pleasantries and competitive verse-spinning, recoiled with the indignant energy of his honest and masculine spirit. "Hunt [he had written in 1818] does one harm by making fine things petty and beautiful things hateful— Through him I am indifferent to Mozart . . . and many a glorious thing when associated with him becomes a nothing— This distorts one's mind—makes one's thoughts bizarre—perplexes one in the standard of Beauty." Under Hunt's touch, fancy was whimsy, and beauty prettiness. Yet the bounce that distinguished Hunt's talk and mannerisms, the air of complacency that irradiated his somewhat pug-like features and sparkled from his dark liquid romantic eyes, were maintained against a constant pressure of work and worry.

He was poor; he had a large family; his health was bad. While Hunt chirped or carolled among his busts and vases, wreathed verses in true-love knots or gaily hummed the *motifs* of an Italian opera, there were often tradesmen at the door and always growing children to stamp or scream in the immediate background.

By temperament the innocent voluptuary was an inveterate optimist—his feeling for beauty and his taste for happiness had not declined—and it seemed merely natural that his friends in Italy should be eager to fly to his rescue. But even Hunt hesitated at the prospect of a long and expensive journey overland, burdened by six children and an ailing wife. He expressed his doubts; to which Shelley responded that they must come by sea. "Put your music and your books on board a vessel [he recommended], and you will have no more trouble." A delightful picture unfolded, bright with the colours of hope; and it was Shelley's visionary advice that Leigh Hunt followed. On November 16, 1821, the whole family embarked at the port of London and by the nineteenth, "amidst rain and squalls," had passed the Nore. Rather less apparent now seemed the advantages of a winter sea-voyage. The cabin in which Leigh Hunt and his wife were obliged to sleep upon the floor while their six children were packed tight in the bunks above was small, wet, and atrociously overcrowded. Let his readers imagine (wrote Leigh Hunt afterward) "the little back-parlour of one of the shops in Fleet Street, or the Strand, attached or let into a great moving vehicle, and tumbling about the waves. . . ." Eventually the captain decided to make for Ramsgate; and there they remained three tedious weeks. On December 11 they left the harbour "in company with nearly a hundred vessels, the white sails of which, as they shifted and presented themselves in different quarters," exhibited "a kind of noble minuet." Then the skies overclouded; a storm swept down; "and there ensued such a continuity and vehemence of bad weather as rendered the winter of 1821 memorable in the shipping annals" and strewed the coasts of Europe with wreckage from Jutland to Genoa. For ten hideous days they were battered and buffeted up and down the Channel. Twice they touched the Atlantic but were driven back again; one gale continued without respite for nearly sixty hours; the vessel "looked like a wash-house in a fit." Excepting Hunt, the whole party was incessantly seasick; but in nothing else that he ever wrote (save perhaps in three deservedly famous sonnets) did Hunt's literary virtues find better employment than in his account of their misery. Puking children, danger and cold and dark could not dull his dispassionate appreciation of all that he felt and suffered; and now he observed the even greater sufferings of the goat they had brought on board ("a present from a kind friend, anxious that we should breakfast as at home"), which he lugged into the cabin and fed on biscuit; now admired the phantasmal appearance assumed by hanging garments which swayed and gestured mysteriously as the vessel laboured; now, when he had struggled up onto the slippery and reeking deck, gazed with delight and awe across a huge perspective of tormented sea space. "The sun [he remembered] rose in the morning, at once fiery and sicklied over; a livid gleam played on the water, like the reflection of lead; then the storms would recommence; and during partial clearings off, the clouds and fogs appeared standing in the sky, moulded into gigantic shapes, like antediluvian wonders, or visitants from the zodiac; mammoths, vaster than have yet been thought of; the first ungainly and stupendous ideas of bodies and legs, looking out upon an unfinished world. These fancies were ennobling, from their magnitude."

On December 22 the Hunts' vessel reached the safety of Dartmouth. Exhausted and woebegone, they clambered ashore; and it was not until five months later, on May 13, when further financial provision had arrived from Italy, that they again dared the perils of a voyage to the Mediterranean. That second voyage, comparatively speaking, proved swift and pleasant. Once more Marianne Hunt was extremely ill; but Hunt, though his confidence was shaken, enjoyed the journey—the waters of the Bay of Biscay "heaving in huge oily-looking fields, like a carpet lifted" or "striped into great ribbons"; the "beautiful lone promontory" of Cape St. Vincent; or the burnished wings of "gold and yellow and rose colour, with a smaller minute sprinkle in one spot, like a shower of glowing stones from a volcano," which shone in the western sky over the hills of Spain as the sun descended. Incessantly he repeated the name of their destination: the Mediterranean, the Mediterranean— sea of Homer, Virgil, Catallus, with its Ἀνήριθμον γελασμα, its innumerable rippling smiles, and marmoreal expanses of unbroken dark blue. By June 13 they were skirting the shores of the Gulf of Genoa and admiring groves and white villages that "looked as Italian as possible." On the twenty-eighth they left Genoa and set sail for Leghorn, where Hunt was to renew old friendships and begin his new life.

In the harbour of Leghorn, he discovered Trelawny, "dark, handsome, and mustachio'd," standing on the deck of Byron's yacht. Leghorn itself appeared a commonplace sea port, a kind of "polite Wapping, with a square and a theatre"; and, after he had installed his wife and children in hotel rooms, Hunt's next move was to make a call at Monte Nero. The day was hot; the road led through hot and dusty suburbs; Monte Nero, when he arrived there, struck Hunt as the hottest-looking house he had ever seen. Its walls, washed a sultry salmon-pink, flared out in the sunshine across the surrounding countryside; but, once he had crossed the threshold, the atmosphere within doors was even more oppressive. A scene in the best Italian manner was rapidly boiling up. On June 28, according to a report prepared by the local authorities, a violent quarrel had occurred between Byron's coachman and the Gambas' cook; during the dispute they had drawn their knives; the entire household was soon involved in meridional pandemonium; and a pitched battle had been fought beneath Byron's windows. Hurrying onto the balcony, with a brace of loaded pistols, he threatened that he would shoot down all the combatants unless they immediately desisted; in spite of which it proved necessary to call the police. Into the aftermath of this tea-cup hurricane poor Leigh Hunt stumbled. Pietro Gamba, unlucky as always, had received a knife-wound from one of his own servants. He was ruffled, extremely indignant, and had his arm in a sling. Teresa also was in a state of the utmost perturbation. Her face was flushed; her eyes were bright; her long hair streamed round her shoulders in wild dishevelment. From an English point of view they were both unusual figures; but just as disconcerting to Leigh Hunt was the sight of the poet himself. Byron had changed considerably since 1816—so much so that at a first glance he was scarcely recognizable.

In place of the "compact, energetic, and curly-headed person" whom Leigh Hunt had expected, stood a man fattish and no longer young, whose greying hair fell "in thin ringlets about his throat." His costume suggested a life of ease and lassitude —a loose nankeen jacket, white trousers, an open neck-cloth; his manner was affable but vague and unconcerned, and he appeared anxious to make light of the whole ridiculous incident. Unfortunately the potential assassin was still outside. Leigh Hunt looked down from the casement; and there he was, "glaring upwards like a tiger," wearing a red cap and "a most sinister aspect, dreary and meagre, a proper caitiff." Monte Nero, in fact, was in a condition of blockade. Luckily, however, the hour had come when Byron and his friends were accustomed to take their evening ride; and it was resolved that this habit must not be interrupted. Byron, meanwhile, had assumed his velvet cap and a "loose riding-coat of mazarin blue," in which (observed Hunt) he looked "more lordly than before, but hardly less foreign"; and together they began to edge toward the doorway. Pietro threatened; Teresa apostrophized; Byron, "metamorphosed, round-looking, and jacketed," did his best to damp down their southern fire "with his cool tones, and an air of voluptuous indolence." As they emerged—Teresa urging "Bairon" to hold back and "all squeezing to have the honour of being the boldest"—the besieger collapsed on a bench and burst into floods of tears. "His cap was half over his eyes; his face gaunt, ugly, and unshaved. . . . To crown all, he requested Lord Byron to kiss him. The noble Lord conceived this excess of charity superfluous." But he excused the man; Pietro Gamba shook his hand; and Teresa looked on in a pitying sort. Before Byron's valet, who had been dispatched for help, returned with a police officer, the scene had ended in dramatic repentance and equally dramatic pardon.

It was an exciting, but disturbing, preface to Hunt's Italian adventures. The following day arrived Shelley from Casa Magni, shrill, rumpled, enthusiastic, kind as ever—a welcome contrast to the affable but languid Byron—though Hunt noticed that he had "less hope" and that his hair was grey-threaded. Rapidly he whirled his friends off from Leghorn to Pisa, where he saw them installed on the ground floor of the Palazzo Lanfranchi, among furniture that he had bought with money supplied by Byron, and called in the physician Vacca to attend to Marianne Hunt. Vacca gave little hope of the patient's recovery. As usual, Shelley's task was to advise and comfort; but for the time being he had promised to return to Lerici, whither he intended to sail with Edward Williams; and after a day's sight-seeing he bade Hunt good-bye and set out for Leghorn. At Pisa he had found a letter from the Magnetic Lady, addressed to her "Dearest Friend" and concluding with a postscript that seems at least provocative. Why did he talk (inquired Jane) "of never enjoying moments like the past? Are you going to join your friend Plato, or do you expect I shall do so soon?" Drawn by the same lodestar, husband and friend were eager to begin the journey. Byron, in the meantime, had left Monte Nero. The recent rumpus had given the authorities the excuse they needed—they had been thoroughly alarmed by Byron's suggestion that, as owner of the *Bolivar*, he should be allowed to embark or land passengers along the Tuscan coast wherever it pleased him—and an order of expulsion was pronounced against both the Gambas. Toward the end of June, they continued their flight to Genoa, while Byron and Teresa retired to the comparative quietude of the Palazzo Lanfranchi.

At Leghorn the weather was sultry and stifling. "Processions of priests and religiosi," with prayers for rain, wound between the dusty house-fronts bearing lights and images; but not a drop had yet descended from the unresponsive sky. On Monday, July 8, Shelley visited his bankers accompanied by Trelawny, made some purchases at a store, and finally embarked just after one o'clock. With the masters of the *Ariel* went a young English seaman, named Charles Vivian, whom Trelawny had engaged. The *Bolivar* was to escort them into the offing; but, when they were under way, the guard-boat boarded them to examine their papers and, since Trelawny had not his port clearance, he was obliged to remain in harbour. Sulkily he gave orders to furl the sails, but did not leave the deck and continued to observe the *Ariel's* progress out to sea, till it had vanished in the heat-mist that veiled the distance. The oppressive warmth and the unusual stillness had made him drowsy. He went below and fell asleep, to be aroused some hours later by the noise of his men getting up the cable chain. Though it was only half-past six, the heavens had darkened. "The sea was of the colour, and looked as solid and smooth as a sheet of lead, and covered with an oily scum. Gusts of wind swept over without ruffling it, and big drops of rain fell on its surface, rebounding, as if they could not penetrate it. There was a commotion in the air, made up of many threatening sounds. . . . Fishing craft and coasting vessels under bare poles rushed by us . . . running foul of the ships in the harbour. As yet the din and hubbub was that made by men, but their shrill pipings were suddenly silenced by the crashing voice of a thunder squall that burst right over our heads. For some time no other sounds were to be heard than the thunder, wind, and rain."

Within twenty minutes the storm had passed; but when Trelawny again examined the sea, the high sails of Shelley's boat had completely vanished. From the tower of the port Captain Roberts had caught a last glimpse of the *Ariel*. It was then some ten miles out, and he noticed that Shelley and his companions were taking in their topsails. More significant is a current story retailed by Taafe. Soon after they had put to sea, they were said to have been sighted by a vessel making for Leghorn, the captain of which, knowing that they "could not long contend with such tremendous waves, bore down upon them and offered to take them on board." But "a shrill voice" returned a decisive "No." Astonished by their foolhardiness, the captain continued to follow them through his telescope. "The waves were running mountains high—a tremendous surf dashed over the boat, which to his astonishment was still crowded with sail." A sailor, using a speaking trumpet, shouted to them to reef their sails or they would be lost. "One of the gentlemen (Williams, it is believed) was seen to make an effort to lower the sails—his companion seized him by the arm as if in anger."

On his own account, Shelley had now "solved the great mystery"—whether involuntarily or by an act of deliberate rashness it is impossible to determine—but the obscurity that surrounds his means of departure can never be cleared up. When *Ariel* was finally dragged from the seabed, there were indications that she had been run down by another vessel—for her "starboard quarter was stove in, evidently by a blow from the sharp bows of a felucca"—and, since the boat was undecked, had foundered instantly. That Shelley was the victim of a piratical onslaught by fishermen who believed that the rich *milord inglese* had embarked with a large sum in gold is a suggestion that has also been put forward; [8] but regarding none of these suggestions can we hope to arrive at certainty. It is plain, however, he had had such a death as he would have himself desired, and no doubt he sank as again and again he had announced that he intended to do—quickly, without protest or ignominious struggle. For nearly a fortnight nothing was heard at Leghorn of the *Ariel's* crew; and on the third day Trelawny rode to Pisa, warned Hunt, then went upstairs to speak to Byron. "When I told him, his lip quivered, and his voice fal-

[8] In 1875, Trelawny, then living in retirement on the South Coast, received through his daughter in Rome a report that an old fisherman who had died near Sarranza twelve years earlier had confessed on his death-bed that he had helped to sink Shelley's boat. Trelawny accepted the story, and a correspondence on the subject took place in the columns of the *Times*.

tered as he questioned me." Soon afterward a punt, a keg, and some bottles that had belonged to the *Ariel* were salvaged along the coast. Ten days later two bodies were thrown ashore, one near Viareggio and the second three miles away at the Bocca Lericcio. The first Trelawny recognized as that of Shelley— not by the features, for both the face and hands were entirely fleshless, but by the tall slight figure, the schoolboy jacket, the volume of Æschylus in one pocket and the copy of Keats's poems, borrowed from Leigh Hunt and hastily turned back at *Lamia*, which had been thrust into another. Particularly horrible was the mutilation of Williams's body, which retained only a sock, a boot, a black silk handkerchief knotted around the throat, and the rags of a shirt pulled over the head, "as if the wearer had been in the act of taking it off." The body of the sailor Vivian was not found till three weeks after the *Ariel's* disappearance and like the bodies of Shelley and Williams was given temporary burial where it had been discovered.

Trelawny at once undertook the problem of how ultimately they were to be disposed of. He it was—with the energy of a natural man of action—who had organized search parties and himself galloped along the coast, while Byron and Hunt remained at Pisa, helpless and dejected. And it was Trelawny now who interviewed the Tuscan authorities and, to avoid any infringement of the strict quarantine laws, persuaded them to agree that the bodies should be disinterred and immediately cremated. By Trelawny's order an iron furnace was built at Leghorn; and on the morning of August 14, Trelawny, Byron, and Hunt met at Williams's grave, together with officials, a party of soldiers, and some of the *Bolivar's* crew. "A considerable gathering of spectators," including "many ladies richly dressed," hovered near by. As the remnants of Williams's body were grubbed from the sea-sand, Byron looked on with horrified interest. "Is that a human body?" he asked. "Why, it's more like the carcass of a sheep. . . . Let me see the jaw. I can recognize any one by the teeth, with whom I have talked. I always watch the lips and mouth: they tell what the tongue and eyes try to conceal." And later: "Don't repeat this with me," followed by a suggestion that they should try the strength of the water that had drowned their friends. Before they were a mile out, Byron was seized with cramp and vomiting, and reached land again, much to his annoyance, only by Trelawny's aid.

Next morning the same party assembled on the beach near Viareggio. It was a cloudless Italian day. On the horizon stood the island shapes of Gorgona, Capraia, and Elba; behind the forest of stunted pine trees that edged the shore rose the white marble crests of the distant Apennines. The sea was very blue and completely calm. As he thought how the prospect would have delighted Shelley, he felt (Trelawny remembered) a kind of reluctance at dragging his body from the deep yellow sand in which it had been interred. For a time the gang of workmen continued to dig in vain; then they were "startled and drawn together" by the dull hollow sound of a mattock striking on the skull. Quicklime or the early effects of decay had discoloured what remained of the flesh a dark ghastly blue. Unlike Williams's, Shelley's limbs did not fall from the trunk when they were touched, and the corpse was lifted whole onto the funeral furnace. Then the wood was kindled; Trelawny threw frankincense and salt into the fire and poured wine and oil over the body. The oil and salt gave the flames a peculiar glistening and quivering brilliance. Watching from Byron's carriage, which he had not had the strength to leave, Hunt observed the "inconceivable beauty" of the shimmering flame-sheet as it "bore away towards heaven in vigorous amplitude.

. . . It seemed as though it contained the glassy essence of vitality." So fierce was the combined radiance of fire and sun that all around them the atmosphere waved and trembled. Meanwhile, the corpse had fallen open, disclosing the heart (which Trelawny claimed afterward to have snatched from the brazier), and the frontal bone of the skull having dropped away, Shelley's brains, cupped in the broken cranium resting on the red-hot furnace bars, "literally seethed, bubbled, and boiled as in a cauldron for a very long time." The last was a detail that deeply impressed Byron and to which in later conversation he often reverted. But after a time the sight sickened him and he swam off to the *Bolivar*. That evening, as they drove homeward through the pine-forests, both Byron and Leigh Hunt experienced one of those moods of hysterical gaiety that sometimes follow hard on the heels of some unbearably painful drama. They drank in the carriage, and sang and shouted like men possessed.

Chapter Eight

WITH Shelley vanished the last possibility of an understanding between Byron and Leigh Hunt. Only Shelley could have succeeded in holding together two characters so inevitably antagonistic, and his extinction threw their differences into a sharper relief. Yet in the letter, if not always in the spirit of their compact, Byron's behaviour toward his friend's protégé was just and generous. After Shelley's death, his first move had been to request that Leigh Hunt would regard him "as standing in Mr. Shelley's place" and declare "that I should find him the same friend that the other had been." But already Hunt had experienced serious misgivings and, according to his subsequent account, written in a mood of retrospective rancour, "my heart died within me. . . . I made the proper acknowledgment; but I knew what he meant, and I more than doubted whether even in that, the most trivial part of friendship, he could resemble Mr. Shelley. . . ." That is to say, Hunt suspected he would prove a more difficult creditor. To Byron, nevertheless, he was indebted not only for the means of coming to Italy, but his accommodation and furniture once he had arrived and various sums of money to help solve his immediate problems. Both men had suffered seriously from the shock of Shelley's death; and the effect on Hunt was to exaggerate some of his most unpleasing traits—to make him more than ever egotistical and vain and pettish. In his attitude to Byron there was neither measure nor dignity; and now he was so effusive and familiar as to overshoot the mark, now so distant and ceremonious as to appear absurd and stilted. In vain Byron addressed him facetiously as "dear Lord Hunt," hoping thereby to limit the excessive frequency of his "dear Lord Byron's." Hunt posed and prated, was tart or sulky, but found it utterly impossible to achieve composure.

Yet outwardly life at the Palazzo Lanfranchi was regular and placid. About the time Hunt began to think of bed, Byron, after a lazy sensuous day, would be marshalling his sluggish faculties to face the evening's work and settling down to literature and gin-and-water. Byron drank heavily and wrote late; Hunt retired early and rose irritable. His study had been fixed in a small room overlooking the courtyard with an orange tree before the window; and from this refuge he would listen to the noises of the floor above, the *piano nobile*, where Byron and his household were established. He came to recognize them; in a short time he had come to hate them. The great man was a leisurely and languid riser, lounging aimlessly about his room while he read and breakfasted, gossiping with the English valet if his temper was good. More exasperating still, he loved to sing. To poor Hunt, rigid with annoyance at his table below (was he not conscious of his own superior musical sensitiveness?), would float the strains of a voice "at once small and veiled" rehearsing snatches of Rossini "in a swaggering style." Then he took a bath; then his valet dressed him. Finally he would appear in the garden courtyard, handsome and prosperous-looking, blithe and self-confident. "Leontius!" he would shout at the study casement and limp up to the windowsill with some provocative pleasantry.

That Byron's behaviour may have been well meant though a little tactless—as so often the attitude of the rich to their dependent acquaintances—passed Leigh Hunt's somewhat limited comprehension. Grudgingly he left his books and his papers; reluctantly he descended into the garden, "very green and refreshing under the Italian sky." Chairs had been placed by the Italian servants, and there he found Byron, in his nankeen jacket, his white waistcoat and trousers, his visored and gold-trimmed velvet cap, expecting him seigneurial and flippant as always. In the small, feminine, heavily beringed hand (which otherwise played with a lace handkerchief) was the snuff-box which he carried to ward off hunger and because he imagined that the taking of snuff helped to preserve his teeth. Presently they would be joined by the poet's mistress. She too had been late in getting up, and her blond tresses, still glossy from combing and brushing, lay sleek and unbraided about her shoulders. Nostalgically Hunt remembered an English poet:

> Yclothed was she, fresh for to devise.
> Her yellow hair was braided in a tress
> Behind her back, a yardè long, I guess:
> And in the garden (as the sun uprist)
> She walketh up and down, where as her list . . .

Alas, the sun had risen many hours ago. And it was not an English garden in which Countess Guiccioli walked, plucking at the orange flowers and the oleanders and the other cribbed domesticated blooms of that urban paradise, but an Italian *hortus conclusus* beneath a meridional sky, so deeply blue as to seem oppressive and almost hostile. No doubt she "was handsome and lady-like, with an agreeable manner . . ." but "none of her graces appeared entirely free from art." Hunt would amuse her by "speaking bad Italian out of Ariosto"; and she, good-naturedly enough, would "troll it over" on her pretty patrician lips, "keeping all the while that considerate countenance, for which a foreigner has so much reason to be grateful." There was no denying that, physically at least, she had many good points; for "her hair was what the poet has described, or rather *blond*, with an inclination to yellow; a very fair and delicate yellow. . . . She had regular features . . . large . . . but without coarseness, and more harmonious than interesting. Her nose was the handsomest of the kind I ever saw; and I have known her both smile very sweetly, and look intelligently, when Lord Byron said something kind to her. I should not say, however, that she was a very intelligent person. Both her wisdom and her want of wisdom were on the side of her feelings, in which there was doubtless mingled a good deal of the self-love natural to a flattered beauty. She wrote letters in the style of the 'Academy of Compliments'; and made plentiful use, at all times, of those substitutes for address and discourse which flourished at the era of that polite compilation. . . ." At a closer glance, Hunt discovered, she did not really please; and he was quick to notice, not without a certain acid satisfaction, that, whereas her head and shoulders were youthful and charming, her legs were abbreviated and her figure was dumpy. He voted her calculating, self-conscious, stilted in movement, "a kind of buxom parlour-boarder, compressing herself artificially into dignity and elegance, and fancying she walked in the eyes of the whole world, a heroine by the side of a poet." She was the personification of showy Italian sentiment; and more and more heavily as the days dragged by, all alike, all sunny, all vacant and calm, the South had begun to weigh on Leigh Hunt's spirit, till its sunshine and its quiet seemed to poison and suffocate him. That Byron should appear so placid merely increased his anger. How dared he loll back in voluptuous ease, while Leigh Hunt, burdened by the cares of a family, tortured by solicitude for an ailing wife, himself in poor health, with indifferent prospects, accepted the odious role of literary pensioner! Was it for this that he had affronted authority and suffered imprisonment? With such a wealth of grievances beneath the surface, their conversation often hovered on the verge of acrimony; and when Byron in his casual and reckless fashion, having heard Hunt that morning "dabbling on the pianoforte," made some splenetic references to the art of music and suggested that musical interests implied effeminacy, Leigh Hunt was provoked to a snappish rejoinder. Who was this oiled and curled dandy that he should call him effeminate? "He, the objector to effeminacy, was sitting in health and wealth, with rings on his fingers, and babywork to his shirt . . . just issued, like a sultan, out of his bath." Hunt replied, therefore, in a tone of carefully maintained reasonableness, that, although there was no question that the love of music might be overdone, he imagined that it would be "difficult to persuade the world, that Alfred and Epaminondas, and Martin Luther, and Frederick the Second, all eminent lovers of music, were effeminate men"; to which Byron did not attempt to produce an answer—his own stock of historical parallels was not extensive. He had been talking, as his habit was, for the sake of talking, in the spirit of moody contradiction that sometimes possessed him. He retired from the unequal contest baffled and irritated.

Toward noon Hunt would rise and go in to dinner, Byron remaining behind in the courtyard or loitering upstairs to his books and his couch. When the heat of the day declined, the pair would again join company and ride out either on horseback or in Byron's open carriage, Trelawny, a heroic mustachioed figure, puffing at a thick cigar and bestriding his large and spirited horse, often cantering beside them as they entered the forest or turned into the vineyard of some peasant acquaintances. There they were greeted by the dark-haired girl whom Hunt had already encountered in the Palazzo Lanfranchi and with whose whole family Byron was on intimate terms. In attendance were the favourite's younger sister, "delicate-looking and melancholy," an honest father who had difficulties with his landlord and heaved deep lugubrious sighs as he retailed his misfortunes, and a loud, hard-faced, swarthy-skinned peasant mother who served them ripe figs under a garden trellis, cracking (Hunt remembered) "some extraordinary jokes" which embarrassed him in so far as they were comprehensible. A patriarchal scene; yet he was glad to leave it. Like everything else he had observed of Italy, the landscape he explored on their rides round Pisa had "a certain hard taste in the mouth." Fondly conjured up from the steel-engraved embellishments to a favourite edition of the Italian poets, Hunt's ideal Italy continually failed to materialize. The real Italy he neither understood nor could learn to delight in; its mountains were "too bare, its outlines too sharp, its lanes too stony, its voices too loud, its long summer too dusty." He was "ill, uncomfortable, in a perpetual fever," longing for the greenness and neatness of the fields round London, from which one returned to one's own prettily appointed suburban parlour with the teacups, the rosewood pianoforte, the busts and vases, or for the snug appealing romanticism of the English Lake District. At home, in the Palazzo Lanfranchi, his consolations were few. Of the kind of inverted snobbery from which her husband suffered, Mrs. Hunt presented even severer symptoms; and she reached Italy armed with the determination on the one hand that she would not condescend to speak the language, on the other that her attitude toward Lord Byron should make it clear that his title left her unimpressed. He was treated, therefore, to an alarming display of middle-class dignity, interspersed with occasional touches of feminine malice, whenever in his efforts to placate her he laid himself open to them. Any suspicion of covert ridicule had always upset him. Educated in the school of Holland House (where manners, if not more Christian, were at least more accountable), he had had no experience of the acerbities of Hampstead, and by Mrs. Hunt and her acidulous sallies he was frequently dumbfounded. "What do you think, Mrs. Hunt?" he had once remarked. "Trelawny has been speaking against my morals! What do you think of that!" "It is the first time I ever heard of them," Mrs. Hunt replied, with a sniff or snicker not difficult to imagine. Byron (Hunt noted with some relish) was "completely dashed, and reduced to silence." On another occasion, when Byron had been speaking disrespectfully of various of the Hunts' acquaintances, "criticizing . . . their personal appearance, and that in no good taste," their injured friend carried the war into the enemy's camp by asking if Byron had heard Marianne's *bon mot* to the Shelleys about the disdainful and romantic portrait that Harlowe had drawn of him. Byron was too sensitive to decline a repetition; and Hunt thereupon explained with quiet gusto that Marianne had said that it "resembled a great schoolboy, who had had a plain bun given him, instead of a plum one." Byron did not smile and "looked as blank as possible." But henceforward he made no attempt to improve the relationship.

Incidentally, he had developed a violent dislike for his visitors' children. Hunt considered their behaviour above reproach. "They had lived in a natural, not an artificial state, and were equally sprightly, respectful and possessed." But Byron thought them dirty, noisy, and mischievous—they were a kraal of Hottentots, he said, a pack of Yahoos—and, since he expected them as soon as they arrived to proceed to the most monstrous acts of vandalism, he had posted his fierce bulldog on the main staircase, with strict orders to keep off "the little Cockneys," lest they should extend their depredations to his first-floor rooms. The same bulldog also savaged the Hunts' goat, a melancholy survivor of storm and shipwreck, and had bitten off one of its ears before the victim was rescued. Hunt was devoted to his children and fond of animals (while Byron's feeling for both species was capricious and self-centred) and his touchiness grew more pronounced as his health deteriorated.

He had begun to suspect—and in this suspicion at least Leigh Hunt was perfectly justified—that Byron's enthusiasm for their paper, now christened the *Liberal*, was rapidly declining. Byron's London friends were furious when they learned of the association. It was not that they objected to Hunt's politics, but they considered that the poet's reputation might suffer irreparable damage if he linked his name with that of the leader of "the Cockney School." Thus Moore started a vigorous campaign against the journal; and Hobhouse (to borrow one of Leigh Hunt's most felicitous phrases) "rushed over the Alps, not knowing which was the more awful, the mountains or the Magazine." In other words Hobhouse, accompanied by his sisters, made an expedition through Italy during the summer months and paid a visit to Byron at the Palazzo Lanfranchi. There he met Hunt and was "very polite and complimentary" but, in private talk, "if his noble friend was to be believed, did all he could to destroy the connexion between us." Byron, however, refused to desert the *Liberal;* nor is it fair to suppose, as Hunt afterward was at some pains to persuade his readers, that, "from the moment he saw the moderate profits" the magazine was likely to bring in, "he resolved to have nothing farther to do with it in the way of real assistance." To this Hunt appended the additional, if somewhat contradictory plaint, that Byron had made use of the paper "only for the publication of some things which his Tory bookseller was afraid to put forth." It was true that Byron had quarrelled with Murray—finally driven to despair by Murray's procrastination—but he would have had no difficulty in finding a publisher elsewhere. Within a week of his arrival at Leghorn, Leigh Hunt had applied for a loan on his brother's behalf, and Byron, since he was short of ready money, gave the Hunts, for publication either in the *Examiner* or in the new journal, as they might decide, his *Vision of Judgment*, warning them that it contained actionable passages.[1] Among other works that he handed to the Hunts during Leigh's stay in Italy were *Heaven and Earth, The Age of Bronze*, and nine cantos of *Don Juan*, from Six to Fourteen. The first number of the *Liberal* appeared on October 15, 1822, and was received by the Tory press with wild invective. "Casting up the account," the *Literary Gazette* discovered "that Lord Byron has contributed impiety, vulgarity, inhumanity . . . Mr. Shelley, a burlesque upon Göthe; and Mr. Leigh Hunt, conceit, trumpery, ignorance, and wretched verses. The union of wickedness, folly, and imbecility is perfect. . . ." The opening number, as it turned out, was not unsuccessful; but three numbers that followed revealed a steady falling-off.

Dogged already by the idea that his star was waning, Byron was in no mood to encounter a new defeat. Besides, he was exasperated by Leigh Hunt's helplessness—the side of his character that Dickens was to portray brilliantly and cruelly in the personage of Mr. Skimpole—and by Hunt's assumption

---

[1] When John Hunt was prosecuted for the publication of this violent anti-monarchical satire, Byron provided the funds to pay for his defence.

that his friends' incomes were as a matter of course his own. ". . . You cannot imagine [Byron was to write to Moore in 1823] the despairing sensation of trying to do something for a man who seems incapable or unwilling to do any thing further for himself—at least, to the purpose. It is like pulling a man out of a river who directly throws himself in again." By the autumn of 1822, the relations of the collaborators had been severely strained; but, notwithstanding recurrent outbreaks of barely disguised hostility—Lord Byron making Marianne Hunt one of his cold and embarrassed bows; Mrs. Hunt snapping or sparking back, to the evident discomfiture of the haughty nobleman who, haughty though he might be, had little experience (she recognized) of dealing with a "woman of spirit"; Moretto the bulldog worrying Mrs. Hunt's goat or growling on the marble staircase at her noisy and dirty children —the intercourse between the two households was not entirely suspended. And when, toward the end of September, Byron finally abandoned the Palazzo Lanfranchi and moved to the Casa Saluzzo, in the hilltop village of Albaro overlooking Genoa, he was accompanied, though in a different party, by the Hunts and their children. With Mary Shelley they shared the neighbouring Casa Negroto. After the half-Oriental existence of the house at Pisa, Hunt appreciated the "English welcome" that Mary gave him; but his dissatisfaction and dejection were beyond repair.

At Albaro he spent "a melancholy time . . . walking about the stony alleys, and thinking of Mr. Shelley." And the more he regretted Shelley, the more he resented Byron; till the spiteful character-sketch he was to give to the world through the *Recollections* had become finally and firmly imprinted on Leigh Hunt's mind. Warped by the author's self-pity and tinged with envy, the portrait would be more amusing and far more damaging if the prejudice that informs it were less solemnly self-centred, and more convincing if it included a greater degree of sympathy. But how should Hunt, impoverished, ailing, worried, feel sympathy for Lord Byron, rich, celebrated, carefree, pampered by his servants, adored by his mistress, spoiled, courted, admonished by his fashionable London friends? In fact, Byron's seeming placidity was the true measure of his disillusionment. At Venice there had been dissipation; at Ravenna, love; and, when love waned, the dreams of a united Italy. At Pisa and Genoa there was nothing—neither love nor hope. Since Shelley's death—Shelley, to whom he was now prepared to pay a magnanimous valedictory tribute: "the *best* and least selfish man I ever knew. I never knew one that was not a beast in comparison"—he had had few associates whom he either respected or admired. Trelawny, of course, was a good fellow; but what a preposterous poseur! With his fierce eyes, his wild moustachios, the tall stories he was fond of telling about his early life, he bore an odd resemblance to one of Byron's own early heroes; and Byron was quick to grasp the situation's essentially comic side. Author and character met face to face! The poet liked to tease Trelawny with his taint of Byronism; and presently through some kind friend it came to Trelawny's ears that Byron had said that it was a great pity he should have read *Childe Harold*, intimating that his youthful Byronic studies had not improved him. Luckily, however, he did not learn that Byron, in a splenetic moment, had also declared that, if they could teach Trelawny to wash his hands and tell the truth, they would have some hope of turning him out a gentleman. But even so he soon revolted against Byron's influence and derived a certain pleasure from the observation of his more blatant shortcomings—Byron's love of money, his physical bravado and nervous weaknesses. He was glad to note that, although proud of his patrician birth, among strangers Byron very often looked flushed and diffident, and, although he delighted in his prowess as a swimmer, his strength was limited. Together they sailed and swam and shot and drank—Byron, Trelawny remarked, had an uncommonly weak head—but the association was forced and the friendship temporary.

Tom Medwin, another boon companion, had already vanished. In his luggage he took a large sheaf of reflections and indiscretions, gathered (according to Shelley's widow) "when Lord Byron was tipsy." Byron had been warned that Medwin was Boswellizing; but this revelation had by no means arrested his flow of confidences. Rather the reverse. When Byron was in the mood to talk, no considerations of ordinary prudence could hold him back, and a comparatively new acquaintance seemed as suitable an auditor as his oldest and dearest friend. A fool Medwin might be; he was at least an excellent listener; and, as they rode out to shoot or rode back in the cool of the evening or sat over their glasses in the Palazzo Lanfranchi, Byron's musical voice meandered irresistibly on and on, reckless of his own credit, unsparing, when an occasion prompted, of the credit of others. That Byron's talk was largely haphazard did not decrease its interest. Characteristic of his fluid and oscillatory temperament (which oscillated, nevertheless, round a number of fixed points) was the exuberance with which he gallivanted from theme to theme. Now women provided his subject, and now religion. Whereas on the latter his opinions were vague and speculative—he loved the music of an English cathedral service and had been "made very uncomfortable" by a little book that purported to prove the truth of Christian doctrine—on the former they had a positive and downright cast. Medwin could not imagine how it disgusted him to see a woman eat! European women were "in an unnatural state of society. The Turks . . . manage these matters better than we do. . . . Give a woman a looking-glass and a few sugar-plums, and she will be satisfied." He had suffered from the opposite sex as long as he could remember; and, besides a detailed analysis of Lady Byron's character and conduct and of the motive that had induced her to become his wife—she had wished to reform and befriend a celebrated wrong-doer: "friendship is a dangerous word for young ladies"—he dwelt in passing on later and earlier love-affairs, on the autumnal charm of Lady Oxford, the crack-brained violence of Lady Caroline Lamb (concerning whom he repeated to Medwin some particularly savage verses),[2] and his unforgettable disappoint-ment by the heiress of Annesley Hall. His memory was prodi-gious, both for joys and for sorrows. But the joys had passed—"almost all the friends of my youth are dead . . ."; and death, from childhood to middle age, had never been far away. Why, only that morning, he had heard of the suicide of poor foolish Polidori! "I was convinced something very unpleasant hung over me last night: I expected to hear that somebody I knew was dead—so it turns out! Poor Polidori is gone! When he was my physician, he was always talking of Prussic acid, oil of amber, blowing into veins, suffocating by charcoal, and compounding poisons. . . . It seems that disappointment was the cause. . . ." He might have added that Polidori had ex-pired of Byronism—too strong and too exciting a drug for weak and unbalanced natures, the excitant he had himself re-jected but had not escaped from.

Yet escape he must, if he was to retain his integrity, perhaps his sanity. Maybe he would purchase a stake in some younger and fresher continent. The idea of a flight to the New World

---

[2] The publication of these verses in Medwin's *Conversations with Lord Byron* did much finally to overset Lady Caroline's always precarious mental equilibrium.

was still attractive; and before he left Leghorn in the spring of 1822 he received with warmth a cultured American traveller, Mr. George Bancroft, who followed in the footsteps of the Bostonian Mr. Coolidge, and had sat to an American painter, William Edward West, whose portrait was destined for the "Academy of Fine Arts at New York." During the same month, an American squadron reached the port of Leghorn; Byron was invited on board, where he was received "with all the kindness which I could wish, and *more ceremony* than I am fond of." Commodore Jones was extremely courteous; Captain Chauncey showed him a "very pretty edition" of his poems published in the United States; and, as he took his leave, an enthusiastic feminine visitor asked him to give her the rose he happened to be wearing, "for the purpose, she said, of sending to America something which I had about me. . . ." Byron had returned home gratified, if a little exhausted. Plainly across the Atlantic there was none of that apathy toward his poems and dramas which he suspected, now and then, must exist in London; but, counterbalancing the attraction of the New World, was the idea of Greece.

The appeal that it exercised was largely an emotional one. He was dominated by images of the past; in the past lay happiness; and at no period of his existence had life been happier, had youth been more real and joy less transitory, than in the two rambling discursive years of Near Eastern travel. The ideas of youth and freedom were closely intertwined. Now Greece, the country of his youth, was struggling to be free, just as he himself was struggling to throw off his servitude; and he listened eagerly to every report that arrived of the Grecian patriots. Those reports, it is true, were at best confusing. During 1822 Greece had flared up into open insurrection; and by the end of that year, with the exception of certain isolated and beleaguered points, including the Acropolis of Athens and various fortresses scattered along the Gulf of Patras, the whole of the Grecian peninsula had been overrun by the insurgent armies. It was only when the Greeks themselves sat down to form a government and frame a constitution that the difficulties of the problem that they confronted became apparent. Such unscrupulous and bloodthirsty military chieftains as Odysseus and Kolokotrones, subtle Phanariot schemers from Constantinople, that nervous parliamentarian and friend of the Shelleys, Alexander Mavrocordato, dignitaries of the Orthodox Church and Western Philhellenes, proved among themselves at least as antagonistic as Christian and Mussulman; and no sooner had Greece been rescued temporarily from its Turkish masters than it split up into a multiplicity of warring political factions.

Yet behind the depressing spectacle afforded by modern Greeks loomed the conception of Greece itself, glorious in history, further glorified by the associations of Byron's early manhood. Returning to Greece he might recapture hope. But, whether it was to Greece that he removed or to South America, one thing was evident—that he needed money; and the signs of avarice that were noticeable while he lived in Venice, at Genoa developed till there was no concealing them. The death of his detested mother-in-law in 1822 had not only entitled him to a second surname—henceforward he would sign himself always "Noel Byron"—but had brought him a share in the fortune of the rich Lord Wentworth, Annabella's uncle, who had died some years earlier; [3] and from that moment his finan-

[3] Contrary to the usual belief, Byron did not "marry an heiress." Annabella Milbanke, however, had expectations through her uncle Lord Wentworth. On his death in 1815 he left his property for life to Byron's mother-in-law Lady Milbanke, who thereupon took the name of "Lady Noel" and, much to Byron's indignation, survived till January 1822.

cial position had been secure. A converted spendthrift is as hard to deal with as a repentant profligate. Hour after hour he would sit over the steward's account-books, pen in hand, puzzling his way through Zambelli's figures, throwing his pen down with an expression of delight if he could save a scudo. Pitiless in small accounts, he was generous in large sums. Never consistent, he no longer concealed his oddities; and the eccentric behaviour of his notorious granduncle, "the Wicked Lord," who had shut himself up with his tame crickets among the ghosts of Newstead, found a mild reflection in the poetic recluse of the Casa Saluzzo. Teresa, of course, was still beside him; but hers was a declining influence. In their relations Byron had now reached that particularly difficult stage where esteem, affection, and gratitude upon the one hand are balanced by an intense emotional fatigue upon the other. Yet toward her his attitude was always mild and considerate. "Lord Byron [Medwin noted] is certainly very much attached to her, without being actually in love"; and among their acquaintances, when they were sitting together beneath the orange trees, he would address her as "Piccinina" or some other endearing diminutive, while she basked in the air of recovered intimacy his phrase created.

Yet he was tired of her—as he had already hinted in talk with Hobhouse—and of the whole existence of which Teresa Guiccioli had formed an essential part. From no point of view were his prospects pleasing. The failure of the *Liberal* had done him little good; and during the spring of 1823 he remarked resignedly that he was now, he supposed, "as low in popularity and bookselling as any writer can be. . . ." Except for Scott, there were few contemporaries whom he could read with satisfaction; both on the field of literature and the field of politics the Tories triumphed.

Byron was not alone in the despair he felt. Survivors of the "gigantic and exaggerated times" that had produced Napoleon, English liberals watched their hopes of change growing steadily fainter and fainter. As the first impetus of the revolutionary movement appeared to have died down, so the first wave of Romantic poetry had broken and spent itself. By June 1822, when Shelley's featureless and decomposing body was scooped up from the sands of Viareggio, Keats had been dead for seventeen months. Coleridge and Wordsworth, however, had respectively twelve and twenty-eight years to live; and the decade that followed, for Coleridge at least, was slow and inglorious. Yet, just as Keats, given different circumstances, might by his sheer poetic gift have bridged the gulf between the Augustan and Romantic traditions, so Coleridge, had his temperament been more happily constituted and the conflict within himself less acute and prolonged, might have dominated the new literature by force of intellect.

Yet his failure was crushing and comprehensive. And here, not for the first time, one is confronted by the paradoxical observation that, although men make up an age, the age itself is contributory in making men. A poet may help to shape the future; he is controlled and shaped, nevertheless, by the immediate past and by the influence with which it bears down upon the present, crystallized in the intangible contemporary "atmosphere." Coleridge and Wordsworth belonged to the generation that had been excited, almost beyond endurance, by the events of 1789, troubled and horrified by the growth of the Terror, and profoundly stirred by the astonishing spectacle of Napoleon's rise. Some had welcomed, some had shuddered at, the Revolution. But, in both instances, the shock went very deep, and the shocks that followed it were demoralizing and, at length, disabling. Thus Wordsworth receded into a graceless conservatism, the youth and strength of his imagination gradually losing ground, enthusiasm giving way to arid prejudice. By 1822, and even earlier, he was regarded, along with Southey, as poetic arch-traitor to the liberal cause and the hireling representative of a Tory government whose principles and pension he had accepted. In Coleridge's development, the effects of contemporary occurrences are perhaps somewhat less easy to discover; but he, too, after a burst of creation at the turn of the century—practically all the poems that deserve to be remembered were written during 1797 and 1798—experienced a curious falling-off of creative strength, till in 1801 he admitted that the poet was dead in him, while the opium-habit began to claim him more and more definitely, soothing his sense of disappointment and lulling his nerves.

Yet opium was not the sole, nor indeed was it the main, cause of Coleridge's failure. Drug-addiction, like chronic alcoholism, is more often a symptom than the disease itself; though the malady of which in Coleridge's case it may have been symptomatic was of a type that baffles analysis and defies cure. In common with many other writers of the early nineteenth century, he suffered from that odd disease of the volition to which mystics have attached the name of *acedia*, a condition of spiritual despondency and mental paralysis that leaves the sufferer still lucid yet entirely impotent. And then, Coleridge had highly developed moral feelings. It is possible that, had those feelings been less highly developed, and his conscience not so squeamish and not so obstreperous, he might have given them fewer occasions to reproach and torment him. But his sense of duty intensified his sense of failure; and it was his sense of failure that, in spite of every prohibition, human or divine, he was obliged to lull by constant recourse to opium, which, temporarily at least, reconciled him to his moral predicament. Disintoxicated, he must justify himself by action. Intoxicated, he found no justification necessary: it was enough that he knew and felt and imagined. For Coleridge, in fact, as afterward for Charles Baudelaire, opium provided an intensification, not so much of sensual as of spiritual experience. It procured the key to one of those *paradis artificiels* that are a visionary equivalent of the tree-embowered, rock-walled garden fastnesses, "enfolding sunny spots of greenery," where the pupils of the Old Man of the Mountain received their training. But he returned to the real world for the most part with empty hands. Alas, of the "two to three hundred lines" that formed the original *Kubla Khan* (a poem for which Byron felt always the deepest admiration), what with the insubstantial nature of such half-fixed reminiscences and the disastrous arrival of the person from Porlock, only an imperfect recollection was ever salvaged; and the fate of *Kubla Khan* was typical of the fate of his other efforts. Remnants, husks, vestiges found their way to the reader; the essential substance remained with Coleridge to furnish his dream life, just out of reach on the wrong side of the ivory threshold—huge epic poems, gigantic treatises, exhaustive commentaries, all unattempted though in the mind's eye vivid and definite. Resolutions piled up till their magnitude terrified him. He groaned—moralized—then slipped back into ruinous reverie.

Yet Coleridge, notwithstanding the tragic diffusion and gradual dispersion of his creative gifts, had the kind of maturity to which Shelley could not aspire and a critical clearsightedness beyond an enthusiast's scope. The enemies that Coleridge dreaded were those within himself. Shelley's adolescent persecution mania filled the world with bogies which assumed now the lineaments of Sir Timothy Shelley, now the pale murderous mask of wicked Lord Castlereagh (that domestic despot but singularly enlightened director of English foreign policy), and now emerged, crudely personified, as Custom and Prejudice. Half the foes he engaged were of his own creation; half the sufferings he endured were self-provoked; and among real opponents he was a desperate but a random hitter. His verse has the same touch of sketchy enthusiasm. The orchestral accompaniment of *Prometheus Unbound* may be supplied by the spheres; but the celestial clockwork is not revolving very smoothly. The voice may be that of an archangel; but, now and then, it cracks on the top register and the result is a singularly appalling dissonance. Shelley confused ecstasy and imagination, just as in the field of politics he confused the hatred of "tyranny" (which may have a private psychological basis) with a defence of the intellectual principles on which freedom has been established. Indeed, his liberalism never quite emerged from the period when, accompanied by the pretty stupid girl whom he had "rescued" from her boarding school, he attempted to launch an English revolution with the help of paper boats, handbills scattered fancifully from high windows, and messages in bottles committed to the waves. His genius is most apparent when he is least declamatory, when he forgets the helter-skelter rush of personified abstractions that went streaming through his mind, "Kings of suns and stars, Daemons and Gods, Aetherial Dominations . . ." gleaming like meteors, blazing like planets, and comes home to the self and the self's perplexities, its loves and its disappointments, the beauty and the misery of a finite universe.

Keats's famous reproof was certainly merited. But then, Keats had already arrived at a balance between the imagination and the intellect—or between the creative and critical aspects of an artist's brain—that Shelley's temperament debarred him from ever achieving. It was his business (Keats knew) to create, not legislate. But nothing could be further from the selfish secluded æstheticism in which the deliberately non-political artist (supported by a small private income) is supposed to pass his days than Keats's dedication of all his powers to the intellectual purpose that suited them best and through which they could be exploited to the greatest advantage. It is our misfortune, however, that the *Letters*, which outline his plan of campaign, should show him usually a step ahead of the campaign itself and that even the *Odes* should strike us, here and there, as an anti-climax.

Yet few poets have accomplished such a remarkable process of self-clarification in so short a space of time. Sensibly, he refused to regret "the slipshod *Endymion*. That it is so [he told a correspondent only six months after its publication] is no fault of mine. No!—though it may sound a little paradoxical. It is as good as I had power to make it—by myself. Had I been nervous about its being a perfect piece, and with that view asked advice, and trembled over every page, it would not have been written; for it is not in my nature to fumble—I will write independently—I have written independently *without Judgment*. I may write independently, and *with Judgment*, hereafter. The Genius of Poetry must work out its own salvation in a man: It cannot be matured by law and precept, but by sensation and watchfulness. . . . That which is creative must create itself." And *Endymion*, though so evidently the product of an adolescent artist, in love with the idea of writing poetry and somewhat befuddled by an overdose of the Elizabethans, has still movements of astonishing ease and amplitude:

> . . . As when heaved anew
> Old ocean rolls a lengthened wave to the shore,
> Down whose green back the short-lived foam, all hoar,
> Bursts gradual with a wayward indolence.

To re-read Keats's *Letters*, having not looked into them for several years, is an experience at once delightful and disconcerting. So much naïveté coexists with so much maturity, so much vulgarity with so much delicacy of imagination. Here is the suburban poetaster, prolific of schoolboy puns, who collaborated with his friend Brown in painfully facetious letters to Mrs. Dilke; and here, embodied in the same person—unselfconsciously sharing the honours upon almost every page—is a writer of adult seriousness and profound intelligence. His mind was peculiarly honest and utterly disinterested. "I never wrote one single line of Poetry [he declared in April 1818] with the least shadow of public thought." The most imperfect and irresponsible artists (he recognized) are those afflicted with a strong sense of public responsibility or public self-importance; and, just as the individual must have begun to understand himself and grasp his own limitations before he can hope to interfere beneficially in the existence of others, so the artist must graduate through self-absorption into any extended sympathy with contemporary problems or the world around him.

There is a great gulf between the poet who, at the age of twenty-four, had decided that "the only means of strengthening one's intellect is to make up one's mind about nothing— to let the mind be a thoroughfare for all thoughts, not a select party," and poets who turned their minds into packed committee rooms or, like Coleridge, into debating societies with a single speaker. Keats's nature was entirely innocent of the taint of salvationism; and for that reason alone his conception

of poetry seems both more modern than the definitions attempted by many nineteenth-century critics and also closer to
the spirit of the previous age. No Augustan poet need have
dissented from his view that "poetry should surprise by a fine
excess, and not by singularity; it should strike the reader as a
wording of his own highest thoughts, and appear almost a
remembrance." And Johnson himself might certainly have
agreed that "its touches of beauty should never be half-way,
thereby making the reader breathless, instead of content. The
rise, the progress, the setting of imagery should, like the sun,
come natural to him, shine over him, and set soberly, although
in magnificence, leaving him in the luxury of twilight."

What happened to prevent the execution of so bold a design?
The student of Keats's *Letters* feels that he is witnessing a tragedy where the enemies of perfection in art and of happiness in
life, repulsed along the whole length of a poet's defences, suddenly re-emerge, disguised, behind the ramparts. To begin
with, there is talk of the "sore throat" that followed the Scottish
and Irish walking tours of 1818. Then there occurs a casual
mention of the daughter of the lady who had moved in next
door—her countenance attractive but wanting in "sentiment,"
her nostrils "fine—though a little painful," her mouth "bad
and good," her profile "better than her full face," her entire
personality fascinating but perplexing, "beautiful and elegant,
graceful, silly, fashionable and strange." From that moment,
death and love work as malicious allies. The earliest letter to
Fanny Brawne is dated July 8, 1819; and, as approaching
death rapidly speeds up the tempo, the tone adopted mounts
in intensity and gains in bitterness. Yet Keats continued to
fight a rearguard action. Again and again he affirmed his desire
for that condition of moral and spiritual independence in
which, he believed, great poetry must find its origin. Deliber-

ately he would deny himself disturbing contacts and hurry through London without a visit to Hampstead, because "I cannot resolve to mix any pleasure with my days. . . . I am a Coward, I cannot bear the pain of being happy. . . ." Very clearly he could see his life as it ought to have been, and only after a prolonged struggle did he abandon himself to his fate as it was. Finally, physical weakness had spoiled his triumph. Death had at once intensified the claims of life and made them impossible either to satisfy in terms of the body or to relegate to their proper place in the world of the mind.

If Keats was a writer who, although not insensitive to the life of his time, was sufficiently strong to withstand its more malignant influences, Coleridge, Shelley, Wordsworth represent the plight of the intellectual in modern society from three widely separated but complementary points of view. Wordsworth is the type of artist who, after an early expedition into revolutionary experiment, allows himself, for reasons part economic and part personal, to drift back to conservatism once the tide has turned. His was the warm nature easily chilled, the magnanimous spirit strangely susceptible to specious argument, cursed with an instinctive appreciation of the main chance, that in every generation is held up to obloquy. Their former associates may revile such artists; but their pride increases. Too intelligent not to see "both sides of the question," they lose their youth, their inspiration, and at last their integrity in the labyrinth they have created round their own self-love. To the evasions and circumlocutions of middle age they still bring the obstinacy and the conceit of youth. They are the arch-renegades who remain unconscious of their own apostasy.

Very different was the spiritual doom of Coleridge, whose predicament seems to have reproduced in waking life an experience we have most of us undergone during the course of a nightmare. Then, as the necessity of making some immediate and drastic move becomes more and more apparent, so does the sensation of complete impotence grow more and more powerful. All Coleridge's vices derived from his virtues. It was the fact that he could imagine with such lucidity, and analyse and discuss with such an easy strength, that made it at first difficult, and afterward quite impossible, to desert the ideal world of reverie and speculation for the disturbing, imperfect world of action. As Shelley said, he had been blinded by an excess of light; as he himself remarked, his illustrations swallowed up his thesis; till every advance in thought became a retreat from reality, and every improvement in the theory of how books should be written a diminution of the ability to set pen to paper. Between his sensitiveness and a universe which, since the breakdown of his early revolutionary enthusiasms and the collapse of his existence as a husband and father, he had discovered that he could neither like nor understand, he raised the massive barrier of his intellect and his erudition.

Shelley no one could have accused of sparing his own sensitiveness; but, because he was enthusiastic rather than critical, and lacked any aptitude for self-discovery, he never succeeded in giving life and literature their respective dues. The connexion of Shelley's love for his sister, and consequent hatred of his father, with his detestation of Prejudice, Priestcraft, Tyranny, is so clear as to demand little additional emphasis. A wrong-headed or foolish man may produce magnificent verse; but a poet who is both high-minded and muddle-headed, and feels the impact of emotion without knowing its origin, mistakes excitement for the faculty of inspiration and emphasis for the gift of poetic clarity. Through a contemplation of the careers of such poets as Shelley, and through the services of such biographers as Thomas Jefferson Hogg—eager to admire but determined to patronize—we have arrived at that identification of Youth and Poetry, according to which every true poet is an adolescent and true poetry is a byproduct of immature feeling rather than a considered statement of our adult discoveries. Shelley's revolt against the age he lived in— an age of industrial growth and political retrogression—would have been more effective had its origins been less confused and his view of the poet's functions been less didactic—had he been content (in Keats's phrase) to sit like Jupiter instead of constituting himself a kind of celestial busybody. His liberalism, though bold and generous in its expression, rested on a basis that was so insecure as to give a strained uneasy note to his poetic utterance. His choric verse has a breathless speed that is occasionally beautiful; it lacks the "comprehension and expansion" of the greatest literature.

At last the stage is cleared for the appearance of Byron. Wordsworth, Shelley, Keats, Coleridge were all of them devoted men of letters, unselfishly absorbed in their self-appointed work; Byron represents the intrusion of the brilliant amateur. It was at once the secret of his enormous popular success and the measure of his æsthetic limitations that he should rely so completely on the guidance of instinct. His capacity for deliberate reasoning was not impressive: but, as Goethe once observed, in an often-quoted passage of *Eckermann's Conversations*, though he understood himself but dimly, he possessed "a high degree of that dæmonic instinct and attraction which influences others independently of reason, effort, or affection, which sometimes succeeds in guiding where the understanding fails." In life and literature he was an unrepentant, indeed an almost unself-conscious, egotist; but, whereas Keats might progress through a knowledge of himself to a love and understanding of the world around him, for Byron the Self was circumambient—something he could no more escape from than he could escape from his Destiny. Both his greatness and his littleness were on the same conspicuous scale; and it is our misfortune that his talents should have been sufficiently dazzling to lend a false dignity to the weaker side of his literary character. His conception of poetry was crude and straightforward. Verse, he said, was the "lava of the imagination"—its canalization into literature prevented its overflow —and, elsewhere, that it was the "dream of his sleeping passions," the direct image of some experience he had actually lived through. The poet, in fact, above all other things, must be a Personality!

Few personalities have more than a pathological interest; and it is to Byron's personal influence on modern literature that we owe the whole tribe of gifted exhibitionists, ranging in scope from Alfred de Musset to Dowson, who have attempted to "live" their poems as well as write them. Contrast Byron's deliberate exploitation of the poetic role with Keats's analysis of the artist's character. "As to the poetical character . . . [Keats wrote during October 1818] it has no self— It is everything and nothing. . . . It enjoys light and shade; it lives in gusto, be it foul or fair, high or low, rich or poor, mean or elevated.—It has as much delight in conceiving an Iago as an Imogen. What shocks the virtuous philosopher delights the chameleon poet. . . . A poet is the most unpoetical of anything in existence, because he has no Identity—he is continually . . . filling some other body. The Sun, the Moon, the Sea, and men and women, who are creatures of impulse, are poetical and have about them an unchangeable attribute; the poet has none, no identity—he is certainly the most unpoetical of all God's creatures. . . ."

Had Byron's demonic example been somewhat less overwhelming, and Keats's lonely voice more sustained and more powerful, how great might have been the benefit to modern poetry and how significant the results that it at length achieved! How different, perhaps, the whole face of contemporary Europe! Nationalism was essentially a Romantic movement, and from nationalism springs the half-baked racial theorist with his romantic belief in the superiority of "Aryan" blood and his romantic distrust of the use of reason. So far-reaching were the effects of the Romantic Revival that they still persist even in shapes under which they are no longer recognized and among writers who have learned to profess themselves devoutly classicist. For Romantic literature appeals to that strain of anarchism which inhabits a dark corner of every human mind and is continually advancing the charms of extinction against the claims of life—the beauty of all that is fragmentary and youthful and half formed as opposed to the compact achievement of adult genius.

Not for Byron was that calm "autumnal felicity" which (in Gibbon's words) had fallen to the lot of "Voltaire, Hume, and many other men of letters" and which Gibbon himself by the accident of physical infirmity alone was prevented from enjoying. In such a constitution as Byron's there could be no completeness. Or rather, there could be no completeness of the Augustan sort—a laborious triumph of intellect and art and will-power over the inevitable inequalities of human existence. The intellectual pattern was at best fragmentary. Yet by a frank recognition of the extraordinarily diverse elements of which his nature is composed and by a surrender, largely deliberate, to the guidance of instinct, a Romantic poet in the pattern of his life and work may achieve a rhythm which, if far less harmonious, is at the same time more arresting and far more tragic. Gibbon's significance is in a mountain of magnificent prose, raised by decades of painstaking and unselfish labour. Voltaire, like his patron and pupil Frederick, impressed his genius by the audacity of his campaigns, the brilliance of his victories. Byron's significance is as much in his weakness as in his strength: it depends as much on what he failed to do—and on the undirected violence of his mismanaged efforts—as on any work of art that he brought to maturity. Old before his time, he retained to the end many of the features of stumbling adolescence. But to the instinctive understanding occasionally possessed by women—Byron's nature included a large number of exceedingly feminine traits—he added a certain strain of cool dispassionate honesty. His opinions were often absurd; in his personal relationships he was sometimes shifty; but through his chaos darted strange gleams of prophetic insight.

Thus, he could not control his direction yet could foresee his destination. Looking back he felt that his itinerary had been foredoomed, and looking on he saw the goal toward which it tended. More and more imperative became the claims of death. He did not run to it, however, with Shelley's eagerness —like a stream to the ocean, a child to its parent—and loitered casually, half reluctantly along the predestined path. . . . His mood might be tragic, but it was not lugubrious. He had never been afraid of appearing to trifle; and with an enthusiasm so pronounced as to be almost childish he welcomed at the beginning of April 1823 the company of a small and brilliant party of English visitors. There had been other tourists at Genoa during the last few months, both congenial and uncongenial: James Wedderburn Webster, an old acquaintance, husband of the ill-fated Lady Frances and more ridiculous than ever in a new glossy black wig of improbable curliness; Lady Hardy, widow of Nelson's captain, an amusing, observant, sharp-tongued woman, to whom Webster made violent and unsuccessful love; and Henry Fox, the Hollands' only legitimate son, whom Byron was attached to for his father's and mother's sake, and because, like himself, Henry Fox had been born lame. But around the Blessingtons hung an effulgence that eclipsed all rivals. Lord Blessington Byron had known during his London period; and he preserved a vivid memory of his fellow-dandy and man-of-pleasure "in all the glory of gems and snuff-boxes, and uniforms, and theatricals. . . ." The former Lord Mountjoy seemed now to be "much tamed." Still rich, pleasure-loving, indolent, incurably good-natured, he was slipping gradually into a condition of vinous sloth which would one day degenerate into chronic alcoholism. Meanwhile, in 1818, he had married again. Marguerite Blessington was an adventurous and amusing personage. The daughter of a petty landowner in County Waterford, at the age of fifteen she had been forced into a miserable marriage with a certain Captain St. Leger Farmer of the 47th Foot. After three months, Mrs. Farmer had left her husband; Lawrence had painted her portrait in 1807; and she next reemerges as the mistress of a Captain Jenkins with whom for several years she had lived in placid domestic retirement. From Captain Jenkins's arms Marguerite Farmer had moved to those of the plutocratic, extravagant, fashionable Lord Mountjoy, and from Stidmanton in Hampshire to a house in Manchester Square. By falling while he was drunk out of the window of a debtor's jail, Captain Farmer had removed the last obstacle to his wife's good fortune, and from that moment she had swept onward with superb assurance. Lord Blessington, an indistinct but kindly figure, was as lavish as he was rich, and as complaisant or unsuspicious as he was devoted. With the Blessingtons travelled that dazzling ephebus Count

Alfred d'Orsay, paragon of elegance and model of manly grace, whom the world regarded, no doubt correctly, as Lady Blessington's lover.

At thirty-five, with her shining dark hair, neatly parted down the middle of the scalp and drawn back from the smooth white forehead, her delicate skin, noble brow, and lustrous expressive eyes, Marguerite Blessington retained all her power of pleasing. To good looks she added a brisk intelligence, and to vivacity and curiosity some touches of literary aptitude. Naturally, she was eager to visit Byron; and, though Tom Moore when she met him in Paris had alarmed her by the announcement that the poet was growing corpulent—"a fat poet is an anomaly in my opinion"—it was full of tremulous interest, not unmixed with awe, that she arrived at Genoa. To her diary she expressed her hopes and fears by means of a rhetorical question: ". . . Am I indeed in the same town with Byron? Tomorrow I may, perhaps, behold him. I never before felt the same impatient longing to see any one known to me only by his work." Next day, with Lord Blessington's help, the longing was gratified; and following her first impressions came a tiny earthquake tremor of disappointment. Faithful to the conception of Byron's character that had been popularized by *Childe Harold*—and, for the vast majority of his admirers, not yet qualified by *Don Juan*—she had imagined there would be some difficulty in obtaining access, and presumably had promised herself the credit of overcoming his defences. But the citadel capitulated before she had had time to lay siege. Byron was delighted to receive his old friend. He was also delighted, yet evidently a little flustered, by the apparition of this talkative, brilliant, disarming creature who brought in her train the aroma of fashion and the perfume of beauty. No reticence, if some trace of shyness, distinguished his almost effusive welcome. Ushered into a large plainly furnished chamber, Lady Blessington "looked in vain for the hero-looking sort of person" whom she had expected. She had imagined Byron "taller, with a more dignified and commanding air. . . ." The real Byron, on the other hand, was slight and nervous. Since a short but sharp illness during the previous autumn—the result of a long swim during a very hot day in the Gulf of Spezia—he had shed the excessive weight gathered at Monte Nero and was now so emaciated as to seem frail and boyish. His coat—much too large for him—might have been several years old; his other garments induced a suspicion that they had been purchased ready-made. From a perpetual consciousness of his lame foot, he was abrupt and awkward. His reddish curls, darkened by macassar oil, were heavily grey-streaked.

"Were I to point out the prominent defect of Lord Byron [concluded the diarist], I should say it was flippancy, and a total want of that natural self-possession and dignity which ought to characterize a man of birth and education." Positively she found it hard to prevent him from talking; and if Lady Blessington had pictured herself in the attractive role of a woman of talent "drawing out" a man of genius or melting the cold reserve of a poetic misanthrope, those expectations were destined to be cruelly cut short. The confidences arrived unsolicited, accompanied by a flood of gossip. Misfortune had saddened him, but he was rarely solemn. Their first talk revolved mostly round London friends and, having handed the lady to her carriage with many elaborate courtesies—already her disappointment had begun to lose its edge and she had decided that, though odd and foreign-looking, he was "remarkably gentleman-like"—he asked permission to call upon them the following day. Next morning, before they expected him, his card was brought up. Then Byron appeared in bubbling good humour and embarked once again on the subject of mutual English friends, concerning whom he spoke with affection not untempered by badinage, in which "none of their little defects" was allowed to escape lightly. Nor was this all. When finally he took his leave, among profuse apologies for having stayed so long—he had lived so much out of the world, he explained, that he had forgotten its customs—he promised that Thursday to dine with the Blessingtons at their hotel, the Albergo della Villa. On the appointed day, he was announced an hour before the usual time. At first somewhat ruffled because he had found the passages and the staircase full of gaping English tourists, he very soon recaptured his previous gaiety, made a large meal which included two helpings of English plum pudding, and, observing that he considered it a *jour de fête*, consented to drink several glasses of champagne. He hoped (he said) they would not be shocked by the extent of his appetite; but the truth was that for several months he had been living almost entirely on vegetables; "and now that I see a good dinner, I cannot resist temptation, though tomorrow I shall suffer for my *gourmandise* as I always do. . . ." In the meantime, he ate with appreciation and talked with gusto, provocative, malicious, gay, ingratiating.

On her side, Lady Blessington was both charmed and disconcerted. Their relationship had a ludicrous but also a pathetic aspect; for whereas the admirer was repeatedly disillusioned and sometimes extremely shocked, till from blind admiration she had fallen back on a kind of tolerant affection, Byron was completely unaware of the effect he made and continued, as he thought successfully, to entertain his visitors. The flow of gossip that amused but disconcerted Lady Blessington was Byron's idea, somewhat distorted in memory, of social small talk; but his conversation, like the cut of his coat, was a little out of date. London had changed considerably since 1816; manners were less licentious and conventions sterner; but Byron kept the pose and prattle of a Regency man of the world. It was as such, rather than as a mere versifier, that (Lady Blessington soon ascertained) he liked to be regarded. Though savage in his criticisms of the London *beau monde*, its tedious crowded balls and stifling evening parties, about all its doings he still evinced the most eager interest. There was no doubt that he had a "decided taste" for aristocracy; and Lady Blessington, when she was conducted around his private apartments, raised her eyebrows at the oddity of the poet's bedchamber, where the bed itself was topped with coronets and wreathed with his family motto, ostentatious and richly gilt but shoddy and gimcrack. Nothing could have been more "un-English" than his clothes and furnishings: they were extravagant but inexpensive, garish but well worn. Byron's taste might have passed without remark in a foreign nobleman. It was unlooked for—indeed horrifying—in a British peer of the realm!

Of these criticisms—or of their possibility—Byron was quite unconscious. But he knew that on other scores he sometimes exposed himself and when, as often happened, he felt that he had gone too far, he would do his best to efface the bad impression with a smile and a pleasantry. Lady Blessington was allowed to lecture him to her heart's content. No one (he declared) disliked being scolded by an attractive woman; and his new friend acquiesced in the compliment and accepted the privilege. From time to time, it was true, she hurt his feelings; and then he would turn pale with anger or suddenly leave her presence, only to return a little later determined to "make it up." About their association hung a pensive autumnal radiance. The tired heart that had ceased to quicken its pace for

Teresa Guiccioli broke into a sedate but pleasing flutter for Marguerite Blessington. Life, long, dull and automatic, became eventful and various. The quiet routine of vegetarian meals and study and exercise—punctuated if not enlivened by visits to Teresa's rooms—was discarded in favour of a regular social round. When he rode out now in the afternoons it was as one of a cavalcade. Byron (his friend noted) was a nervous rider; and the figure he cut on horseback was at least surprising, for his mount was "literally covered with various trappings, in the way of cavessons, martingales, and Heaven knows how many other (to me unknown) inventions. The saddle was *à la hussarde* with holsters, in which he always carried pistols." As for his costume—that was as outlandish as it was characteristic, combining a touch of inappropriate splendour with an indication of the wearer's economical habits. His nankeen coat and trousers "appeared to have shrunk from washing," the jacket being "embroidered in the same colour" and embellished with "three rows of buttons; the waist very short, the back very narrow, and the sleeves set in as they used to be ten or fifteen years before." The ensemble was completed by a dark blue velvet cap, with eye-shade, rich gold band, and large gold tassel, a pair of blue spectacles, and nankeen gaiters. Sometimes, in place of the white coat he wore his Highland jacket, liberally befrogged, in the green tartan of his mother's clan.

Thus equipped, he would jog with the Blessingtons along the road to Nervi, usually talkative and (except when they encountered English sight-seers and he blushed nervously and muttered irritably at the sound of their whispered comments) affable, entertaining, in high good humour. Or he would spend the evening with them and, after tea, sit out on the balcony. From other balconies drifted the fragrance of southern night flowers; the blazing *fanale* cast fiery reflections upon passing sails; and fishing boats crossed the moonlit water, each with a flare at the prow. Beneath their windows "were crowded an uncountable number of ships from every country, with their various flags waving in the breeze, which bore to us the sounds of the various languages of the crews." But neither at this nor at any other time did Byron rouse the suspicion that he aspired to a lover's role. Love might colour his emotions; it did not cloud them. "I am worn out in feelings [he had told Marguerite Blessington]. . . . Though only thirty-six, I feel sixty in mind. . . ." Nowadays he was content with the pleasures of friendship. He liked the sympathy of this attractive experienced woman, whom he could shock, then conciliate, then shock again, feeling all the while that he continued to hold her interest and perhaps to touch her heart. Above all, she provided an excuse for his favourite mental indulgence. He could give way to the joys of recollection and incessantly remember aloud.

Not even to Marguerite Blessington did he uncover the whole of his past. But, as he talked, either in his flippant social manner or in the more serious and sententious style that he adopted when they were alone, name after name and episode after episode would come floating up to the surface of his conversation. For so self-conscious a man he was remarkably downright; and topics that his friend might have herself avoided were introduced and discussed by the poet at their earliest meetings. Lady Byron's conduct he was never tired of analysing and describing. After eight years he could hardly forgive her for the blow she had dealt him; yet when he spoke of her it was usually in a respectful and sometimes an affectionate tone, as though he half admired, much as he resented, her inflexible righteousness. His daughter, too, he mentioned often, and always regretfully. Her miniature portrait hung over his writing-desk. It was a kind of talisman—the symbol of permanence in a life that had been otherwise diffuse, overcrowded, and chaotic. As he talked, how many were the names, how many the faces! Lady Melbourne—there was a woman he had been really fond of. "She was a charming person—a sort of modern Aspasia, uniting the energy of a man's mind with the delicacy and tenderness of a woman's. . . . I have often thought that, with a little more youth, Lady Melbourne might have turned my head. . . ." And "Poor dear Lady Jersey!" Did she (he wondered) "still retain her beautiful cream-coloured complexion and raven hair?" Madame de Staël was the cleverest woman he had ever met. She had been kind to him, moreover, and given him good advice. But he could not forget how at a large London dinner party the famous blue-stocking had had trouble with her corset and had appealed to the footman behind her chair to pull out an obtrusive whalebone! Madame de Lieven was another hostess for whom he felt affection and gratitude: she and Lady Jersey had rallied to his support during the separation scandal when the rest of the London *beau monde* conspired to cut him. "Of all that coterie, Madame de Lieven, after Lady Jersey, was the best. . . ." Then his reminiscences would slide back again to the more immediate past, and he would speak with tender regard of Teresa Guiccioli, her beauty and virtues, her exalted birth and the fortune that she had given up. ". . . She must know that I am sincerely attached to her; but the truth is, my habits are not those requisite to form the happiness of any woman. . . ." Through his references to his mistress sounded a hollow obituary note.

She belonged already to the past: she would have no share in his future life. It seemed to have been settled (he would sigh) that he must go to Greece; and if he went there he did not expect that he would return alive. But Hobhouse wished it, and the Greek Committee continued to bother him. . . . In fact, since February 1823, when he had finally decided for Greece and against the Americas, Byron's feelings had been subject to considerable fluctuation. What had been attractive in fancy became alarming when it was translated to the plane of practical reality. Besides, there was an uncomfortable suspicion that he had perhaps been cornered! It was one thing to decide that he would go to Greece, and quite another to learn that the Greek Committee, a body of earnest liberal gentlemen which included Jeremy Bentham, Hobhouse, Douglas Kinnaird, and several others bonded together to promote the cause of the Greek insurgents, had elected him to deputize for them on the field of glory. The idea of death might leave him calm; he shuddered, nevertheless, at the prospect of moving house. Heaped around him was the treasure-trove of so long a period! "Byron [Trelawny was to write] never sold or gave away anything he had acquired" and was surrounded by "all the rubbish accumulated in the many years he had lived in Italy, besides his men, women, dogs, and monkeys, and all that was theirs." He was usually "bedevilled for a week after moving"; the removal from Pisa to Genoa had completely knocked him up; and it was now suggested that he should transplant himself to some Grecian wilderness. Yet from every side his well-wishers appeared to be closing in. During 1823 a representative of the Greek patriots, Andreas Luriottis, had arrived in London. The Committee had held its first meeting on February 28 and Edward Blaquière had volunteered to travel to Greece and review the position. Blaquière and Luriottis had broken their journey to visit Byron and he had welcomed them to the Casa Saluzzo on the fifth of April. During May he learned that by a unanimous vote he had been elected a member of the Greek Committee, to whom he responded that he was desirous of going to the Levant in person and that the only difficulty was "one of a domestic nature." The obstacle he referred to was, of course, his mistress; but (as Trelawny noted) he did not "seem disposed to make a mountain of her resistance" and had promised that Pietro Gamba should bear him company.

From that point, there was no hope or possibility of turning back. But the more he thought of Greece, the more convinced he felt that this expedition was to be his ultimate journey. To Medwin he had already expressed the conviction that he would not survive it, and to Lady Blessington again and again he spoke of his approaching death. But in this, as in everything else, his attitude was disconcerting. Lady Blessington would have applauded a heroic pose. There was something (she mused) "so exciting in the idea of the greatest poet of his day sacrificing his fortune, his occupations, his enjoyments—in short, offering up on the altar of Liberty all the immense advantages which station, fortune, and genius can bestow—that it is impossible to reflect on it without admiration." But Byron gave his gesture of sacrifice a flippant and cynical cast, talked at length of the uniforms he meant to wear, of the loans he proposed to advance, and the worthlessness of the modern Greeks whose cause he championed, "entering into petty details . . . always with perfect sang-froid." In another mood, he would say that he longed to return to England, to bid good-bye for the last time to his wife and daughter, or speak of the "grey Greek stone" that might mark his burial place, lost in some wild valley of the Thessalian uplands, within sight perhaps of the snowy crest of unforgotten Olympus, where eagles screamed and wheeled against a brilliant Aegean sky. Lady Blessington was vexed and puzzled, then wondered and admired again. Byron seemed positively to flourish on her naïve discomfiture.

From April 1 to June 2 their idyll lasted. Two long months went by in rides, visits, dinner parties, endless conversation. Hard as she tried to conventionalize it, in Lady Blessington's mind Byron's portrait was still strangely nebulous; in spite of earnest attempts she had found it impossible to define his character. Generous yet avaricious, flippant yet tender-hearted, sceptical yet irremediably haunted by superstition—was there a single aspect in which he achieved consistency? But one thing was plain—that he believed in fate. "There was a helplessness about Byron, a sort of abandonment of himself to his destiny, as he called it, that commonplace people can as little pity as understand"; and when fate spoke to him clearly he always answered the call. With a certain reluctance, however, he took his leave of happiness. At the beginning of June the Blessingtons made ready to depart, and on June 2 for the last time he called at their hotel rooms, looking out from their flower-filled balcony across the harbour of Genoa. He wept and made no effort to conceal his tears. To each of them he presented a parting gift—to Lord Blessington, benevolent but indistinct; to "*le beau Alfred*," tall, splendid, Apollonian, who had done his pencil likeness to embellish a sketch-book, with the world before him; to Lady Blessington, still a little puzzled but no doubt deeply touched; to Miss Power, Lady Blessington's unmarried sister—and from each asked a corresponding *gage d'amitié*. Then he dried his eyes and uttered "some sarcastic observation on his nervousness," though at the same time his lip quivered and the words were tear-fogged. Behind him was a glimpse of the contentment he had always aspired to: it would pass away from him in the Blessingtons' travelling carriage on the road to Lucca. The hardest stage of his journey still stretched ahead.

London, May 23, 1941

Index

271